S0-AAD-567

virginia woolf

4/77

For Valerie & Menaleus —
I listened to your shells,
and this is my reply.

Mom

virginia woolf
a critical reading

AVROM FLEISHMAN

the johns hopkins
university press
baltimore
& london

Copyright © 1975 by The Johns Hopkins University Press
All rights reserved. No part of this book may be reproduced or
transmitted in any form or by any means, electronic or mechanical,
including photocopying, recording, xerography, or any information
storage and retrieval system, without permission in writing from
the publisher.

Manufactured in the United States of America

The Johns Hopkins University Press, Baltimore, Maryland 21218
The Johns Hopkins Press Ltd., London

Originally published, 1975

Johns Hopkins paperback edition, 1977

Library of Congress Cataloging in Publication Data

Fleishman, Avrom.
    Virginia Woolf: a critical reading.

    Includes bibliographical references and index.
    1. Woolf, Virginia Stephen, 1882–1941—Criticism and interpretation.
PR6045.072Z63   1975   823'.9'12   74-24375

ISBN 0-8018-1616-5
ISBN 0-8018-1958-X (paperback)

Avrom Fleishman is professor of English
at The Johns Hopkins University. His
other published works include *A Reading
of Mansfield Park, Conrad's Politics,*
and *The English Historical Novel.*

In memory of

EARL REEVES WASSERMAN

*Mit deinem Meister zu irren
ist dein Gewinn.*

A NOTE ON THE TEXT. References to Virginia Woolf's works are, unless otherwise stated, to the standard edition (untitled as a whole) published by The Hogarth Press (London). (Dates in the text refer to the initial publication of each work.) Page references are made parenthetically at the end of quotations; in a few cases where confusion is possible, a footnote with the title of the work quoted is introduced. The edition of Woolf's essays used is the four volume Hogarth Press edition, *Collected Essays* (London, 1966–67; hereafter cited as *Collected Essays*). The edition of Woolf's diaries used is the Hogarth Press edition, *A Writer's Diary: Being Extracts from the Diary of Virginia Woolf*, edited by Leonard Woolf (London, 1965 [1953]; hereafter cited as *Diary*). References to works not available in the standard Hogarth Press edition are given full bibliographical identification in the notes.

contents

foreword

*If only (one finds oneself feeling in re-reading these novels), if only
these dissolved units of understanding had been coordinated into a
system; if only, perhaps, there was an index, showing what had been
compared with what; if only these materials for the metaphysical
conceit, poured out so lavishly, had been concentrated into crystals
of poetry that could be remembered, how much safer one would
feel.*—William Empson[1]

The plaint once sounded by Woolf's first perceptive critic has been
answered by many studies, yet even the fearless reader may feel no
safer in the presence of her texts. The "dissolved units" have been
coordinated in a number of systems—psychological, philosophic, feminist—but only fragmentary views of the individual works have
emerged from their rubrics. Much of the recent outpouring has failed
to respond to Empson's call for an account of "what had been compared with what"—with the notable exception of James Naremore's
The World Without a Self. The appearance of this fine literary treatment—and also of a number of sensitive essays in the recent Woolf
issue of *Modern Fiction Studies*—suggests that the moment is propi-

[1]"Virginia Woolf," in *Scrutinies II*, ed. Edgell Rickword (London, 1931), p. 216.

tious for esthetic contemplation.[2] Under scrutiny of this kind, I believe, Woolf will be more firmly placed not only among the writers who established a distinctive style in the modern novel but also among the enduring masters of fictional art.

As Woolf was both the contemporary and at some points the literary confrère of Eliot, Joyce, Pound, and Yeats, it is not surprising that her imagination worked in much the same way as theirs. Hers is a fundamentally literary sensibility: she is a creature of books. Fathered by an intellectual and his library, sustained by constant reviewing for *The Times Literary Supplement* and other periodicals, at home in a notoriously bookish milieu, Woolf lived her life in the marketplace of literary ideas and objects. Into that forum went the classics, all of "English lit," and the contemporary outpouring— good, bad, and in limbo. Constantly educating herself—and chafing at being deprived, as a woman, of a solid classical education—Woolf became a *learned* author, not in Milton's sense, perhaps, but at least in Arnold's.

This lifelong bout of reading was to lead Woolf to form her works around metaphors, allusions, and quotations drawn from the classics— ancient and modern. In the process, she made a cumulative synthesis of the sentiments, values, and perceptions of her tradition; she incorporated Sophocles, Montaigne, Shakespeare, and much, much else into her way of seeing the world. The marks of this assimilation are to be found not only in works of parodic cultural history like *Orlando* and *Between the Acts* but in everything she wrote. They are to be found in the very tissue of her mind, which she held to be a function of all the minds with which she had engaged—in books as well as in life. More radical than Eliot's theory of "tradition and the individual talent," less artificial than Yeats's notions of the artist's formation of identity from masks inspired by his predecessors, Woolf's view of a cultural spirit shaping the artist's imagination

[2]Naremore's book (New Haven and London, 1973) is the most sustained literary study of Woolf to appear since James Hafley's *The Glass Roof: Virginia Woolf as Novelist* (Los Angeles and Berkeley, 1954). Naremore's searching commentary on Woolf's style relieves her critics—at least for the immediate future—of the obligation to focus on its qualitative impact and its reflection of the author's sensibility. Her narrative voice, however—"the voice of everyone and no one" that Naremore labors to define— comes close, in his formulation, to a belletristic chattiness, the result of "Mrs. Woolf's fondness for the sketch, her tendency to list [her own] impressions" (p. 101). These suggestions are less convincing than the critic's fine observations on the world view from which Woolf's style proceeds and which it in turn embodies in the texts. And his subsequent discussion of this world view as it mingles with the ethos of love and death in *To the Lighthouse* constitutes the closest approximation to the essential themes of that fiction that I have read.

was drawn from her own experience in furnishing the chambers of her mind. And that view led her—as similar views led Eliot, Yeats, Pound, and Joyce—to practice what may be called an encyclopedic style: the network of allusion that stands as the dominant mode in modern British literature.

To place Woolf in this company is not to bestow accolades but to establish an appropriate context for reading her works. As with novelists like Fielding or George Eliot, it is important to know what Woolf read and what she thought of it as she shaped her ideas of fiction. But to set up an intellectual context is only preliminary to the criticism of individual works of art, in which learned background is made esthetic foreground. At the very least, the critic should discover the sources and determine the relevance of Woolf's numerous quotations and references—a task that has been left largely undone. The present work proposes no "source study" or intellectual biography; it is simply a reading of Woolf's nine major fictional works.

Woolf was fairly explicit about the way her mind worked when she wrote, and described it operating at a high degree of effectiveness in the writing of *The Waves*: "What interests me in the last stage was the freedom and boldness with which my imagination picked up, used and tossed aside all the images, symbols which I had prepared. I am sure that this is the right way of using them—not in set pieces, as I had tried at first, coherently, but simply as images, never making them work out; only suggest" (*Diary*, page 169, 7 Feb. 1931). Her exultation in this freedom of imagination and her resistance to allegorical consistency should not obscure the fact that she names image and symbol as the essential materials of her activity. It is with them, therefore, that this study will be most often occupied.

When the use of image and symbol becomes so thoroughgoing, it becomes harder to speak of *novel* in any pre-Woolfian, pre-Joycian sense. One easy, question-begging gambit is to speak of her novels as poetic, but Woolf sought more precise terms to account for her generic innovations: "I have an idea that I will invent a new name for my books to supplant 'novel.' A new_____ by Virginia Woolf. But what? Elegy?" (*Diary*, page 80, 27 June 1925). Elegy is a genre that figures mightily in Woolf's fiction, but only as an end—remembrance and propitiation of the dead—rather than as a set of conventional means. Means and ends are inseparable among the other genres with which her works have dealings: biography, satire, comedy, are all present in force. Adopting an approach that Northrop Frye has proposed for works like those of Joyce, which mix the traditional genres in reaching toward a comprehensive fictional world, we

may call Woolf's genre as well as her style encyclopedic,[3] although
the implied magnitude is more in keeping with the sum of her oeuvre
than with any one of its component works. In what follows, I shall
indicate the genres whose traits seem most in evidence in specific
works, and allow the evidence of an encyclopedic genre to emerge of
itself. I often use the term "fictions" rather than "novels" to name
these works neutrally—and without any of the mystique that has recently been attached to it.

My own critical interests are somewhat eclectic, and I can defend
them only as a principled, rather than unprincipled, eclecticism. The
psychologically oriented may regret my occasional sallies into the history of Woolf's time, older new critics may disparage my biographical
excursuses, and tough-minded historicists may deplore my seduction
by myth. In defense, I shall be able to allege only that I made these
notations of the historical, mythic, and other meanings of Woolf's
works because I believe them to be demonstrably present at certain
points in the text. Such an assemblage of truths—if they are indeed
such—can at best be considered a guide to reading Woolf, rather
than a systematic statement about her or her work. Hence the sub-
title of this book.

Among the things this eclectic approach will not readily assimilate is a philosophical analysis of, or generalization about, Woolf's
writings. Although I have joined in the discussion of such matters to
offer an alternative view,[4] I shall not undertake to substantiate it
further by applying it uniformly to Woolf's fictions. Although explanatory in varying degrees when dealing with Woolf's enterprise
as a whole, philosophic theories will be found wanting when asked to
account for the multifarious verbal events in a work of fiction. They
will account for *some* observable features but not others; from this
fact derives the persistence of extraliterary controversy and a tendency toward interpretive fads.[5]

---

[3]Cf. Harvena Richter, *Virginia Woolf: The Inward Voyage* (Princeton, 1970), pp. 7–8,
where Frye's lesser form, "anatomy," is invoked to describe Woolf's syncretism.
[4]"Woolf and McTaggart," *ELH*, xxxvi (1969), 719–38.
[5]A good summary of the literature on the Bergson and Moore influences on Woolf
can be gleaned from Jean Guiguet, *Virginia Woolf and Her Works*, trans. Jean Stewart
(London, 1965 [1962]), pp. 32 ff., 382 ff. The most important recent addition to the
Moore view is S. P. Rosenbaum, "The Philosophical Realism of Virginia Woolf," in
English Literature and British Philosophy, ed. Rosenbaum (Chicago and London,
1971), pp. 316–56. In addition, a number of critics have approached Woolf from the
standpoint of recent trends in Continental thought, e.g., Maxime Chastaing, *La
Philosophie de Virginia Woolf* (Paris, 1951); Maurice Blanchot, "La Vocation de Vir-
ginia Woolf," *La Nouvelle NRF*, vi (1958), 865–73; Geoffrey H. Hartman, "Virginia's
Web," *Chicago Review*, xiv (1961), 20–32 (reprinted in his *Beyond Formalism:
Literary Essays, 1958-1970* (New Haven and London, 1972).

Another thing the present study will not do is take account of all the Woolf manuscripts. Although I have examined some of the manuscripts at the New York Public Library, British Museum, and Knole, I must confess to finding the enterprise one of diminishing returns. Once the broad outlines of Woolf's proceedings on a given book are ascertained, analyses of specific variants usually arrive at a conclusion that she changed it and improved on it—didn't she? The publishing of the many beautiful, omitted passages is, of course, desirable in itself, but I have done this only where it seemed useful for explanation.[6] For the gross facts about a number of the manuscripts, a series of articles by Charles G. Hoffman may be employed.[7] As for the manuscript diaries in the Berg Collection, I am confident that the Quentin Bell biography has given us a fair assessment of the facts they contain, although I look forward to fuller treatment of their meditative passages. Though the evidence on Woolf's behavior as a writer and person is not all in, enough of it can already be adduced to make a study of the literary objects fairly secure.

As my last preparatory remark, I rest on Borges's dictum: "There is no intellectual exercise which is not ultimately useless." I take courage from that "ultimately."

□

It remains to acknowledge the help others have generously given: my students, James Sherry and Penelope Cordish; my former colleagues, J. Hillis Miller and Robert M. Slusser; and particularly my colleague, Arnold Stein, who read the manuscript with care and penetration. Quentin Bell, the British Museum, and the Henry W. and Albert A. Berg Collection of the New York Public Library (Astor, Lenox and Tilden Foundations) have kindly given permission to make quotations from manuscript materials. Part of my research has been done under a grant from the American Council of Learned Societies, and while on research leave granted by The Johns Hopkins University; I am grateful for this support. Several sentences have previously appeared in a review-essay on Woolf criticism published in *Studies in the Novel*; the editors have kindly allowed me to reprint.

[6]See Richter, *Inward Voyage, passim*, for valuable quotations from the Berg Collection manuscripts in the New York Public Library, some of which will be discussed below.
[7]" 'From Lunch to Dinner': Virginia Woolf's Apprenticeship," *Texas Studies in Literature and Language*, x (1969), 609-27 [on *The Voyage Out, Night and Day*, and *Jacob's Room*]; "From Short Story to Novel: The Manuscript Revisions of Virginia Woolf's *Mrs. Dalloway*," *Modern Fiction Studies*, xiv (1968), 171-86; "Fact and Fantasy in *Orlando*: Virginia Woolf's Manuscript Revisions," *Texas Studies in Literature and Language*, x (1968), 435-44; "Virginia Woolf's Manuscript Revisions of *The Years*," *PMLA*, LXXXIV (1969), 79-89.

virginia woolf

the voyage out

"They seemed
to be thinking
together"

Virginia Woolf's first full-length fiction resembles a conventional novel in being largely taken up with personal relations among the British middle class—specifically, the love affair of a shipping magnate's daughter and a young novelist (with an independent income of £700 a year). But by the curious choice of setting—a South American city, presumably in Brazil, for the steamer *Euphrosyne* does business on "the Amazons" (39)—its social portraiture is modified by strains of another fictional type: the novel of tropical adventure, in vogue at the time (1915).[1] Although the work initially resembles W. H. Hudson's *Green Mansions* (1904) in romantic tone, it is structurally much closer to Conrad's "Heart of Darkness" (1899). Action begins with a movement down the Thames—with a distancing from contemporary England and a reminder of its past imperial glories— continues with a trip by small steamer up a jungle river ("They seemed to be driving into the heart of the night. . . . The great darkness had the usual effect of taking away all desire for communication . . ."

---

[1] The probable source of this story of love in the tropics was one of Leonard Woolf's romantic experiences in Ceylon, which he later recounted in *Growing: An Autobiography of the Years 1904-11* (London, 1961), pp. 150-56; the girl in that work was named Rachel, too.

1

[325]),[2] and reaches a climax in an extended death scene involving both the central figure and the chief observer. Yet *The Voyage Out* is no more an exotic novel of the colonies than it is a traditional social novel; in this first work, Woolf exposed a number of the themes that make her fiction distinctive and important.

The work's principal theme is manifested in its structure. A first group of six chapters is devoted to the ocean voyage, during which Rachel Vinrace makes her debut in the modish society of the Dalloways and the intellectual milieu of the Ambroses (the Cambridge scholar Ridley Ambrose is her mother's brother, as indicated on pages 15 and 20). The progression moves on land when her Aunt Helen, determined to bring Rachel out, invites her to stay at the villa the Ambroses have taken for the winter and spring.[3] A second group of six chapters sets the scene at the fictional Sta. Marina, particularly at the hotel where the English stay. These characters are the stock-in-trade of English satirists from the Augustans to Waugh: e.g., the bluestocking Miss Allan, the socially responsible Thornburies, the Francophile Hughling Elliot. Two social activities in this section move Rachel's coming-out further along: the ascent of Monte Rosa and the dance, at both of which she and Terence Hewet are brought together. The third section, of seven chapters, is a neatly arranged sequence of stages in the growth of love: first Rachel (chapter XIII) and Hewet (XIV) are shown meditating on their feelings, then their friends (XV) and the principals themselves (XVI) are shown discussing them, and finally—after a chapter in which Rachel goes to chapel and loses her faith—first Hewet (XVIII) then Rachel (XIX) are shown fully in love. The final section of eight chapters follows the more externalized events of the river voyage, the illness and death of Rachel, and the responses to it of those at the hotel.

---

[2]Conrad's story is also recalled in the vision of Britain as the Romans saw it, in *Mrs. Dalloway* (28), even more strikingly (with the quoted title) at the climax of *The Years* (418), and at the conclusion of *Between the Acts* (256).

[3]The time scheme of the novel is fairly clear, although only lightly sketched in: the ocean voyage begins in October (1) and ends four weeks later (100); three uneventful months bring the story to the beginning of March (108); Helen and Rachel discover the hotel and eavesdrop there on March 15 (113); the river voyage occurs in April (204); and Rachel falls ill and dies in May (420).

The historical time of the action is not specified but is limited to the first decade of this century by the fact that Alexandra is queen (13); a *terminus ad quem* is provided by Helen's reading of G. E. Moore's *Principia Ethica*, published in 1903 (a passage from chapter I is read out by Dalloway on p. 82). The discussion of an election involving Asquith and Austen Chamberlain (109) and the mention of possible British action in Morocco (373) place the date near 1906, which saw both a general election and the Algeciras conference on the African situation.

The form of the action, from an initial state of innocence to the social initiation, love, and death of a young woman, is accompanied by a movement in space: from the known world of England, to the transient realm of English tourists on the coast of South America, and finally into the interior where Rachel reaches the farthest verge of her journey and of her development—discovering her love and contracting her death in the jungle at virtually the same time. This movement in geographical space and in personal life is accompanied by a third "voyage out," and this latter may be considered the deeper theme of the novel, that which makes it more than a tale of maturation and more than a journey of discovery. The main journey is a mental one, for this is a fiction of metaphysical depth of the same order as those which follow it in the Woolf canon. Rachel's voyage is a series of moments of vision in which she progressively sees less from the conventional perspective in which she has been educated and more in accord with the rhythm of life and death which underlies the lesser rhythms of daily affairs. In focusing on this change, *The Voyage Out* represents a turn in the tradition of the English *Bildungsroman*—one of the major strains in the novel's tradition—toward the tracing of a metaphysical education.

□

Another look at the plot of *The Voyage Out* will reveal a number of striking peculiarities. A young girl—twenty-four years old, but emphatically described as naive—makes a journey, first by sea, then to a mountaintop, and finally up a river, in the course of which she achieves a degree of experience, flowers into first love, and contracts her death. The form of the action, the major symbols, and the dealings with innocence and enlightenment, love and death, all conspire to make this a story of initiation, in line with the mythos of heroic quest. No doubt the initiation will be more readily perceived than the quest; Rachel Willoughby's introduction to the ways of the world is more evident than her heroic destiny and ultimate elevation. Yet the two patterns are frequently linked in the history of literature, as they are in that of religion, and a tissue of literary allusions in this text establishes them jointly as the donnée on which inventive modern variations are to be played.

Northrop Frye has described the literary form of mythic quest in his account of the structure of romance:

> The complete form of the romance is clearly the successful quest, and such a completed form has three main stages: the stage of the perilous journey and the preliminary minor adventures; the crucial struggle, usually some kind of battle in which either the hero or his foe, or both, must die;

and the exaltation of the hero. We may call these three stages respectively, using Greek terms, the *agon* or conflict, the *pathos* or death-struggle, and the *anagnorisis* or discovery, the recognition of the hero, who has clearly proved himself to be a hero even if he does not survive the conflict.[4]

This formulation suggests the possibility that *The Voyage Out* may be a story of initiation and heroic quest even though its protagonist dies at the close: our *anagnorisis*, which comes in witnessing her state of mind as she achieves a vision of death, is simultaneous with her *pathos* or death struggle. The structure also proves applicable in assigning relative importance to the novelistic parts: the body of the action—going to South America, encountering the Ridleys, the Dalloways, and the society of the hotel, climbing a mountain, falling in love—is a series of adventures in the "perilous journey" leading up to the major action, the "crucial struggle" with death itself. And the fact that this romance ends tragically rather than comically does not diminish the clarity of the mythic design; as Frye describes another version of this plot, it is "the tragedy of innocence in the sense of inexperience, usually involving young people. . . . the archetypal tragedy of the green and golden world, the loss of the innocence of Adam and Eve. . . ."

No matter how much afflatus we ascribe to the climactic action of Rachel's death, the fiction will not seem a heroic romance unless we also find the heroine undergoing a process of initiation. Modern anthropological research has developed the relation of heroic myths to initiatory rituals (without establishing the primacy or the precedence of either) and it is inevitable that a story of a young girl's entry into the world of sex, society, and death will be as readily homologous with the patterns of ritual as with those of myth. In a summary of initiation rituals by Mircea Eliade, the relevance of heroic myth is clearly evident: "The majority of initiatory ordeals more or less clearly imply a ritual death followed by resurrection or a new birth. The central moment of every initiation is represented by the ceremony symbolizing the death of the novice and his return to the fel-

---

[4]*Anatomy of Criticism: Four Essays* (New York, 1968 [1957]), p. 187. It may be worthwhile to recall Frye's counsel on the limited explanatory power of mythic parallels: ". . . any attempt to prove that a romantic story does or does not resemble, say, a solar myth, or that its hero does or does not resemble a sun-god, is likely to be a waste of time. . . . If the hero of a romance returns from a quest disguised, flings off his beggar's rags, and stands forth in the resplendent scarlet cloak of the prince, we do not have a theme which has necessarily descended from a solar myth; we have the literary device of displacement. . . . If we are reading the story as critics, with an eye to structural principles, we shall make the association, because the solar analogy explains why the hero's act is an effective and conventional incident" (p. 188). It goes

lowship of the living. But he returns to life a new man, assuming another mode of being. Initiatory death signifies the end at once of childhood, of ignorance, and of the profane condition."[5]

Not only is the initiation rite a reenactment and reaffirmation of the death and rebirth of a god, king, or hero, but it transmits to the novice the meaning, value, and perhaps, in intention, even the immortality—of the original mythic event: "By virtue of this ritual . . . death, too, is itself sanctified, that is, is charged with a religious value. Death is valuated as an essential moment in the existence of the Supernatural Being. By dying ritually, the initiate shares in the supernatural condition of the founder of the mystery. Through this valuation, death and initiation become interchangeable. And this, in sum, amounts to saying that concrete death is finally assimilated to a transition rite toward a higher condition." Whether or not Eliade is justified in ascribing an impulse toward transcendence to all such rituals and mythologies, there is an equivalent of this religious ethos in *The Voyage Out*. The focus of the novel toward the heroine's death is not a denial of her initiation but a confirmation of it. Her death is not to be seen merely as the entry of the absurd which cuts off the steady development of the heroine but as the last and highest stage of that development itself. It is not necessary to regard Rachel's death as "sanctified" or to guarantee its issuance in immortality to see it as part of a transition toward a "higher condition," a final unfolding of potentiality, a refinement of consciousness. In this sense, Rachel's "death and initiation become interchangeable," and the tragic conclusion of the novel is elided with its romantic treatment of her adventures and development.

No one would claim that Rachel Willoughby is to be regarded as a subject for literal initiation, involving a confirmation of her standing in the tribe; she is no primitive in modern dress, repeating the age-old mysteries of temporary segregation, moon-identification, and sexual purification. Yet such analogues do not seem entirely unrelated to a novel which moves not merely to a tropical country but into what is still the most unexplored of regions, to an avowal of love in a dark jungle forest, and to direct encounter with a native village at the farthest point of a "voyage out."

without saying that this is as much a statement of the usefulness of mythic interpretation as it is a put-down of its excesses. The quotation from Frye in the text below is from p. 220.

[5]*Rites and Symbols of Initiation: The Mysteries of Birth and Rebirth*, trans. Willard Trask (New York, 1965 [1958]), p. xil. Quotations below are from pp. 131 and 42, respectively.

The symbolic burden of the river voyage is introduced as early as the second chapter in a description of Helen Ambrose during the ocean crossing:

She chose a thread from the varied tangle that lay in her lap, and sewed red into the bark of a tree, or yellow into the river torrent. She was working at a great design of a tropical river running through a tropical forest, where spotted deer would eventually browse upon masses of fruit, bananas, oranges, and giant pomegranates, while a troop of naked natives whirled darts into the air. Between the stitches she looked to one side and read a sentence about the Reality of Matter, or the Nature of Good. (30)

The fact that Helen is reading Moore's *Principia Ethica*, with its corrosive treatment of traditional metaphysics, does not conflict with the impression of philosophical weight in her embroidery. The primitive setting with river, fruit, and deer is linked with a violent scene of natives in arms to compose a picture of some comprehensiveness: it is "a great design," suggesting a generalized image of nature and society. We are thus early given a symbolic model or map of the estate of life and death to which the heroine gradually becomes privy in the course of her growth.

A closer approach to the significance of the primal forest and river occurs when the band of tourists makes an ascent of Monte Rosa. With the progressive distancing of this elevation ("Higher and higher they went, becoming separated from the world" [150]), they achieve a new perspective on the immediate country, on the earth in general, and on themselves: "Before them they beheld an immense space—grey sands running into forest, and forest merging into mountains, and mountains washed by air, the infinite distances of South America. A river ran across the plain, as flat as the land, and appearing quite as stationary. The effect of so much space was at first rather chilling. They felt themselves very small, and for some time no one said anything" (153). Given this enlarged perspective on nature and man, we can assess the mountaintop revelation as yielding access to the significant and the perdurable in reality, if not to the numinous and "wholly other" which initiates have perceived on mountains. The chosen members of the group are here made ready to pursue a deeper penetration by way of the river.

The plan for a river journey is, indeed, an appropriate touristic enterprise, and in this context it can even be seen as a form of colonial exploration. It is described in a time scale based on earlier English explorations, a perspective which emphasizes the endurance of the land and river beyond historical change:

6

Since the time of Elizabeth very few people had seen the river, and nothing had been done to change its appearance from what it was to the eyes of the Elizabethan voyagers. The time of Elizabeth was only distant from the present time by a moment of space compared with the ages which had passed since the water had run between those banks, and the green thickets swarmed there, and the small trees had grown to huge wrinkled trees in solitude. Changing only with the change of the sun and the clouds, the waving green mass had stood there for century after century, and the water had run between its banks ceaselessly. . . . (323)

Just as in the previous passage the sublimity of space awes the beholder, now the intimation of infinite time comes forward with similar effect. The inevitable association of the *panta rei* theme with the river is not allowed to dominate the scene, for the stronger note is the permanence of the land beside the passing water.

The journey brings the civilized group out of a stable condition and into another system of experience; it creates a form of ritual isolation in which profound changes can occur. The account of Terence Hewet, for example, mingles his falling in love with his movement in space, so that his journey into the jungle and into a special state of mind are made one:

In some strange way the boat became identified with himself, and... it [was] useless for him to struggle any longer with the irresistible force of his own feelings. He was drawn on and on away from all he knew, slipping over barriers and past landmarks into unknown waters as the boat glided over the smooth surface of the river. In profound peace, enveloped in deeper unconsciousness than had been his for many nights, he lay on deck watching the tree-tops change their position slightly against the sky, and arch themselves, and sink and tower huge, until he passed from seeing them into dreams where he lay beneath the shadow of vast trees, looking up into the sky. (326)

As Hewet moves "from all he knew" into "profound peace," "deeper unconsciousness," and dreams of doing what he is in fact doing, he becomes open to the natural world, to another person, and to the underlying rhythm of life and death.

As Rachel and Terence walk off into the jungle, with an admonitory "Beware of snakes" from his friend Hirst (330), they enter a realm made significant by readily recognized *topoi* of the Garden (and also by underwater associations to be discussed below):

As they passed into the depths of the forest the light grew dimmer, and the noises of the ordinary world were replaced by those creaking and sighing sounds which suggest to the traveller in a forest that he is walking at the bottom of the sea. The path narrowed and turned; it was hedged in by dense

7

creepers which knotted tree to tree, and burst here and there into star-shaped crimson blossoms. . . . The vast green light was broken here and there by a round of pure yellow sunlight which fell through some gap in the immense umbrella of green above, and in these yellow spaces crimson and black butterflies were circling and settling. Terence and Rachel hardly spoke. (331)

As will be seen repeatedly in Woolf's work, the butterfly and moth are associated with the human soul in an emblem of long tradition, though with a burden of personal associations that will be described in connection with *Jacob's Room*. Here the appearance of butterflies serves to focus the scene's significance: this is a primal garden in which two sexes meet and, as in the beginning, discover their mutual destiny. The encounter is thus established not merely as a pure union of souls but as a repetition of the mythical behavior of the race's heroic models. As in Eden, the initiation into sexual life has its consequences in bringing death into the world, for Rachel apparently contracts her fatal disease at this point: "She appeared to be very tired. Her cheeks were white" (333). The scene comes about as a fulfillment of a previous intimation, when Rachel had asked, "What is it to be in love?" in the presence of a great yellow butterfly. "Hypnotised by the wings of the butterfly, and awed by the discovery of a terrible possibility in life" (207), she has anticipated, and now finds, her own mortality in the midst of love and joy.

The heightened rhetoric and wide reference of the scene are dissipated with the lovers' return to the group and the continuation of their voyage but emerge again at their entry into the native village, "the goal of their journey" (348). The natives are rendered with anthropologically sophisticated restraint but with suggestions of mysteriousness that point to a further dimension in the scene:

The women took no notice of the strangers, except that their hands paused for a moment and their long narrow eyes slid round and fixed upon them with the motionless inexpressive gaze of those removed from each other far far beyond the plunge of speech. . . . When sweetmeats were offered them [the visitors], they put out great red hands to take them, and felt themselves treading cumbrously like tightcoated soldiers among these soft instinctive people. But soon the life of the village took no notice of them; they had become absorbed into it. . . . Peaceful, and even beautiful at first, the sight of the women, who had given up looking at them, made them now feel very cold and melancholy. (348–49)

Again an encounter with the structures of nature and society in the tropics yields an intimation of an ongoing and enduring life, but now the revelation serves to exclude the observers, who are "absorbed" but not assimilated into the native community.[6] Although the journey to the native society is thus a partial enactment of the patterns of initiation, affording another moment of access to the enduring rhythm of life, even the specially favored observers are not allowed to master that rhythm themselves. Their sense of standing outside the tribal life thus sharpened, they quickly withdraw from the village and the chapter closes with a summary account of the return trip.

□

Although the journey up the river leads at least two of the characters to a heightened awareness of the world and of each other, a development which I have called a form of initiation and which I have described by drawing on mythological and ritual analogues, it cannot be concluded from the river and jungle scenes alone that an actual movement from one condition to another takes place. The metaphysical education of which I have spoken takes in a much larger succession of scenes and may be considered the major action of the novel as a whole. The first change in Rachel's consciousness occurs when the ship puts out to sea and her perspective can take in all of England (and even entire continents):

Not only did it appear to them to be an island, and a very small island, but it was a shrinking island in which people were imprisoned. . . . Finally, when the ship was out of sight of land, it became plain that the people of England were completely mute. The disease attacked other parts of the earth; Europe shrank, Asia shrank, Africa and America shrank, until it seemed doubtful whether the ship would ever run against any of those wrinkled little rocks again. (29)

The effect of this metaphoric distancing, from a national to a global perspective, is to render the observer not so much international in attitude as newly free:

. . . an immense dignity had descended upon her [the ship]; she was an inhabitant of the great world, which has so few inhabitants, travelling all day across an empty universe, with veils drawn before her and behind. . . .

---

[6]The flatness of this anticlimax is rendered in a strikingly similar way in Claude Lévi-Strauss, *Tristes tropiques* (Paris, 1955), pp. 297–98. In this passage the anthropologist describes his arrival at a Tupi village in Brazil after a river journey: "Pourtant, cette aventure commencée dans l'enthousiasme me laissait une impression de vide. . . . Que je parvienne seulement à les deviner et ils se dépouilleront de leur étrangeté; j'aurais aussi bien pu rester dans mon village. Ou que, comme ici, ils la conservent: et alors, elle ne me sert à rien, puisque je ne suis pas même capable de saisir ce qui la fait telle. . . ."

The sea might give her death or some unexampled joy, and none would know of it. She was a bride going forth to her husband, a virgin unknown of men; in her vigour and purity she might be likened to all beautiful things, for as a ship she had a life of her own. (29)

While this is spoken of the *Euphrosyne*, its obvious anticipation of Rachel's career makes the images of entering a new world and accession to a higher life apply to her as well. And Rachel is later specifically identified with the ship and its symbolic properties: "She became a ship passing in the night—an emblem of the loneliness of human life . . ." (99). Thus, the voyager acquires in the course of the voyage certain properties of life—both the perspectival freedom and the lonely moribundity—which she is fully to reach only at the end of her journey in the passage to death.

The next stage of Rachel's development is reached on coming to South America. In the changed climate and surroundings, Rachel's mind expands in the first of what can be called her "moments of being" (analogous to similar states of mind in the short story that bears that phrase as its title):

The morning was hot, and the exercise of reading left her mind contracting and expanding like the mainspring of a clock. The sounds in the garden outside joined with the clock, and the small noises of midday, which one can ascribe to no definite cause, in a regular rhythm. It was all very real, very big, very impersonal, and after a moment or two she began to raise her first finger and to let it fall on the arm of her chair so as to bring back to herself some consciousness of her own existence. She was next overcome by the unspeakable queerness of the fact that she should be sitting in an armchair, in the morning, in the middle of the world. Who were the people moving in the house—moving things from one place to another? And life, what was that? It was only a light passing over the surface and vanishing, as in time she would vanish, though the furniture in the room would remain. Her dissolution became so complete that she could not raise her finger any more, and sat perfectly still, listening and looking always at the same spot. It became stranger and stranger. She was overcome with awe that things should exist at all. . . . The things that existed were so immense and so desolate. . . . She continued to be conscious of these vast masses of substance for a long stretch of time, the clock still ticking in the midst of the universal silence. (144–45)

In this remarkable record of subjectivity, Rachel first synthesizes the activity around her into a "regular rhythm" and then assimilates it to her own mental rhythm, marked by the "contracting and expanding" assimilations of reading. Though partially fused with the world around her, she maintains by an effort of will the distinction between the "very big, very impersonal" world out there and the self that can

10

move and feel its own finger. She then discovers the fact of her own existence with fresh force, and her new sense of ego reduces the world to an arrangement around her: she is "in the middle of the world." But she perceives both spatial movement and a temporal dimension by noticing the passage of light in that world and thereby intuits the similarity of her own passage and disappearance to the light's. This thought leads to a "dissolution" in which the conscious observer relaxes, the world around becomes "stranger and stranger," and the only emotion is that awe "that things should exist at all" which Heidegger calls the beginning of philosophy. Finally, the external world returns in its simplest rhythm, the ordinary pulse of clock time: ". . . the clock still ticking in the midst of the universal silence." Coming back to ordinary reality, Rachel may be said to have achieved not merely a flash of insight but a mode of perception which can comprehend "vast masses of substance," the "immense" and "desolate" existence of things, and "the universal silence."

Rachel's movement of consciousness in this exotic setting is extreme but not unusual, for the other English at the hotel experience something of the kind in their two communal experiences, the mountain trip and the dance. At the first: "Before them they beheld an immense space—grey sands running into forest, and forest merging in mountains, and mountains washed by air, the infinite distances of South America. . . . The effect of so much space was at first rather chilling. They felt themselves very small, and for some time no one said anything" (153). This initial tendency to be overawed by the spectacle of the world is partially overcome at the dance; significantly, they are transformed with the help of Rachel herself through the medium of her art, the piano. She turns from dance tunes to Bach: "They sat very still as if they saw a building with spaces and columns succeeding each other rising in the empty space. Then they began to see themselves and their lives, and the whole of human life advancing very nobly under the direction of the music. They felt themselves ennobled, and when Rachel stopped playing they desired nothing but sleep" (196). Although this enlargement of perspective is only partly successful, the ordinary men and women of the hotel crowd preferring sleep under the burden of such consciousness, its achievement bears witness to Rachel's heightened powers of communicating something of her vision—employing the esthetic resources of Bach, to be sure.

Rachel achieves a further stage of enlargement under the influence of her love for Hewet. After the dismal chapel service and a series of uninvited intimate revelations in the rooms of women at the hotel, she flees to the end of a hallway and looks out a high window:

She had now reached one of those eminences, the result of some crisis, from which the world is finally displayed in its true proportions. She disliked the look of it immensely—churches, politicians, misfits, and huge impostures. . . . Vaguely seeing that there were people down in the garden beneath she represented them as aimless masses of matter, floating hither and thither, without aim except to impede her. What were they doing, those other people in the world?

"Nobody knows," she said. The force of her rage was beginning to spend itself, and the vision of the world which had been so vivid became dim.

"It's a dream," she murmured. . . .

. . . She went out of the hall door, and, turning the corner of the hotel, found herself among the people whom she had seen from the window. But owing to the broad sunshine after shaded passages, and to the substance of living people after dreams, the group appeared with startling intensity, as though the dusty surface had been peeled off everything, leaving only the reality and the instant. It had the look of a vision printed on the dark at night. (315–16)

The effect of her withdrawal from ordinary people and their conventional behavior is to see them first as artificial and unreal, then as mere matter aimlessly moving, but finally as realities in their own right, for she seizes them more vividly than ever before. So intense is this grasp of ordinary things that it comes with both the shock of waking and the strangeness of a dream: the surface is peeled off, "leaving only the reality and the instant," but at the same time the world wears the appearance of "a vision printed on the dark."

The penultimate moment of intense consciousness occurs as Rachel travels up the river: "As they passed into the depths of the forest the light grew dimmer, and the noises of the ordinary world were replaced by those creaking and sighing sounds which suggest to the traveller in a forest that he is walking at the bottom of the sea" (331).[7]

[7]The image of undersea life is used a number of times in this text to suggest a state of consciousness outside the ordinary, yet offering an eerie simulacrum of it. In shipboard conversation, Mr. Pepper describes "the white, hairless, blind monsters lying curled on the ridges of sand at the bottom of the sea, which would explode if you brought them to the surface" (18); Mr. Grice, the steward on the *Euphrosyne*, shows Mrs. Dalloway his collection of "treasures which the great ocean had bestowed upon him—pale fish in greenish liquids, blobs of jelly with streaming tresses, fish with lights in their heads, they lived so deep" (57); reacting to a storm at sea, "after their view of the strange under-world, inhabited by phantoms, people began to live among tea-pots and loaves of bread with greater zest than ever" (80); exhausted after the ball, Rachel feels "like a fish at the bottom of the sea" (198); finally, in her illness, "She saw nothing and heard nothing but a faint booming sound, which was the sound of the sea rolling over her head. While all her tormentors thought that she was dead, she was not dead, but curled up at the bottom of the sea. There she lay, sometimes seeing darkness, sometimes light, while every now and then some one turned her over at the bottom of the sea" (416).

In the perfect equality of love, Rachel draws Hewet into her mode of vision, returning to the heightened perception she had achieved at the hotel: "Up through the sultry southern landscape they saw the world they knew appear clearer and more vividly than it had ever appeared before. As upon that occasion at the hotel when she had sat in the window, the world once more arranged itself beneath her gaze very vividly and in its true proportions" (344). In this shared vision, they are able to distinguish some of their finer perceptions, such as the identification of self with light which Rachel had made in her first moment of vision:

> "Does it ever seem to you, Terence, that the world is composed entirely of vast blocks of matter, and that we're nothing but patches of light—" she looked at the soft spots of sun wavering over the carpet and up the wall— "like that?"
>
> "No," said Terence, "I feel solid; immensely solid; the legs of my chair might be rooted in the bowels of the earth." (358)

He will learn, in due course, that he is not—and Rachel is not—merely solid matter but temporal and ephemeral, like light.

Rachel reaches her final stage of vision when she expresses a desire to go beyond her intensified awareness of the given world, to get behind it to a sight of some other world, presumably the realm of death, which is approximated by the images of life at the bottom of the sea. The only alternative to passage further into the realm of death is a return voyage to England, marriage, and life, and Rachel contemplates the two alternatives: "What's so detestable in this country . . . is the blue—always blue sky and blue sea. It's like a curtain—all the things one wants are on the other side of that. I want to know what's going on behind it. . . . Just by going on a ship we cut ourselves off entirely from the rest of the world. I want to see England there—London there—all sorts of people—why shouldn't one? why should one be shut up all by oneself in a room?" (369-70). The thought is confused, or confusedly expressed, but she seems to be after a vision of England and ordinary life under the aspect of the undersea, deathlike consciousness she has been acquiring. In her meditation, the horizon becomes a boundary or "curtain" which marks the furthest extent of her vision of the world; she hopes to look beyond it to another order of being and back again from that perspective.

It is this tendency toward abstraction from life that Hewet senses in Rachel as it alienates her from him: "She seemed to be able to cut herself adrift from him, and to pass away to unknown places where she had no need of him" (370). When he expresses his sense of alienation, she is willing to acknowledge it: "It seemed to her now that what he was saying was perfectly true, and that she wanted many more things than the love of one human being—the sea, the sky. She turned again and looked at the distant blue, which was so smooth and serene where the sky met the sea; she could not possibly want only one human being" (370). Under these circumstances, it seems inevitable that she pass beyond their relationship to some realm of her own at the horizon of life—perhaps the state that is meant by the word "death." In this sense, the title of *The Voyage Out* extends its reference beyond the conventional meaning—an outward-bound passage—to suggest the course of Rachel's life as a voyage out of life toward death.

□

Although it is structured on the archetypes of journey and initiation, *The Voyage Out* is not a mythological novel of the kind that was to become a major strain in modern fiction—a strain to which later Woolf fictions are linked. The elementary narrative of a heroine's development is here given greater universality by being treated as a journey in quest; her social maturation and growth of consciousness are informed by their relations with widespread patterns of initiation; and her experience of love and death is heightened by being set in a landscape of primal nature and primitive man. But the expansion provided by these symbolic elements is not by itself sufficient to lift the novel from its predominantly realistic and even satirical mode. Superimposed upon this conventional imitation-of-life, there runs a tissue of quotations from literary works of all sorts, which continually counterpoints the themes of love and death.

As much as any of the fictions to follow in the Woolf canon, this is a literary work about a literary world; literary taste forms a part of the substance of its characters, an index in its narrative mode of portraying them, and an aspect of the author's point of view on the world. The array of literary quotations is, moreover, significant of one of the work's structural themes. In its treatment of a young girl's education, *The Voyage Out* provides her with a short course in Western literature, thereby embodying her cultural as well as emotional growth. Much of the conversation on ship and at the villa is concerned with questions of what to read, what to make of one's reading, and what value to assign to one's books. Indeed, the choice of reading matter becomes an index of character, as the major and minor characters at the villa and hotel give accounts of their literary taste and experience. They range from the omnivorous Miss Allan, marshaling stock phrases to compose her survey of English literary history, to the iconoclastic Mrs. Flushing, who remains aloof from the literary chitchat until Hirst shows her a scurrilous passage of Swinburne.

Beyond displaying the range of middle-class literary taste, the literary objects examined by the characters repeatedly engage the central themes of the novel—love and death. In the course of her reaction to these quoted texts, the heroine undergoes a gradual adjustment of sensibility. The first of Rachel's readings to figure in this way is from a translation of *Tristan und Isolde*:

> "In shrinking trepidation
> His shame he seeks to hide
> While to the king his relation
> He brings the corpse-like Bride.
> Seems it so senseless what I say?"

She cried that it did and threw down the book. (33)[8]

Rachel is not reacting merely to the inept translation but to the exaggerated postures of the romantic legend, popularized at the time by Wagner's opera. (A performance of *Tristan* at Covent Garden figures similarly in *Jacob's Room*.) In her rejection of the legend's grand passion, duplicity, and morbidity, all hinted in this quotation, Rachel also rejects the Wagnerian score, which she has been practicing (48). Her preference is for strictly classical works thereafter, culminating in her performance of Bach at the ballroom scene.

A distaste for the ethos (and accompanying music) of *Tristan* is not peculiar to the heroine; it is shared by Clarissa Dalloway, whose first conversation with Rachel takes up this very subject. Mrs. Dalloway begins her approach to Rachel by picking out some of the themes from the opera score, then goes into raptures about Bayreuth, but concludes by scorning other people's ecstasies over Wagner ("I don't think music's altogether good for people . . ." [49]). It might be possible to equate Rachel's or Clarissa's responses with the criticism that Denis de Rougemont makes of the legend's correlation of love and death, but even without this, something more seems at work in this dialogue than a sample of current attitudes to art. De Rougemont emphasizes the tale's origins in Manichean, Gnostic, and Cathar dualisms which venerate love above all and yet consign it to a rejected world of the flesh, and he finds a reconciliation of this tension in the impulse toward a death-in-love as a withdrawal from the world.[9]

[8]The text is the same as that in the Metropolitan Opera edition of the libretto, which names no translator. The words are spoken "jeeringly" by Isolde of Tristan as he conducts her to King Mark in act 1, scene 2.

[9]Denis de Rougemont, *Love in the Western World*, trans. Montgomery Belgion (Garden City, N.Y., 1957 [1939]).

15

It is retrospectively easy to see Clarissa Dalloway, in this first version of the character, both attracted by but also ultimately drawing back from so decisive an emotional commitment and its implied rejection of the social world. It is also possible to see Rachel making uncertain movements of approach to and retreat from grand passion and life-denying surrender. But it will turn out that love and death are, at least for her, simultaneously achieved, and her rapture in the jungle may be seen as her moment of *ascesis*. In a way that strikingly resembles the use that Eliot in *The Waste Land* and Joyce in *Finnegans Wake* were later to make of the Tristan theme, Woolf manages to scorn the *Liebestod* motif and affirm it, too. (And this having-it-both-ways is in keeping with the contradictory impulses conveyed by the legend.)

To return to Rachel's reading tastes: she drops *Tristan* only to pick "Cowper's Letters, the classic prescribed by her father which had bored her" (33), but this reversion to paternal paths is soon ended. She turns to *Wuthering Heights* (61, 83), like *Tristan* a tale of love impossible under the conditions of earthly life and fulfilling itself only in death but one mediated by a more complex perspective. Mrs. Dalloway next exposes Rachel to another version of transcendence in death, Shelley's "Adonais," quoting from lines 352–56:

> "He has outsoared the shadow of our night,
> Envy and calumny and hate and pain—
> . . . .
> Can touch him not and torture not again
> From the contagion of the world's slow strain." (62)

(She later remembers part of the omitted line 354: "Unrest which men miscall delight" [63].) Clarissa's attitude to the poem and the rejection of the world emphasized in these lines is abruptly registered: "How divine!—and yet what nonsense! . . . I always think it's *living*, not dying, that counts" (62). But she had previously said, "I feel that there's almost everything one wants in 'Adonais' " (45). These conflicting attitudes toward life and death, social engagement and chaste isolation, are to be writ large in the fiction Woolf was subsequently to write around this character. (The poem also serves as a touchstone for Richard Dalloway's characterization, as he responds to his wife's rapture: ". . . whenever I hear of Shelley I repeat to myself the words of Matthew Arnold, 'What a set! What a set!' " [45].) The effect of these attitudes on Rachel is less clear; she does not take to reading Shelley, but the pairing of love and death is further established as a prefiguration of her career.

The heroine does, however, respond to another of Mrs. Dalloway's suggestions: to read Jane Austen. Rachel is initially prejudiced

16

against her as being "so like a tight plait" (62), and she cannot be much encouraged by Dalloway's priggish pronouncement that Austen is "incomparably the greatest female writer we possess . . . and for this reason: she does not attempt to write like a man" (66) (moreover, Clarissa immediately reveals that "she always sends [him] to sleep!" [67]). But while Dalloway dozes off after a few lines of *Persuasion* are quoted (67), Rachel's attention is aroused. Her subsequent dalliance with Dalloway is accompanied by his recommendation to read Burke, just before he snatches a kiss from her (84), and a similar irony accompanies Clarissa's parting gift of her copy of *Persuasion* as the Dalloways leave the ship (87).

It does not appear that Rachel reads the novel, although the charm of the Dalloways persists and leads her to ask her uncle for Burke's "Speech on the American Revolution" (202). The shift in her taste toward the eighteenth century is abetted by meeting St. John Hirst, who recommends Gibbon and sends her the first volume of the *Decline and Fall* (203), but she concludes that she has been "horribly, oh infernally, damnably bored" (251). Meanwhile, she has picked up other works of fiction (Balzac's *Cousine Bette* [202]) and drama (Ibsen's *Doll's House* [142-43]), but the sum of her literary experience is taken when she brings it to bear on her first romantic challenge: ". . . none of the books she read, from *Wuthering Heights* to *Man and Superman*, and the plays of Ibsen, suggested from their analysis of love that what their heroines felt was what she was feeling now" (272).

While Rachel develops her literary taste, in line with her larger course of development, the cultural atmosphere around her remains fairly constant. It is the culture of the English middle classes, classicist in its better-educated strata, broadly based on the English authors, and popular in its everyday tastes. From the outset of the voyage, we are greeted by the marks of high culture on the prow of the ship: the *Euphrosyne*—one of the Graces, whose name is associated with happiness. Shipboard conversation is dominated by the presence of the professional classicist Ridley Ambrose—who is working on an edition of Pindar that has reached at least three volumes and who has also published a "commentary on Aristotle" (20)—and his Cambridge crony, the apparently nonprofessional scholar Pepper, who "devoted January to Petronius, February to Catullus, March to the Etruscan vases perhaps" (21).

Their learning is not a salient element in the novel, except at one point: when the Dalloways come aboard and are introduced to the company, Clarissa puts on her little act of admiration for the classics, and Pepper strikes up with a quotation from the *Antigone* (46). In Jebb's translation these lines (332-37) from the famous chorus on man run: "Wonders are many, and none is more wonderful than man; the power that crosses the white sea, driven by the stormy south wind, making a path under surges that threaten to engulf him." The lines are well chosen, of course, as a snatch of mellifluous Greek and have an appropriate relation to the setting in which the party of sea voyagers finds itself. But Pepper does not go on to quote the rest of the chorus (which the same editor summarizes): "Man is master of sea and land; he subdues all other creatures; he has equipped his life with all resources, except a remedy for death." (At the end of this chorus, Antigone is brought in to face Creon and eventually her doom.[10]) For those on ship or off with a knowledge of the chorus's import, it would act as a premonition of an ultimate fatality, as well as a congratulation on joining an adventurous voyage. To put the matter in thematic terms, the citation from the Greek serves to universalize the novel's action as a voyage of human enterprise and a passage in man's mortality.[11]

The classics figure in the culture of the younger generation of characters but are marked by the special features of contemporary taste. St. John Hirst indulges in the turn-of-the-century appeal to the classics for sensuous and intellectual values free of traditional Christian trappings (what Stephen Dedalus calls "new paganism"). We find Hirst at chapel service with Swinburne's translation of Sappho, and he manages to interest the unconventional Mrs. Flushing in it: "She gulped down the Ode to Aphrodite during the Litany . . ." (280) (Ambrose has less success in recommending the *Symposium* to her, perhaps because the subject is man's independence of women [235]). Hirst's reading of Gibbon moves in the same direction and helps to fix this as an early version of Woolf's later portrayals of Lytton Strachey, whose tastes and idiosyncrasies ran on similar lines.

For the budding novelist, Hewet, on the other hand, poetry is grist for his mill, and we find him reading Hardy, Whitman, and Milton, each with reference to his personal preoccupations. He first quotes the final stanza of Hardy's "He Abjures Love," from *Time's Laughingstocks*:

> "I speak as one who plumbs
> Life's dim profound,
> One who at length can sound

---

[10]For Woolf's persistent return to the image of Antigone, see Jean Guiguet, *Virginia Woolf and Her Works*, trans. Jean Stewart (London, 1965 [1962]), pp. 419 and 464. The subject will come up again in discussing *The Years*.

[11]A similar prefiguration of death in a literary allusion occurs on the ocean voyage, as the steward, Mr. Grice, quotes "Full fathom five thy father lies" (59).

> Clear views and certain.
> But—after love what comes?
> A scene that lours
> A few sad vacant hours
> And then, the Curtain." (127)

Hewet is a young man weighing his hopes and prospects in love, and the Hardian bitterness of abjuration comes readily to him, even though not yet tested by experience. But there is also in the quotation a premonition of death and the emptiness of life after love (in the poem, to be sure, it is the death of the abjuring lover rather than that of the beloved which is anticipated). Moreover, a number of earlier lines that Hewet fails to quote have a subsequent relevance to his (or his beloved's) life and death: "But lo, love beckoned me./ And I was bare,/And poor, and starved, and dry,/And fever-stricken." We need not ascribe prescience to Hewet, in selecting this poem, if we are to grasp its significance; it repeatedly conjoins the notes of love and death in literary form before they are brought together in the lovers' experience.

Terence's next burst of poetry occurs on the river journey:

> "Whoever you are holding me now in [your] hand,
> Without one thing all will be useless." (327)

This is Whitman, giving fair warning to the universe of his ineradicable individuality—"I give you fair warning before you attempt me further,/I am not what you supposed, but far different"—in a poem from *Calamus* that draws its title from the first line (which Terence misquotes by adding the bracketed word indicated above). Terence presumably would refer this evocation of the one-thing-needful to Rachel, of whom he is thinking while reading, but in the context of the novel's journeyings it would seem to have a range of reference commensurate with Whitman's own: "Carry me when you go forth over land or seas." Hewet has been experiencing a sense of passage from the known to the unknown, finding it "useless for him to struggle any longer with the irresistible force of his own feelings. He was drawn on and on away from all he knew . . ." (326). The poetic utterance here serves to underscore a movement of heightened transaction with life to which Hewet, like Rachel, is led in the course of his journey by the force of love and the hovering presence of death.

The final expression of Hewet's poetic strain is his use of a famous lyric in the course of his wooing of Rachel. He reads to her from "Comus":

19

"There is a gentle nymph not far from hence,
That with moist curb sways the smooth Severn stream.
Sabrina is her name, a virgin pure . . ." (398)

After quoting this description of the tutelary deity, he goes on to read the song that calls her forth in the masque:

"Sabrina fair,
    Listen where thou art sitting
    Under the glassy, cool, translucent wave,
. . . .
    Goddess of the silver lake,
    Listen and save!" (399)

In the ongoing action of the novel, Rachel responds by noting the first signs of her illness: she feels hot, her head aches, and she can hardly bring herself to the effort of interrupting the reading. In this context, then, the famous song points the irony of Rachel's demise: like the Lady of the masque, she has been a virgin wooed by a river, but instead of being aided by a divine force she goes down to her death.[12] The extended quotation (of which I have given only part) operates powerfully to generate the atmosphere of death itself, as couched in the imagery of underwater withdrawal recalled by Rachel in her feverish imaginings:

"Under the glassy, cool, translucent wave,
    In twisted braids of lilies knitting
    The loose train of thy amber dropping hair." (402)

Again literary quotation counterpoints the threnody that increasingly becomes the main motif of the text: Rachel's descent into death is rendered as a final immersion in the river of her journeying.

The final quotations of poetry are made by Ridley Ambrose and appear to be merely rhythmic aids to his pacing, while passing the time waiting for Rachel to die:

"Peor and Baalim
    Forsake their Temples dim,
        With that twice batter'd God of Palestine
    And mooned Astaroth—" (428)

These lines from Milton's ode "On the Morning of Christ's Nativity" (197-200) prove, however, not merely rhythmical (like the ballad he

[12]Harvena Richter also comments on this irony in *Virginia Woolf: The Inward Voyage* (Princeton, 1970), pp. 124-25, concluding: "At the novel's end, Rachel and Sabrina join as the sheets of her bed turn to water. . . . Sabrina, the water spirit, a lovely death-wish, has come for her." I do not identify Sabrina as an agent of mortality, and am therefore unpersuaded that the water-spirit is an active force in Rachel's undoing.

mouths on page 427) but functional. They refer to the triumph of the new dispensation over the pagan gods of the East, but the gospel comes into the present text at a singularly unconvincing moment, at the point of Rachel's demise. There is no hint of resurrection or of any other form of transcendence at the close of the fiction; the blank fact of death alone remains, as Hewet is led away from the dead body with which he had found himself in communication, and the rhythm of daily life picks up again at the hotel.

□

In a letter to Lytton Strachey, Woolf stated her intention for the conclusion of *The Voyage Out*:

What I wanted to do was to give the feeling of a vast tumult of life, as various and disorderly as possible, which should be cut short for a moment by death, and go on again—and the whole was to have a sort of pattern, and be somehow controlled. The difficulty was to keep any sort of coherence, —also to give enough detail to make the characters interesting—which Forster says I didn't do. I really wanted three volumes. Do you think it is impossible to get this sort of effect in a novel;—is the result bound to be too scattered to be intelligible? I expect one may learn to get more control in time.[13]

Yet she had already achieved one of the finest first works by any author, one which approaches the limits of art in its climactic scene:

Once he held his breath and listened acutely; she was still breathing; he went on thinking for some time; they seemed to be thinking together; he seemed to be Rachel as well as himself; and then he listened again; no, she had ceased to breathe. So much the better—this was death. It was nothing; it was to cease to breathe. It was happiness, it was perfect happiness. They had now what they had always wanted to have, the union which had been impossible while they lived. . . .

It seemed to him that their complete union and happiness filled the room with rings eddying more and more widely. He had no wish in the world left unfulfilled. They possessed what could never be taken from them. . . .

As he saw the passage outside the room, and the table with the cups and the plates, it suddenly came over him that here was a world in which he would never see Rachel again.

"Rachel! Rachel!" he shrieked, trying to rush back to her. But they prevented him, and pushed him down the passage and into a bedroom far from her room. Downstairs they could hear the thud of his feet on the floor, as he struggled to break free; and twice they heard him shout, "Rachel, Rachel!" (431–32)

---

[13]*Virginia Woolf and Lytton Strachey: Letters,* ed. Leonard Woolf and J. Strachey (London and Toronto, 1956), p. 57, 28 Feb. 1916.

night and day

"Words with short

wings for their heavy

body of meaning"

Night and Day (1919), Virginia Woolf's ostensibly conventional love story, discovers its mode of celebrating love in the comic—particularly the Shakespearian—tradition.[1] The winey spirit that pervades its lovers' illusions and transformations resembles that of the early comedies, while the mystic aura of its denouement is that of the late romances. When defining her sense of love, and contrasting it with that of the traditional psychological novel, Woolf opted for a mystery and vivacity akin to Shakespeare's:

The psychological novelist has been too prone to limit psychology to the psychology of personal intercourse; we long sometimes to escape from the incessant, the remorseless analysis of falling into love and falling out of love. . . . We long for some more impersonal relationship. We long for ideas, for dreams, for imaginations, for poetry.

And it is one of the glories of the Elizabethan dramatists that they give us this. The poet is always able to transcend the particularity of Hamlet's relation to Ophelia and to give us his questioning not of his own personal lot alone but of the state and being of all human life. In *Measure*

---

[1]Perhaps some of the *brio* of *Night and Day* derived from the author's response to her recent marriage. For other autobiographical aspects of the fiction, see Quentin Bell, *Virginia Woolf: A Biography* (London, 1972), I, 185-86 and II, 4 ff; also II, 9, where Leonard Woolf's similar fictional response to the marriage is described.

for Measure, for example, passages of extreme psychological subtlety are mingled with profound reflections, tremendous imaginations.[2]

Shakespeare's presence in the text—by direct reference, thematic derivation, and parodic echo—is strong enough to make this the most traditional work of an otherwise consistent experimentalist. Its traditionalism should not be seen as a return to the realistic conventions of nineteenth-century fiction; those who see it so may dismiss it as a relapse into a style that Woolf had already rejected instead of savoring its more radical reversion. We shall examine it as a systematic attempt to rework comic conventions when dealing with the generic themes of illusion and reality, the compact of lunatic, lover, and poet, and the miraculous transforming power of love. When we recall that among Woolf's nine fictions of substantial length are two other comic works which operate largely by literary parody on similar themes, it becomes clear that an important strain in Woolf's experimentalism was the parodic mode of her major contemporaries. She uses the past, including the literature of the past, for the purposes of ironic contrast, organizing mythos, and cultural integration. If *Orlando* and *Between the Acts* may be said to derive from the same literary impulses as *The Waste Land* and the *Cantos, Night and Day* will be found to anticipate them in the way that "Prufrock" and "Mauberly" prefigure their creators' later work. Such a view would assign this fiction a place in the Woolf canon more prominent than it has yet been accorded.[3]

It has been generally observed that the title establishes a duality between a night-world of love and imagination opposed to a day-world of contemporary reality. The fact that several Shakespearian comedies are organized around this polarity—with two of them incorporating the imagery of night in their titles—suggests that the fiction's dual structure is found rather than created, that the freely inventive character of the work is best seen as a manipulation of comic conventions. In other Woolf works, quotations from Shakespeare are made the focus of dramatic scenes, as with sonnet 98 in *To the Lighthouse,* or become thematic refrains by insistent repetition, as does the dirge

---

[2]"The Narrow Bridge of Art," *Collected Essays,* II, 225. This essay was published in 1927, but its general line, if not its detailed reference to Shakespeare, is anticipated in Woolf's numerous statements on modern fiction.

[3]Others have perceived the novel's relation to Shakespeare: Josephine O. Schaefer, *The Three-Fold Nature of Reality in the Novels of Virginia Woolf* (The Hague, 1965), p. 50, points out the affinity of its action to that of *Twelfth Night*; and Jean O. Love, *Worlds in Consciousness: Mythopoetic Thought in the Novels of Virginia Woolf* (Berkeley, Los Angeles and London, 1970), p. 118, remarks on Mrs. Hilbery's place in the tradition of the "wise fool."

from *Cymbeline* in *Mrs. Dalloway*. In *Night and Day*, no one Shakespearian element is allowed to predominate; even the plot has analogues in several of the plays.

The formula for the action is familiar; beginning with two young couples, we find one pair (Katharine Hilbery and William Rodney) unstably engaged and the other fractured by its relationship to the first (Mary Datchet loves Ralph Denham, but he, instead of returning her love, loves Katharine). Such an imbroglio can be manipulated in a number of ways, and the pattern Woolf chose was one that might be called the "shuffle": a new character is introduced, causing a realignment of relations, with one of the original members left out in the cold (in this case, Mary, partly through her own acceptance of the situation, when she rejects Ralph's proposal). In schematic form:

Part I   [Mary] Ralph   Katharine—William
Part II   Ralph—Katharine   William [Cassandra]

Although the basic movement of the action falls into two parts, the actual working of the plot breaks down into five "acts":

Chapters	*Climax*
I–XI	Katharine's acceptance of William's proposal
XII–XIX	Mary's refusal of Ralph
XX–XXV	Katharine and Ralph's friendship pact
XXVI–XXX	Their mutual declaration of love
XXXI–XXXIV	Their vision of ideal union

Although the distribution of chapters among these five acts is unequal, it should be noted that the length of the first two acts is almost equal to that of the last three, with about 270 pages in each half. The midpoint in the text falls at the transition from act two to act three at the critical moment of Mary's refusal of Ralph. The shuffle of lovers, involving the dropping of Mary and the addition of Cassandra, is free to begin at this central point.

More explicitly than in the geometrical arrangement of relationships and formal patterning of the plot, the presence of Shakespeare is felt throughout the text in a series of references to his life, works, and symbolic lordship over art and love. Not only Katharine's mother but her aunt, Mrs. Millicent Cosham, are his devotees. Their perpetual reference to him is initially placed within a satire of their late-Victorian upper-middle-class "arty" estheticism: Mrs. Cosham "carried her pocket Shakespeare about with her, and met life fortified by the words of the poets. How far she saw Denham, and how far she confused him with some hero of fiction, it would be hard to

say. Literature had taken possession even of her memories" (157).
Mrs. Cosham goes on to consult Ralph about "an obscure passage in
'Measure for Measure,' " reading out from her pocket volume:

> "*To be imprison'd in the viewless winds,*
> *And blown with restless violence round about*
> *The pendant world. . . .*" (159)

Meanwhile Ralph overhears a conversation that confirms Katharine's engagement to William. We find running through these apparently irrelevant literary punctuations of the main action a cumulative identification of Ralph with one variety of romantic hero. Here,
as he suffers the near-tragic emotions registered by the imprisoned
Claudio in his vision of death (act 3, scene 1, ll. 124–26), the comparison only slightly reduces Ralph's buffetings by love toward banality.
Shakespeare's imaginative and disturbed heroes are the models here,
much as Hamlet is for Stephen Dedalus in *Ulysses.*

A more complex response is generated by the more elaborate satire
of Mrs. Hilbery's devotion to Shakespeare. At first this motif is
limited to characterization, bolstering the impression of Mrs. Hilbery
as an ineffectual poetaster, busily failing to write the biography of
her father, the great poet "Richard Alardyce." As late as chapter
xxiv this characterization is maintained with amusing simplicity,
but at that point Mrs. Hilbery's significance begins to be complicated
through an account of her interest in Shakespeare:

Beginning with a perfectly frivolous jest, Mrs. Hilbery had evolved a theory
that Anne Hathaway had a way, among other things, of writing Shakespeare's sonnets; . . . she had come half to believe in her joke, which was, she
said, at least as good as other people's facts, and all her fancy for the time
being centered upon Stratford-on-Avon. She had a plan . . . for visiting
Shakespeare's tomb. Any fact about the poet had become, for the moment,
of far greater interest to her than the immediate present. . . . (322)[4]

That Mrs. Hilbery's idolatry carries a hint of the mystical as well
as a touch of the ridiculous is suggested by her wish to set up as a
prophet in the street, commanding: "People, read Shakespeare!"
(323). She then announces her own relationship to Shakespeare's
characters, thereby prefiguring her dramatic and mythic role in the
denouement of the love plot: "Your father's Hamlet, come to years
of discretion; and I'm—well, I'm a bit of them all; I'm quite a large bit
of the fool, but the fools in Shakespeare say all the clever things"
(324). As Mrs. Hilbery rattles on, trying to find a particular quotation

[4]The bizarre theory of the sonnets' authorship fixes Mrs. Hilbery's life model as Lady
Anne Ritchie, Woolf's aunt and Thackeray's daughter; see Bell, *Virginia Woolf*, i, 11.

in Shakespeare about love, her fantasy begins to invade the sober, rational mind of her daughter, so that Katharine starts to woolgather at her work and finds that "a quotation from Shakespeare would not have come amiss" (326).

The attribution of comic roles to the characters is temporarily suspended but not dissipated. In chapter xxxi, Mrs. Hilbery fulfills her intention to visit the Shakespeare country, explaining: " 'I've been dreaming all night of you and Shakespeare, dearest Katharine' " (453). When she returns at the final arrangement in the lovers' reshuffling, she does so surrounded with Shakespearian attributes which effectively transform her from an object of satire into a master of festivities. In archetypal terms, she plays the role of fairy godmother or cook-doctor who arranges the lovers' union and removes all obstacles in their path (in this case, primarily, the blocking action of her husband, who is disturbed by the lovers' departure from "civilization" in abruptly changing their engagements). Mrs. Hilbery's flower-laden entrance establishes her ritual role as sanctifier of fertility: " 'From Shakespeare's tomb!' exclaimed Mrs. Hilbery, dropping the entire mass upon the floor, with a gesture that seemed to indicate an act of dedication. Then she flung her arms wide and embraced her daughter" (508).

When Katharine expresses her distrust of the feelings she and Ralph share—"an illusion—as if when we think we're in love we make it up—we imagine what doesn't exist" (513)—Mrs. Hilbery explains with authority, " 'We have to have faith in our vision. . . . Believe me, Katharine, it's the same for every one—for me, too—for your father' " (513). In response to this manifestation of universal, if not divine, authority, "Katharine looked at her as if, indeed, she were some magician" (513). From this placement among the masters of festivity and magicians of transformation, Mrs. Hilbery returns to the comically realist mode as the scene closes: "She swept up her flowers, breathed in their sweetness, and, humming a little song about a miller's daughter, left the room" (514).

Mrs. Hilbery's regenerative comedy becomes an active force as she performs her office of bringing the lovers together—literally collecting them from various parts of London in her carriage. The process is accompanied by a ritualistic instruction in her mysterious doctrines: "She went on talking; she talked, it seemed to both the young men, to some one outside, up in the air. She talked about Shakespeare, she apostrophized the human race, she proclaimed the virtues of divine poetry, she began to recite verses which broke down in the middle" (520). Although the burden of the mystery is never made clear, it is nonetheless effective for her novitiates: "The gesture with which she dismissed him had a dignity that Ralph never forgot. She seemed to make him free with a wave of her hand to all that she possessed" (520). The fullest revelation of her tutelage is made when she croons over the united lovers:

Either Mrs. Hilbery was impervious to their discomfort, or chose to ignore it, or thought it high time that the subject was changed, for she did nothing but talk about Shakespeare's tomb. "So much earth and so much water and that sublime spirit brooding over it all," she mused, and went on to sing her strange, half-earthly song of dawns and sunsets, of great poets, and the unchanged spirit of noble loving which they had taught, so that nothing changes, and one age is linked with another, and no one dies, and we all meet in spirit, until she appeared oblivious of any one in the room. (526)

When Mr. Hilbery is finally reconciled to the shuffle of his daughter's engagements, this imaginative advance, too, is sanctioned by Shakespearian authority. As he comes upon the united lovers, his wife puts him in touch with the mood of the occasion by asking, "Oh, Trevor, please tell me, what was the date of the first performance of *Hamlet?*" (528). The practical effect of the question is to divert attention from personal life to literature, at which not only Hilbery but William Rodney is considerably more adept: "Rodney felt himself admitted once more to the society of the civilized and sanctioned by the authority of no less a person than Shakespeare himself. The power of literature, which had temporarily deserted Mr. Hilbery, now came back to him . . ." (528).

For these literati Shakespeare provides a set of verbal substitutes for direct participation in love, but for Katharine the effect is in line with the invasion of her life by the spirit of romantic comedy: "All this talk about Shakespeare had acted as a soporific, or rather as an incantation upon Katharine" (529). And so in their closing embrace, the lovers are surrounded by elements of an Elizabethan finale or masque: ". . . they had been borne on, victors in the forefront of some triumphal car, spectators of a pageant enacted for them, masters of life" (532). There is an even more marked acquisition of Shakespearian attributes as their thoughts turn to the future: " 'As you like,' she replied. . . . it seemed to her that the immense riddle was answered; the problem had been solved; she held in her hands for one brief moment the globe which we spend our lives in trying to shape, round, whole, and entire from the confusion of chaos" (533). Here the language and imagery of two of the best-known expressions in the tradition of romantic comedy are brought to the service of these modern lovers: the freedom of *As You Like It*, and the globe of Prospero's world-creating imagination.

Not only the persistent reference to Shakespeare, as the patron of comic vision and imaginative transformation by love, but a number of more general references to the Elizabethan stage add to the novel's buildup of a traditional mode. Two of the characters are formal students of the subject: Rodney, who presents a paper on "the Elizabethan use of metaphor in poetry," (47) with special reference to "Shakespeare's later use of imagery" (51); and Ralph's sister, Hester, who will talk on for hours "if you start her upon Elizabethan dramatists" (402). In other characters, Elizabethan qualities are the points of reference for personality traits, e.g., Henry Otway (Katharine's cousin and Cassandra's brother): "He had a fine head, the brow arched in the Elizabethan manner, but the gentle, honest eyes were rather sceptical than glowing with the Elizabethan vigour" (206). The most sweeping presence of the Elizabethan age is seen as a point of view or way of looking at the world, as with Katharine: "No doubt much of the furniture of [her dream] world was drawn directly from the past, and even from the England of the Elizabethan age. . . . It was a place where feelings were liberated from the constraint which the real world puts upon them" (145).

Like Shakespearian festive comedies in which an interruption of ordinary life allows the exceptional to emerge—or otherwise put, when the harsher realities of the daytime world are abandoned for the imaginative life of the night realm—*Night and Day* is a comedy of transformation under the spell of love's illusions. That these illusions are akin to the illusions fostered by art, and that illusions are not mere errors but a means of access to certain realities unavailable to ordinary experience, are themes in the novel owing their form and much of their substance to Shakespeare. And the trials, illuminations, and purgations worked out in the plot, the range in mode from social satire to mysterious suggestions of sorcery, the modeling on ritual and archetypal patterns, are means as appropriate for embodying these themes in fiction as they have been shown by modern criticism to be for the Shakespearian stage. Just as some of the more practical characters look askance at the star-struck behavior of the lovers, we too may find this the story of a "season of lunacy" (436)—yet all the more acceptable because of it. In this context, the fiction can be seen as adumbrating an apocalyptic vision of personal happiness, social unity, and racial regeneration at the ritual meal that celebrates the lovers' union: ". . . before the meal was far advanced civilization had triumphed, and Mr. Hilbery presided over a feast which came to wear more and more surely an aspect, cheerful, dignified, promising well for the future" (531).

□

"It was a Sunday evening in October," the text begins, "and in common with many other young ladies of her class, Katharine Hilbery was pouring out tea. Perhaps a fifth part of her mind was thus occupied, and the remaining parts leapt over the little barrier of day which interposed between Monday morning and this rather subdued moment, and played with the things one does voluntarily and normally in the daylight" (1). From the outset a distinction is drawn between two realms of day and night, but the distinction is not as simple as twelve-hour stretches of daylight and darkness. The "little barrier of day" between Monday morning and Sunday evening must indicate the entire week, the time of normal and voluntary activities; while the remaining time is Sunday night, the time that Katharine has already entered, when four-fifths of her mind lives in the realm of imaginative activity where one "plays" with "the things one does . . . in the daylight." For Katharine, this night-world is preeminently the world of mathematics, of abstract reason divorced from concrete objects, of pure possibility rather than limited actuality: "It was only at night, indeed, that she felt secure enough from surprise to concentrate her mind to the utmost. . . . She would not have cared to confess how infinitely she preferred the exactitude, the star-like impersonality, of figures to the confusion, agitation, and vagueness of the finest prose" (40).[5]

This withdrawal into imaginative life is also an escape from historical existence, not only from the exigencies of writing her grandfather's biography with her flighty mother, but from being a particular person and living among others: ". . . as the night was warm, she raised [the window] in order to feel the air upon her face, and to lose herself in the nothingness of night. . . . She cast her mind out to imagine an empty land where all this petty intercourse of men and women, this life made up of the dense crossings and entanglements of men and women, had no existence whatever" (106). The image of the isolated heroine who lives in her imaginings is a familiar one not only in Elizabethan romance but throughout the history of enchanted maidens; indeed, Katharine here resembles the Lady of Shalott: "At this moment she was much inclined to sit on into the night, spinning her light fabric of thoughts until she tired of their futility . . ." (108). There is even a touch of the Cinderella about her, especially in the association of periods of enchantment and grim reality with the

---

[5]The most inclusive treatment of the light-and-dark pattern, taking in the images of star, flame, sun (as in Ralph's drawing), etc., is Melinda F. Cumings, "Night and Day: Virginia Woolf's Visionary Synthesis of Reality," *Modern Fiction Studies*, XVIII (1972), 339–49.

imagery of night and day; as she puts it, "At twelve my horses turn into rats and off I go. The illusion fades. But I accept my fate. I make hay while the sun shines" (374-75).

Given such associations, it becomes less fanciful that Katharine be described at length in the act of stargazing:

> . . . she changed the focus of her eyes, and saw nothing but the stars.
>
> To-night they seemed fixed with unusual firmness in the blue, and flashed back such a ripple of light into her eyes that she found herself thinking that to-night the stars were happy. . . . And yet, after gazing for another second, the stars did their usual work upon the mind, froze to cinders the whole of our short human history, and reduced the human body to an apelike, furry form, crouching amid the brushwood of a barbarous clod of mud. This stage was succeeded by another, in which there was nothing in the universe save stars and the light of stars; as she looked up the pupils of her eyes so dilated with starlight that the whole of her seemed dissolved in silver and spilt over the ledges of the stars for ever and ever indefinitely through space. (204-5)

The ensuing conversation with her cousin Henry Otway develops some of the implications of her withdrawal from mundane affairs to a stellar distance. The mere presence of another person involves a loss of relation to the stars: ". . . directly Katharine got into his presence, and the sense of the stars dropped from her, she knew that any intercourse between people is extremely partial . . ." (207). She tries to express her Menippean perspective on man's finitude amid the infinite but is rebuffed: " 'When you consider things like the stars, our affairs don't seem to matter very much, do they?' she said suddenly. 'I don't think I ever do consider things like the stars,' Henry replied" (208). And he turns to jeering: " 'What about the stars?' he asked. 'I understand that you rule your life by the stars?' " (209).

Henry's implied criticism is, of course, right: looking at human life from the perspective of the cosmos is corrosive of personal relations, and Katharine's vision of the stars at Stogdon, the Otway home, is a step in her disengagement from her fiancé, which occurs during their visit there. Back in London, after some twists and turns in their relationship, her withdrawal into the imaginative realm is completed: "She looked away into the fire; it seemed to her that even physically they were now scarcely within speaking distance; and spiritually there was certainly no human being with whom she could claim comradeship; no dream that satisfied her as she was used to be satisfied; nothing remained in whose reality she could believe, save those abstract ideas—figures, laws, stars, facts, which she could hardly hold to for lack of knowledge and a kind of shame" (299). In this state of abstraction, Katharine identifies herself with the moon: ". . . all the time she was in fancy looking up through a telescope at white shadow-cleft disks which were other worlds, until she felt herself possessed of two bodies, one walking by the river with Denham, the other concentrated to a silver globe aloft in the fine blue space above the scum of vapours that was covering the visible world" (317). But a new element has been added to her perspective on the moon—or from the moon—and it returns her to earth again: "There was no reason, she assured herself, for this feeling of happiness; she was not free; she was not alone; she was still bound to earth by a million fibres; every step took her nearer home. Nevertheless, she exulted as she had never exulted before" (317). The new element is, of course, her growing love for Ralph; instead of projecting herself beyond the earth, she finds herself rooted to it. The imagination, which had taken her up in a night-world beyond the social realm, now finds itself occupied by another human being—"but that her condition was due to him . . . she had no consciousness at all" (317).

From this point on, Katharine's relation to her two worlds is less escapist, less magnetized in one direction: "Why, she reflected, should there be this perpetual disparity between the thought and the action, between the life of solitude and the life of society, this astonishing precipice on one side of which the soul was active and in broad daylight, on the other side of which it was contemplative and dark as night?" (358). The opposition between day and night is drawn now as an opposition not of crude fact and ethereal imagination but of two more nearly commensurate states of mind—the traditional terms for which, used by Woolf, are "active" and "contemplative." Given her new impatience with the sharp dichotomy between day and night, Katharine can begin to take another human being into her imagination, and she accepts Ralph's "terms of friendship" (359). Katharine continues her visions of night, stars, and moon, but they become associated with her love for Ralph and with a function of the imagination more creative than is allowed by a sharp cleavage between day and night.[6]

For Ralph Denham, the night is from the outset a more complicated medium than it is for Katharine. On the one hand, it invites him to "indulge" his imagination: ". . . reaching the Underground station, he

---

[6]An anticipation of this association of imaginative love with the figures of the night sky is given in an earlier quotation in the novel from Sidney's *Astrophel and Stella* (sonnet 31).

> "With how sad steps she climbs the sky,
> How silently and with how wan a face." (63)

(Sidney's text reads: "With how sad steps, O Moon, thou climb'st the skies!") The source is noted in Alice van Buren Kelley, *The Novels of Virginia Woolf: Fact and Vision* (Chicago and London, 1973), p. 46, where Sidney's Platonically two-tiered view of love is related to the novel.

blinked in the bright circle of light, glanced at his watch, decided that he might still indulge himself in darkness, and walked straight on" (17); on the other, it reveals a tawdry reality: ". . . in the night, bereft of life, bare places and ancient blemishes [of his house] were unpleasantly visible" (29). It is the former experience that prevails as his feeling for Katharine grows: "The night was very still, and on such nights, when the traffic thins away, the walker becomes conscious of the moon in the street, as if the curtains of the sky had been drawn apart, and the heaven lay bare, as it does in the country" (60). With the invasion of love into his imaginative life, the mixture of dream and reality in his night-world is polarized, so that day comes to be occupied by grubbing middle-class actualities, night by their opposite: ". . . he thought he could pride himself upon a life rigidly divided into the hours of work and those of dreams; the two lived side by side without harming each other" (130).

Ralph is wrong, of course. As his dream of Katharine comes to dominate his mind and as he finds himself separated from her by class and at least partially by temperament, his satisfaction with the night-and-day division of his life decreases. Katharine is no longer an incorporeal vision for him but a living being, in whom illusion and reality are thoroughly mingled: "His eyes were bright, and, indeed, he scarcely knew whether they beheld dreams or realities. . . . He stood watching her come towards him, and thought her more beautiful and strange than his dream of her . . . she overflowed the edges of the dream . . ." (150–51). His working day is no longer purely prosaic but is invaded by dreams and unfulfilled desires: "His brain worked incessantly, but his thought was attended with so little joy that he did not willingly recall it . . ." (165).

The sharp demarcation between day and night, dream and reality, thus eroded, a striking revelation comes to Ralph at about the midpoint of the novel. He is sitting with Mary in a tea shop at Lincoln (while both he and the Hilberys are paying Christmas visits in the region) when Katharine walks by on the street: "This sudden apparition had an extraordinary effect upon him. It was as if he had thought of her so intensely that his mind had formed the shape of her, rather than that he had seen her in the flesh outside in the street. And yet he had not been thinking of her at all. The impression was so intense that he could not dismiss it, nor even think whether he had seen her or merely imagined her" (242–43). This interwoven working of imagination and perception operates in a more pragmatic way for his companion: " 'Katharine Hilbery!' Mary thought, in an instant of blinding revelation; 'I've always known it was Katharine Hilbery!' She knew it all now" (243).

When Katharine enters the shop, the mingling of dream and reality becomes more intimate: "Thus confronted at a distance of only a few feet by the real body of the woman about whom he had dreamt so many million dreams, Ralph stammered; . . . but he was determined to face her and track down in the cold light of day whatever vestige of truth there might be in his persistent imaginations. . . . He realized suddenly that he had never seen her in the daylight before" (246). (The scene and its aftermath may have been inspired by the situations of Shakespearian characters who suddenly find their illusions of the beloved made real, as in *A Midsummer Night's Dream*.) Ralph interprets his experience not as a mere wish fulfillment but as an epistemological problem: he is startled by the involuntary, yet apparently effective, action of his imagination and determined to bring it into harmony with his daytime criteria of truth. The care with which the problem is stated indicates that Woolf conceived this comic scene as a phase in a drama of the imagination.

Ralph's epistemological probings lead him to be suspicious of his dream-workings, and in a moment of despair he concludes: "No good had ever come to him from Katharine; his whole relationship with her had been made up of dreams; and as he thought of the little substance there had been in his dreams he began to lay the blame of the present catastrophe upon his dreams" (262). But his declaration of love to Katharine is still based on the exclusive claims of the imagination: "I've made you my standard ever since I saw you. I've dreamt about you; I've thought of nothing but you; you represent to me the only reality in the world" (313). A more complex way of posing the relation between imagination and reality is to follow, as he begins to accept the necessary transaction between the two realms in the course of an actual love affair:

He was now conscious of the loss that follows any revelation; he had lost something in speaking to Katharine, for, after all, was the Katharine whom he loved the same as the real Katharine? She had transcended her entirely at moments. . . . He felt a mixture of disgust and pity at the figure cut by human beings when they try to carry out, in practice, what they have the power to conceive. How small both he and Katharine had appeared when they issued from the cloud of thought that enveloped them! (319)

This complication of Ralph's ideas of illusion and reality inevitably leads to an enrichment of his governing metaphors, day and night: "Looking at his watch, he seemed to look deep into the springs of human existence, and by the light of what he saw there altered his course towards the north and the midnight" (347). The mingling of light and dark with geographical terms suggests a new way of imag-

33

inatively grasping facts to mark them out as a direction in life. To be
sure, his course of action is subject to confusion and a sense of "distance": ". . . it was long before he could realize these facts; the immense desire for her presence churned his senses into foam, into froth,
into a haze of emotion that removed all facts from his grasp, and gave
him a strange sense of distance, even from the material shapes of
wall and window by which he was surrounded" (407). Nevertheless he
wins through to a resounding affirmation of his love and the knowledge derived from it: "I say I do know you, Katharine. . . . I swear to
you that now, at this instant, I see you precisely as you are. No one
has ever known you as I know you. . . . Could you have taken down
that book just now if I hadn't known you?" (447). His claim here is
not merely to grasp her essential reality through love but even to
project her into active being by the force of his imagination. In the
midst of their flowering love, Katharine continues to distrust his perception of her ("Reality—reality. . . . I cease to be real to you" [500–
501]), but he is willing to surrender the metaphysical term and its
claims if a better can be found: ". . . Ralph expressed vehemently in
his turn the conviction that he only loved her shadow and cared
nothing for her reality" (501).

With this growth of imaginative power, he is able to interweave his
visions with his prosaic law practice in an amusing but effective way:
"The partition so carefully erected between the different sections
of his life had been broken down, with the result that though his eyes
were fixed upon the Last Will and Testament, he saw through the page
a certain drawing-room in Cheyne Walk. . . . By degrees, a pulse or
stress began to beat at regular intervals in his mind, heaping his
thoughts into waves to which words fitted themselves, and without much consciousness of what he was doing, he began to write on
a sheet of draft paper what had the appearance of a poem lacking
several words in each line" (514–15). The authenticity of Ralph's
movement toward art is underscored by the similarity of his rhythmic
impulse to Woolf's other accounts of the creative mind, e.g., the
genesis of Lily's painting in *To the Lighthouse*, where another wave
image connects the artist's rhythm of creation with the pulsations of
human life.[7] The portrait of Ralph as incoherent poet is lightly mocked
here, suggesting that the compact of lunatic, lover, and poet is not
only inevitable but inevitably comic; but the authority of art is never
doubted in Woolf—any more than it is in Shakespeare.

□

[7]Other occasions on which wave imagery is connected with the dominant themes of
Night and Day occur on pages 117, 118, 145, 185, 251, 285, 291, 338, 416, 514, and
533. But the wave imagery does not here become a theme in its own right, as it does in
To the Lighthouse and *The Waves*.

In this sequence of the protagonists' imaginative development—and of the corresponding transformations in the predominant metaphors of night and day—the thematic action of the novel accords with its generic and parodic models. In these concerns, *Night and Day* stands in a tradition that extends from Shakespeare through certain of the Romantics and on to such modern figures as Yeats, for all of whom the imagination is similarly envisioned as the formative power not only of art but of human character. Without dilating on the stature which such an association implies for Woolf, we may support it in tracing the implications of her vision of the imagination's action in love and art.

One of the focal points in the novel occurs early in Katharine's development, at the moment of her decision to marry William. She is described as falling

. . . into a dream state, in which she became another person, and the whole world seemed changed. Being a frequent visitor to that world, she could find her way there unhesitatingly. If she had tried to analyse her impressions, she would have said that there dwelt the realities of the appearances which figure in our world; so direct, powerful, and unimpeded were her sensations there, compared with those called forth in actual life. There dwelt the things one might have felt, had there been cause; the perfect happiness of which here we taste the fragment; the beauty seen here in flying glimpses only. . . . two qualities were constant in it. It was a place where feelings were liberated from the constraint which the real world puts upon them; and the process of awakenment was always marked by resignation and a kind of stoical acceptance of facts. . . . there certainly she loved some magnanimous hero, and as they swept together among the leaf-hung trees of an unknown world, they shared the feelings which came fresh and fast as the waves on the shore. (144–45).

A number of characteristics of the Woolfian imagination may be discerned here: the fragmentariness of sensation in "actual life" and the possibility of another way of perception, in which sensations are "direct, powerful, and unimpeded"; the volitional character of this perceptual mode ("she could find her way there unhesitatingly") and the sense of freedom entailed ("feelings were liberated"); and the perceiver's tendency to credit his experience as revelatory ("there dwelt the realities of the appearances"), while acknowledging the necessary return to a "stoical acceptance of facts." Such descriptions of experience in Woolf have an obvious appeal for Bergsonian and other somewhat mystical critics, but they habitually leave out the pragmatic qualifications that Woolf always places on heightened moments of vision. The day-world is always "the real world"; "the process of awakenment" regularly follows the "dream state"—at least in dealing with lovers and poets, if not lunatics.

It is, of course, true that the lover in Woolf's fiction sometimes finds himself in a lunatic state, as Ralph does in his passion: "He lost his sense of all that surrounded him; all substantial things—the hour of the day, what we have done and are about to do, the presence of other people and the support we derive from seeing their belief in a common reality—all this slipped from him" (235). The language of this and other such descriptions makes clear that these states are to be regarded with sympathy, comic indulgence, and attention to detail, but there is no doubt that they are deluded, lonely, and burdensome—lacking "the support we derive from seeing [others'] belief in a common reality." To the sober realist, especially when his reality is unrewarding, the escape into delusion can be tempting. Thus Mary finds her feminist associate Clacton enviable: "She read Mr. Clacton's statement with a curious division of judgment, noting its weak and pompous verbosity on the one hand, and, at the same time, feeling that faith, faith in an illusion, perhaps, but, at any rate, faith in something, was of all gifts the most to be envied" (271). On the other side of the coin is the curious isolation of the realist and his failure at love, for love demands a projection of imagination beyond oneself (even to the creation or distortion of the love object). William discovers something like this in falling out of love with Katharine: " 'I think you're a trifle cold, and I suspect I'm a trifle self-absorbed. If that were so it goes a long way to explaining our odd lack of illusion about each other. I'm not saying that the most satisfactory marriages aren't founded upon this sort of understanding' " (302). William perceives not only his own personal shortcomings but also a set of truths the fiction underscores: there is a necessary illusion in love, and it requires a mutual "understanding" in several senses of the word—a more or less explicit agreement to love, an intimate knowledge of another person, and a commitment not only to one's own illusion but to another's. It is over this "understanding" that Mrs. Hilbery presides, generalizing it as the ruling form of successful marriages—she offers her own as example—and invoking the master of those who love, Shakespeare.

With this insight gained and her absurd engagement broken, Katharine has a second revelatory moment:

She looked out of the window, sternly determined to forget private misfortunes, to forget herself, to forget individual lives. With her eyes upon the dark sky, voices reached her from the room in which she was standing. She heard them as if they came from people in another world, a world antecedent to her world, a world that was the prelude, the antechamber to reality; it was as if, lately dead, she heard the living talking. The dream nature of our life had never been more apparent to her, never had life been more certainly an affair of four walls, whose objects existed only within the range of lights and fires, beyond which lay nothing, or nothing more than darkness. She seemed physically to have stepped beyond the region where the light of illusion still makes it desirable to possess, to love, to struggle. (373)

Here the ordinary world is held to be charged with illusion but animated by it "to possess, to love, to struggle." The Renaissance *topos* of life as a dream becomes explicit in the image of this illusory realm as lit by "lights and fires," which derives ultimately from the Platonic myth of the cave (*Republic* vii). But the Platonic (or Keatsian) image of the chambers of reality demands a closer reading; indeed, part of the passage's difficulty lies in its triple image of the room. On the literal level, Katharine is in a room with other people; she imagines herself apart from them in a state like death, to which their living realm is an "antechamber"; and she generalizes about life as "an affair of four walls." If we align the terms that go along with these images, we find ordinary life characterized by light and illusion, while the imaginative state she temporarily inhabits is associated with death and nothingness. But this state is also seen as *reality*—the realm of other people is "the antechamber to reality." The day-world, then, turns out to be the evanescent and illusory, while the night-world comes to be seen as the real—yet also as emptiness and death.[8]

The perception of life as an illusion surrounded by nothingness, the ultimate reality, is a common one in Shakespeare, from Prospero's comic vision of "our little life . . . rounded with a sleep" to Macbeth's tragic "tale told by an idiot, . . . signifying nothing." That this perception should come to the heroine of a fiction in the Shakespearian mode requires us to see it as a serious and focal one. The imagination that has been found to govern love is now rendered suspect by its connection with the meaningless life of possession and struggle. Love and illusion are both anterior to an encounter with dark reality, in which one can forget one's own and other "individual lives." But it is also by virtue of the imagination that Katharine has her vision of reality, hears human voices as if *d'outre-tombe*, and sees things under the aspect of eternity.

However somber the tenor of this vision, it remains possible to put it into relation with other truths gathered in the process of the dramatic

[8]This awareness cuts across but does not dispel the affirmative emphasis derived from Dostoyevsky: "It's life that matters, nothing but life—the process of discovering—the everlasting and perpetual process, not the discovery at all" (132; cf. 138). The source of this quotation in *Night and Day*, Constance Garnett's translation of *The Idiot*, has been noted by Nancy T. Bazin, *Virginia Woolf and the Androgynous Vision* (New Brunswick, N.J., 1973), pp. 87, 232 n. The passage appears in the fifth paragraph of part 3, chap. 5 of Dostoyevsky's text. Bazin also notes other references to Dostoyevsky in *Night and Day* and elsewhere in Woolf.

action. For a while, Katharine is dominated by the negative aspects of her vision and tries to argue Ralph out of his love on the strength of it: "Being yourself very inexperienced and very emotional, you go home and invent a story about me, and now you can't separate me from the person you've imagined me to be. You call that, I suppose, being in love; as a matter of fact it's being in delusion" (404). It becomes evident that she is really speaking to herself, as she goes on to say: "You're going to go on dreaming and imagining and making up stories about me as you walk along in the street, and pretending that we're riding in a forest, or landing on an island—" (406). We remember that these are the favorite scenes of Katharine's own dream, for the images are present in her first revelatory vision, where they adumbrate a realm not of mere delusion but the more imaginatively viable one of romance.

The course of this love affair is, more than most others, the story of a change of heart, detailed here as a change in the processes of thought, even of the metaphors by which the lovers have been guided. Night is no longer opposed to day in a simple antithesis offering escape from the given: "The fresh air of spring, the sky washed of clouds and already shedding warmth from its blue, seemed the reply vouchsafed by nature to the mood of her chosen spirits" (487-88). Acknowledging the value of day and light and the common life of man, Katharine accepts from Ralph a new image of reality. She takes up a picture he has drawn amid his poetic ramblings, a "little dot with the flames round it":

He was convinced that it could mean nothing to another, although somehow to him it conveyed not only Katharine herself but all those states of mind which had clustered round her since he first saw her pouring out tea on a Sunday afternoon. It represented by its circumference of smudges surrounding a central blot all that encircling glow which for him surrounded, inexplicably, so many of the objects of life, softening their sharp outline, so that he could see certain streets, books, and situations wearing a halo almost perceptible to the physical eye. . . . But it did not occur to her that this diagram had anything to do with her. She said simply, and in the same tone of reflection: "Yes, the world looks something like that to me too."

He received her assurance with profound joy. Quietly and steadily there rose up behind the whole aspect of life that soft edge of fire which gave its red tint to the atmosphere and crowded the scene with shadows so deep and dark that one could fancy pushing farther into their density and still farther, expanding indefinitely. Whether there was any correspondence between the two prospects now opening before them they shared the same sense of the impending future, vast, mysterious, infinitely stored with undeveloped shapes which each would unwrap for the other to behold; but for the present the prospect of the future was enough to fill them with silent adoration. (522-23)

A number of preliminary points must be made about this climactic scene. Although set up to introduce the final lyrical union of the lovers, it is at the same time an intelligible step in their imaginative development. It is also distinct from earlier revelatory passages in being a collective experience, the product of their "thinking together" (as a similar relation of lovers is called in *The Voyage Out*). The world picture thus derived is a fusion of light and dark imagery, of the fires of Ralph's romantic passion and the dark spaces of Katharine's vision of the *néant*. It also introduces a new dimension into the protagonists' thought: the temporal. For the first time, apparently, they begin to think of themselves as having a future, their perception is now a "prospect," and they can think of living in the way existentialists have taught us to think of it: as a *projet*. The particular form of this expansive possibility and its corresponding life style is, however, not equatable with existentialism but invokes an ideal of transcendence, love's philosophy in this fiction.

□

In the midst of Ralph's growing love, a phenomenon occurs in the text that opens doors on the extraordinary events to follow. While visiting with Mary at her parents' home in Lincolnshire, "he thought of Katharine, the thought of her being surrounded by the spaces of night and the open air . . ." (200). He is also "constraining himself . . . to limit his thoughts to this one room." Unbeknown to Ralph, Katharine is also visiting not far away, at Stogdon (she, too, is unaware of his proximity): "Into that same black night, almost, indeed, into the very same layer of starlit air, Katharine Hilbery was now gazing . . ." (201). This is more than a conventional transition from one chapter to another or from narrative focus on one character to focus on another. It is the first trace of "thinking together," a phenomenon that is further spelled out by Ralph himself: "Without knowing you, except that you're beautiful, and all that, I've come to believe that we're in some sort of agreement; that we're after something together; that we see something. . . . I've got into the habit of imagining you; I'm always thinking what you'd say or do . . ." (315). "Imagining you" is clearly more than a matter of visualizing or idealizing the beloved object; it seems to involve inhabiting the mind of the other, being in "agreement" so as to be acting or perceiving identically, and being "after something together"—not simply a project but a condition of mutuality in which the life processes of two persons fuse to make one process. As the lovers come closer to acknowledging their union, for Ralph "the illusion of her presence became more and more complete. They seemed to pass in and out of each other's minds, questioning and answering. The utmost fullness of communion seemed to be theirs. Thus united, he felt himself raised to an eminence, exalted, and filled with a power of achievement such as he had never known in singleness" (409). When Katharine comes to feel this intimacy and the "power of achievement" which it confers, the union is effected and the final lyrical movement of the fiction can occur.

Ralph instructs her in this lovers' doctrine by writing a philosophic letter in the penultimate chapter:

. . . he tried to convey to her the possibility that although human beings are woefully ill-adapted for communication, still, such communion is the best we know; moreover, they make it possible for each to have access to another world independent of personal affairs, a world of law, of philosophy, or more strangely a world such as he had had a glimpse of the other evening when together they seemed to be sharing something, an ideal—a vision flung out in advance of our actual circumstances. If this golden rim were quenched, if life were no longer circled by an illusion (but was it an illusion after all?), then it would be too dismal an affair to carry to an end. . . . This conclusion appeared to him to justify their relationship. But the conclusion was mystical. . . . (515-16)

The passage does a great deal to clarify a number of themes and images that have slowly been developing. The point with a circle around it is interpreted here as the relation of fact to illusion—a desirable penumbra of significance which the imagination adduces to the given. The question whether this illusion is real or unreal is left a question ("but was it an illusion . . .?"); what is more significant is that it is now expanded to take in the major activities of culture: law, philosophy, and other activities that a Cassirer would call the "symbolic forms." The imaginative processes seem more powerful, more adept in arriving at their end, when conducted in common with others or with another. This joint effort is described first as "communication," then as "communion"—a quasi-religious fusion—rather than as the bridging of a gap between discrete individuals (the latter process being one for which "human beings are woefully ill-adapted"). This doctrine may be derogated even by its proponents as "mystical," but that is only a term to hide our embarrassment when confronted with modes of living outside the ordinary.

At this stage, we are brought to an extended account of the state of communion so long and carefully prepared:

a) "As if the forces of the world were all at work to tear them asunder they sat, clasping hands, near enough to be taken even by the malicious eye of Time himself for a united couple, an indivisible unit" (521). Here the special nature of the lovers' communion is seen opposed to "the forces of the world"—characterized not simply as mundane social life but as the archetypal figure of Time, with its burden of death. The unity created by the lovers' imaginations is thus not a mere withdrawal from other men but an attempt to steal something from reality, where Time and death preside.

b) With Ralph "giving her by a sudden impulse his own unfinished dissertation, with its mystical conclusion, they read each other's compositions in silence. . . . They came to the end of their tasks at about the same moment, and sat for a time in silence" (521). The fact that Ralph cannot understand all of Katharine's mathematical figures, or that Katharine cannot be expected to follow Ralph's "unfinished dissertation, with its mystical conclusion," is less important than the fact of their mutual absorption in each other's writings. Their coming to an end in their reading at "about the same moment . . . in silence"— just as they have been reading "in silence"—suggests that their harmonious activity in thinking together is more important than any thought they may think.

c) "The moment of exposure had been exquisitely painful—the light shed startlingly vivid. She had now to get used to the fact that some one shared her loneliness" (521). This beautiful sentence expresses an idea that other writers have known—that D. H. Lawrence spent so much effort to get at—but that has never been so simply or precisely put. Communion is not a surrender of personality but a mutual recognition of it; the individual remains alone in his new state—fated to be himself but now sharing that fate with another.

d) ". . . she had committed no sacrilege but enriched herself, perhaps immeasurably, perhaps eternally. She hardly dared steep herself in the infinite bliss" (522). The language of theology comes readily to hand when we are faced with the problem of describing such experiences, but it can be seen in the repeated "perhaps" that this is a putative, metaphoric conclusion.

At this point, when Katharine and Ralph identify themselves with the same world picture—the "little dot with the flames round it" (522)—and discern the "correspondence" between their projections of the future, Mrs. Hilbery enters and sings "her strange, half-earthly song of dawns and sunsets, of great poets, and the unchanged spirit of noble loving" (526). But Katharine and Ralph have transcended the conventions of comedy and their night walk in the closing chapter brings them to a state of mind reserved for the heroes of divine comedies and prophetic illuminations.

The lovers move out of the house and into the night, seeking "movement, freedom from scrutiny, silence, and the open air" (531) (although Ralph looks back at the house and its lights as to "the shrine of so much adoration" [532]). The couple moves across the city, in one of the many traversals of London in Woolf's work. But vision takes on the features of the world picture they have agreed to share: "She looked at his face isolated in the little circle of light" (532), and "he appeared to her a fire burning through its smoke, a source of life" (533). At this point Woolf's imagination expands the picture in terms of the *Paradiso's* vision of the heavenly company: "She thought of him blazing splendidly in the night, yet so obscure that to hold his arm, as she held it, was only to touch the opaque substance surrounding the flame that roared upwards" (534). To this Dantean language is added the Shakespearian imagery of the "globe which we spend our lives in trying to shape, round, whole, and entire from the confusion of chaos" (533). Finally, the world picture is seen as a paradigm of apocalyptic transcendence to an obscure but obviously finer state of being: ". . . she spoke of the dark red fire, and the smoke twined around it, making him feel that he had stepped over the threshold into the faintly lit vastness of another mind, stirring with shapes, so large, so dim, unveiling themselves only in flashes, and moving away again to the darkness, engulfed by it" (534-35).

The result of this expansion of the lovers' world picture is to enforce a carefully qualified claim of enlightenment:

They brought themselves by these means, acting on a mood of profound happiness, to a state of clear-sightedness where the lifting of a finger had effect, and one word spoke more than a sentence. They lapsed gently into silence, travelling the dark paths of thought side by side towards something discerned in the distance which gradually possessed them both. They were victors, masters of life, but at the same time absorbed in the flame, giving their life to increase its brightness, to testify to their faith. (535)

Here, communion is conceived of as a journey rather than as a fusion of substance; it is an active state of living together in the world rather than a withdrawal into a nocturnal realm of pure contemplation. The lovers are, of course, happy in a way that only the saved soul has been held to be happy, but their "faith" has no object beyond themselves and their "giving their life" is a mutual interchange rather than a sacrificial act. What Woolf has conceived here is a secular state of personal fulfillment on the model of—even borrowing the imagery of—religious transcendence.

The lovers are inclined to make more of their experience than the narrator allows it: Ralph is unwilling to "resign his belief" (532) in his ideal vision of Katharine, even after their shared laughter at the comedy of their imaginations; and Katharine takes the fact that Mary's light is burning as evidence of some kind of permanence in life: ". . . the light was not moved. It signalled to her across the dark street; it was a sign of triumph shining there forever, not to be extinguished this side of the grave" (536). She goes on to see all London "set with fires, roaring upwards" (536), but this is set down as a dramatically appropriate fantasy. In the same way, Ralph's imagination tries to piece together all the lives with which they have had contact: "They appeared to him to be more than individuals; to be made up of many different things in cohesion; he had a vision of an orderly world" (536). But the sentence preceding has already rendered its judgment of his imaginative leap: "He stopped in his enumeration, not finding it possible to link them together in any way that should explain the queer combination which he could perceive in them, as he thought of them" (536). The imagination here exceeds rational explanation, and the two mental activities are each given their due without excessive claims for either.

The heightened life of the lovers is conceived, then, as a triumph neither of imagination nor of daylight vision but as their synthesis—just as the synthesis of the two minds partly accounts for their triumphal state. The process of synthesis is extended further:

> She felt him trying to piece together in a laborious and elementary fashion fragments of belief, unsoldered and separate, lacking the unity of phrases fashioned by the old believers. Together they groped in this difficult region, where the unfinished, the unfulfilled, the unwritten, the unreturned, came together in their ghostly way and wore the semblance of the complete and the satisfactory. The future emerged more splendid than ever from this construction of the present. (537)

The synthesis contains not only elements of a faith but the persistence of doubt, not only a vision of the whole but the fragmentary parts, not only idyllic success but all the failures of living. It is not a leap into the ideal but a "construction of the present" which, by human effort and power of mind, can be made to shape the future. The lovers sketch their future in a medium that had apparently been rejected in the movement toward nocturnal imagination but which is now revived to serve as an image of their mental activity—the medium of light: the future "swam miraculously in the golden light of a large steady lamp" (537).

43

The final paragraph of *Night and Day* gathers to a crescendo all
that has gone before, and it may be read from sentence to sentence as
a summation of the imagistic strains, mythic analogues, and philosophic suggestions of the text as a whole:

a) "They dismounted [from a bus] and walked down to the river."
The image of the lovers' life quest is here elaborated by placing them
in association with the traditional symbol of the river, marking the
course of human life.

b) "She felt his arm stiffen beneath her hand, and knew by this
token that they had entered the enchanted region." That romantic
region is not, of course, a place but a state of mind—the mutually
creative imagination.

c) "She might speak to him, but with that strange tremor in his
voice, those eyes blindly adoring, whom did he answer? What woman
did he see?" The union of the lovers is accompanied by the continued
tendency of the imagination to move beyond the actual to an ideal of
its own making. There is a hint of fallacy and flaw in even this
beautiful marriage of true minds.

d) "And where was she walking, and who was her companion?"
There is a further suggestion of mythological import in the dark river
now; if it is to be seen as one of Hades's streams, "her companion"
would be not only her lover but her death (a Hades-like figure, who
will emerge fully in *To the Lighthouse*).

e) "Moments, fragments, a second of vision, and then the flying
waters, the winds dissipating and dissolving; then, too, the recollection from chaos, the return of security, the earth firm, superb and
brilliant in the sun." Here the language suggests the limits of the
flashes of illumination that are allowed the mind; there follows a
return to the actual, accepted now not as a fall into darkness but
rather as the assumption of a heritage—the endowment of the entire
earth, "brilliant in the sun."

f) "From the heart of his darkness he spoke his thanksgiving; from
a region as far, as hidden, she answered him." The phrase, drawn
from Conrad's title, was to stay with Woolf from *The Voyage Out* to
Between the Acts; here it points to the ultimate loneliness that is
aligned with the imagery of imagination and night throughout the
novel. But proceeding from it is a song of thanksgiving which
recognizes the inheritance not merely of the soul's joy but of the
entire earth.

g) "On a June night the nightingales sing, they answer each other
across the plain; they are heard under the window among the trees in
the garden." These images—introduced into a description of lovers
by a river—probably derive from a number of Arnold's poems, par-

ticularly "To Marguerite—Continued": "And in their glens, on starry nights, /The nightingales divinely sing;/ And lovely notes, from shore to shore, / Across the sounds and channels pour—." Woolf's sentence carries a suggestion of Keatsian "natural magic" and an intimation of imaginative sympathy within nature, which was lost to Arnold, but apparently still available to Woolf's imagination at this stage of her career.

h) "Pausing, they looked down into the river which bore its dark tide of waters, endlessly moving, beneath them." The archetype of the river is now used to emphasize temporal transiency, particularly as a dark reflection of the human lives that are mirrored in it.

i) "They turned and found themselves opposite the house. . . . The light lay in soft golden grains upon the deep obscurity of the hushed and sleeping household." The return to ordinary life is seen as a continued fusion between the images of light and dark.

j) "For a moment they waited, and then loosed their hands. 'Good night,' he breathed. 'Good night,' she murmured back to him." A temporary parting is accomplished with the conventional phrase, but it now conveys an affirmation of the nocturnal realm, which has been successfully mingled with the diurnal course of life.

□

In the year in which *Night and Day* appeared, Woolf also published one of her first short stories as a slim volume from the Hogarth Press called "Kew Gardens." It contains the following description of a pair of young lovers:

. . . the fact that his hand rested on the top of hers expressed their feelings in a strange way, as these short insignificant words also expressed something, words with short wings for their heavy body of meaning, inadequate to carry them far and thus alighting awkwardly upon the very common objects that surrounded them, and were to their inexperienced touch so massive; but who knows (so they thought as they pressed the parasol into the earth) what precipices aren't concealed in them, or what slopes of ice don't shine in the sun on the other side? Who knows? . . .

Thus one couple after another with much the same irregular and aimless movement passed the flower-bed and were enveloped in layer after layer of green blue vapour, in which at first their bodies had substance and a dash of colour, but later both substance and colour dissolved in the green-blue atmosphere.[9]

---

[9]*A Haunted House and Other Short Stories*, pp. 37–38.

jacob's room

"A tiny bead
of pure life"

Jacob's Room, published in 1922—the year of *Ulysses* and *The Waste Land*—joined with them in establishing a uniquely modern style in English literature. Its characterization of the putative hero as a "problem" in identity, its narration of a man's life by a synthesis of multiple points of view, its extension of the *Bildungsroman* form into a fitful sequence of unachieved experiences rather than a coherent process—these were innovations as distinctive in the history of fiction as those of *A Portrait of the Artist* had been less than a decade before. Moreover, the congruence of the work's discontinuous techniques with its theme—the cutting off of a young man's growth in individuality by the First World War—enabled its stylistic experiments to convey the horror which modern war has placed near the center of our experience. *Jacob's Room* is not only an experimental work, showing all the sketchiness of a first attempt to embody the dynamic insubstantiality of character, but also a fully realized symbol of the meaningless waste of fragile human qualities that has become endemic to modern life.

Although *Jacob's Room* resembles the traditional novel in single-mindedly following an individual's transactions with his world, it is written according to a revolutionary theory of fiction; and it incorporates that theory, in the form of essayistic passages, into its narrative line. The theory is that of Woolf's essays of the period, from

"Modern Fiction" to "Mr. Bennett and Mrs. Brown" (1919-24). The text's principal statement of its norms of psychological realism—and its concomitant skepticism of traditional theories of personality— follows a parody of typical fictional characterization: "Then his mouth—but surely, of all futile occupations this of cataloguing features is the worst. One word is sufficient. But if one cannot find it?" (69). The intercalated essay continues: "And why, if this and much more than this is true, why are we yet surprised in the window corner by a sudden vision that the young man in the chair is of all things in the world the most real, the most solid, the best known to us—why indeed? For the moment we know nothing about him. Such is the manner of our seeing. Such the conditions of our love" (70-71). The paradox of personality is its juncture of vivid presence and resistance to knowledge—its invitation to intuition and escape from language.

A more defensive statement of the ultimate mystery and unavoidable interest in individual personality is later made:

It is no use trying to sum people up. One must follow hints, not exactly what is said, nor yet entirely what is done. Some, it is true, take ineffaceable impressions of character at once. Others dally, loiter, and get blown this way and that. . . . There is also the highly respectable opinion that character-mongering is much overdone nowadays. . . . So we are driven back to see what the other side means—the men in clubs and Cabinets—when they say that character-drawing is a frivolous fireside art, a matter of pins and needles, exquisite outlines enclosing vacancy, flourishes, and mere scrawls. . . . It is thus that we live, they say, driven by an unseizable force. They say that the novelists never catch it; that it goes hurtling through their nets and leaves them torn to ribbons. This, they say, is what we live by—this unseizable force. (153-55; the first two sentences are also stated on page 29.)

It will be seen that the argument shifts in the course of these authorial comments on her procedure: from defending her method of indirection and brief flashes of portraiture against traditional schemes of physiognomic interpretation, Woolf turns to a defense of the novel against those men of affairs who see it as ineffectual in rendering the brute force of reality. Character is both too varied to be reduced to fictional conventions and too subtle to be captured by hearty generalizations about the life-force. If we are to have genuine visions of human life in fiction, then it is likely to be when indirections find directions out: "One must follow hints, not exactly what is said, nor yet entirely what is done."

The method that lies readiest to hand is perspectivism, for if an author cannot simply posit his character's personality by godlike fiat, he may accumulate evidence of that character from other witnesses, whom he must in turn create. Thus, we have a series of views of Jacob in the eyes of his mother and his teacher, his friends Clara and Timothy Durrant, the Durrants' housemaid and his own chambermaid, stray acquaintances like Julia Eliot, and even Jacob himself: "I'm twenty-two. It's nearly the end of October. Life is thoroughly pleasant, although unfortunately there are a great number of fools about. One must apply oneself to something or other—God knows what" (70-71). But if Woolf's principle of relativistic skepticism— "It seems that a profound, impartial, and absolutely just opinion of our fellow-creatures is entirely unknown" (70)—holds for self-knowledge as well, then Jacob's view of himself is not to be taken as definitive but only as valuable testimony by a close participant in his career.

The strength of the impulses to know and to create character is, then, independent of the difficulty of the task; in art as in life, we all are condemned to make the attempt, in full acknowledgment of its futility. The impulse here may be found to derive from love: the vision of a young man's life nipped in the bud haunted Woolf after the death of her brother, Thoby Stephen (who died in 1906 at the age of twenty-five, after a trip to Greece and Turkey much like Jacob's).[1] Besides this loving impulse to capture the identity of others, there is the egoistic impulse to self-discovery, particularly in young men: "the obstinate irrepressible conviction which makes youth so intolerably disagreeable—'I am what I am, and intend to be it,' for which there will be no form in the world unless Jacob makes one for himself" (34). Identity is seen here as a matter of self-creation, by force of will and intelligence, like creation in art; but unlike art, the self is never fixed, always in process, and therefore indefinable.

Beyond Jacob himself, whatever he may be, there is that in which he is mixed, his *Lebenswelt*, as it has been called by phenomenologists like Husserl and Binswanger. "But though all this may very well be true—so Jacob thought and spoke—so he crossed his legs— filled his pipe—sipped his whiskey, and once looked at his pocketbook, rumpling his hair as he did so, there remains over something which can never be conveyed to a second person save by Jacob himself. Moreover, part of this is not Jacob but Richard Bonamy—the room; the market-carts; the hour; the very moment of history. Then

[1]Jean Guiguet, *Virginia Woolf and Her Works*, trans. Jean Stewart (London, 1965 [1962]), pp. 91-93, points out that *The Waves*, too, was written amid strong recollections of Thoby and his death, so that the pressure to create an image of Jacob's self may be seen to be part of a continuing effort in Woolf's fiction to recapture the dead— as will be discussed below.

consider the effect of sex . . ." (71). Although the feeling of what it is to be Jacob is best conveyed by Jacob himself, Jacob is not made up entirely of that feeling or even of his attributes alone. He extends into the places around him, is constituted by the world he interacts with. This life space, then, may be considered—if not as Jacob himself—as Jacob's "room," the space of Jacob's living that is the larger denotation of the fiction's title. And it is this medium, rather than Jacob himself, that is the object of description in *Jacob's Room*, so that the title accurately indicates its limited knowable realm.

□

The narrative record of Jacob's world exhibits both the impulses outlined above: to tell the story of a man's life with something like the disparateness of his experiences, including the sudden spurts of consciousness in which personal growth occurs, and to convey the shock of the absurd as it breaks in on the normal rhythms of life. It is only toward the close that we can fix a firm date for the events and an age for Jacob: he is twenty-six (153) in the spring of the year in which war breaks out, 1914. From this we derive a birth date, 1888 (although this and all dates derived from it may be off by one year). We cannot know Jacob's age at the time of his first childhood vacation in Cornwall (although the date is given as September 3 on page 5) or during the period in which the decision is taken to send him to Rugby (20). The first firm age we can assign is at his entry into society, as it were: "Jacob Flanders, therefore, went up to Cambridge in October, 1906" (27), i.e., at eighteen. Although his age is given as nineteen just two pages later, we must take the occasion—a faintly comic episode with an anxious lady on the train to Cambridge—to be of the following year, with Jacob showing something of the aplomb of a sophomore. He is "about the age of twenty" (34) when punting in May with Timothy Durrant, who is laying plans for their sailing trip in the coming vacation that July (47). We may therefore take the main narrative of Jacob's Cambridge experience to occur in 1908. His first experiences when settled in London after graduation—particularly of *Tristan und Isolde* in the autumn season (66)—thus are probably of 1910.

From the sequence of the months given in the text, we can group his later encounters into the four years 1911–14. His contemplated proposal to Clara in July (70) (or is this only her supposition?), his pickup of Florinda on Guy Fawkes night (72), and his nocturnal walk with Timothy on November 6 (74) belong to 1911. (When Lady Hibbert asks anxiously, "What is going to happen to us, Mr. Salvin? With all my experience of English politics—" [85], she may be referring to the wave of labor unrest which reached an almost anarchic height in the years 1911-12.) His discovery of Florinda's infidelity in January (94) occurs just before the Prime Minister's 1912 Home Rule bill (97); Asquith actually introduced the bill on April 11, although it is a "very cold night" when Jacob reads of it. He is twenty-five (102) at his visit to the wealthy Miss Perry and reads the *Phaedrus* on February 22 (108) the same year, presumably 1913. The rush of events in Jacob's last year is as follows: a bohemian party in Hammersmith in January (110); Fanny Elmer's falling in love with him in February (117); his announcement of his trip to Greece in April (the month in which Fanny reads *Tom Jones*) (122); forcing him to miss the dance at the Slade Art School in May (122); his meeting the Williamses in Patras and again in Athens in May (156); and the medley of figures in Hyde Park that summer (163), while the enthusiasm for war mounts in Whitehall.[2]

When the sum of his activities is taken, what do we know about Jacob? Jacob Alan Flanders (89): son of Seabrook (deceased) and Elizabeth (aged about forty-five) (13), of Scarborough, Yorkshire (6), with two brothers, the elder Archer (later of the Royal Navy), and the younger John (15). His father is euphemistically described in his epitaph as a merchant, but he is hardly middle class, having qualities of both gentleman and roustabout: ". . . he had only sat behind an office window for three months, and before that had broken horses, ridden to hounds, farmed a few fields, and run a little wild—well, she had to call him something. An example to the boys" (14). In class and occupation, the father does set an example to his middle son; Jacob exhibits no professional interests, though he holds an office job (89), but he moves in society at a fairly high level; he is the guest not only of a banking family (the Durrants) but of the wealthy Miss Perry and Lady Rocksbier (with whom he is rumored to be connected) (154). These two strains in his background—bohemian and gentleman—are reflected in his manners and are thus the chief facts others (including the reader) know him by: " 'That young man, Jacob Flanders,' they would say, 'so distinguished looking—and yet so awkward.' Then they would apply themselves to Jacob and vacillate eternally between the two extremes" (154). At any rate, there seems to be no difficulty in his pursuing the standard education of the upper classes: Rugby (20), Trinity College, Cambridge (with rooms in

[2]Alice van Buren Kelley, *The Novels of Virginia Woolf: Fact and Vision* (Chicago and London, 1973), p. 75, posits that episodes of successive years are dated by month so as to form a seasonal cycle—from the opening scene in September to the scene in Hyde Park at end of summer. Even by her own evidence, the cycle is not contained in "little more than a year"; there are at least two full sequences, ending with the leaves of autumn rising and sinking at Jacob's death (176).

Neville's Court) (36), and a grand tour—a deceased cousin having left him a hundred pounds (124).

One of Jacob's more persistent features is an intractability that typifies the resistance of young men to making their peace with the world's follies. The text begins with Jacob's refusing to play and straying away from his mother on the beach. "Tiresome little boy," she mutters (5).[3] A butterfly collector in youth, he corrects his handbook in the margin, showing some respect for its authority by using a fine pen point (21). Invited to luncheon by a don, he reacts to the conventionally intellectual and social-climbing family with four "Oh Gods" and concludes: " 'Bloody beastly,' . . . summing up his discomfort at the world shown him at lunchtime . . ." (33). He enjoys a huge joke at the thought of his gentlemanly friend Masham, and the interrupted tale of Masham's aunt seems particularly funny in his state of deshabille on Durrant's boat (49). His first-mentioned literary endeavor is a review exposing the Bowdlerization in a new edition of Wycherley, although "even as Jacob copied his pages, he knew that no one would ever print them" (68). He judges severely his high social contact, the Countess of Rocksbier, who tears her chicken bones with her hands: "A rude old lady, Jacob thought" (99). He also judges Everard Benson, whom he meets at Miss Perry's: ". . . to win [puzzle] prizes, remember parrots, toady Miss Perry . . . all this, so Jacob felt without knowing him, made him a contemptible ass" (102). He projects a political-historical essay "with some pretty sharp hits at Mr. Asquith [then Prime Minister]—something in the style of Gibbon" (135), and believes the government to be run by "fools." The image of him that rises in the mind of Sandra Wentworth Williams—who is perhaps not the best of judges but who does try to capture a whole view of him—is that of the misanthrope Alceste: "She meant that he was severe. She meant that she could deceive him" (169).

The other side of Jacob is less rebellious and peremptory—less, it might be ventured, Stracheyan—and typifies other qualities in the Bloomsbury milieu: qualities generally associated with the British upper-middle-class intelligentsia, including a mystical bent, a sense

---

[3] The opening vacation scene in Cornwall is reminiscent of the Stephens' childhood and was to be developed in the semiautobiographical portions of *To the Lighthouse*. Specific elements of *Jacob's Room* that are expanded in the later work are the painter Steele's violet-black dab to represent Mrs. Flanders (6), her brown wool knitting, which is present when she soothes a child to sleep during a storm at sea (10), the sheep's jaw which first frightens Jacob and then lies in the children's room (12) (in *TTL*, a pig's skull), a chair that creaks when there's no one about (37, 176), the changing view of the land from a boat (47), the movement of the lighthouse's beam over the water (50–51), and Julia Eliot's setting up her easel to paint on the lawn (62).

of cultural tradition, a high valuation of friendship, an ethical tolerance combined with a kind of innocence regarding sex, a classical strain, and a willingness to assume a political career despite some satirical distance from men of affairs. Punting on the Cam brings Jacob's eyes on a level with cows and children in a field, and his soul is drawn to that age-old symbol of the soul, the butterfly: " 'Jacob's off,' thought Durrant . . ." (35). He looks out the window of his college room and hears "the sound of the clock conveying to him (it may be) a sense of old buildings and time; and himself the inheritor . . ." (43). At a bull session among his friends, "the words were inaudible. It was the intimacy, a sort of spiritual suppleness, which mind prints upon mind indelibly" (44). He approves of Florinda's sexual frankness: "Thus did all good women in the days of the Greeks" (75); after sex, he appears "in his dressing-gown, amiable, authoritative, beautifully healthy, like a baby after an airing, with an eye clear as running water" (91) (his visit to a high-class prostitute is even more swaddled in innocence [103]). He is able to pursue his reading of the *Phaedrus* and its images of the soul, despite the drunken woman in the street crying, "Let me in! Let me in!" (108); and his visit to Greece is suitably momentous, despite the "illusion" of "the Greek myth" (136-37) and the banality of modern Greece and its tourists (149-51). The Greek experience also inspires political reflections—"Why not rule countries in the way they should be ruled?" (149)—and furthers Jacob's bent toward a political career: "But then there was the British Empire which was beginning to puzzle him [probably with doubts about its presumed iniquity]; nor was he altogether in favor of giving Home Rule to Ireland" (138).

These qualities place Jacob in a certain class at a certain time and place, and they are in turn typical of the universal characteristics of young men in the twin processes of individuation and socialization. But apart from these historical and generic traits, the portrait of Jacob illustrates the doctrine of individuality cited above; after all classifications, there is always something left over which marks the self as unique. These residues of identity are most clearly observed in the paraphernalia of living, the concrete objects which come to represent the traits or interests of the individual who selects and uses them:

Jacob's room had a round table and two low chairs. There were yellow flags in a jar on the mantelpiece; a photograph of his mother; cards from societies with little raised crescents, coats of arms, and initials; notes and pipes; on the table lay paper ruled with a red margin—an essay, no doubt—"Does History consist of the Biographies of Great Men?" There were books enough. . . . There were books upon the Italian painters of the Renaissance, a *Manual of the Diseases of the Horse,* and all the usual textbooks. Listless is the air in an empty room, just swelling the curtain; the flowers in the jar shift. One fibre in the wicker arm-chair creaks, though no one sits there. (37)

The student "digs" has a fair proportion of randomness to reasonableness in its selection of objects. The pipes and cards and photo of mother are characteristic, but why the yellow flags? The essay on history and biography is appropriate to one busily defining his own identity and with historical interests of his own (he may well be prepared for it by the volume of Carlyle in his library—"a prize") (37), but why the veterinary manual? Part of this randomness is the result of conscious choice—and therefore expresses character in its own way—for Jacob makes it a principle that "any one who's worth anything reads just what he likes, as the mood takes him, with extravagant enthusiasm" (37) (the narrator here assumes Jacob's voice).[4]

The most unusual items in the catalogue of Jacob's room are those that express the inhabitant's presence even when he is physically absent: not merely fragile things like air, curtains, and flowers, but wicker fibers, whose shape and movement are hypothetically ascribable to Jacob's impress. We are not given as detailed a scrutiny of Jacob's more permanent room, his London flat in Lamb's Conduit Street (69), nor of the only other room described, his hotel room at Patras (138). But the phrases used of the Cambridge dormitory come back when the London room is described after his death: "Listless is the air in an empty room, just swelling the curtain; the flowers in the jar shift. One fibre in the wicker arm-chair creaks, though no one sits there" (176) (not only are these sentences repeated, but also the architectural remarks on page 69).

Having learned this much about Jacob, in his social context, material surroundings, and immaterial presence, we begin to sense that we haven't captured him at all. So we begin to list attributes and make the deductions from behavior that are given the name "character-mongering" in the text. Jacob is named "The silent young man" by Julia Eliot (58); he is not only modest, e.g., about his knowledge of music (87), but monumentally shy, as in the amusing encounter with Sir Jasper Bigham (88). Yet there is also buoyancy and enthusiasm:

[4]Sometimes what seems a vagary has deeper, or at least wider, roots, e.g., the presence of a number of biographies of the Duke of Wellington seems to reflect a wayward choice of reading matter, for Jacob's historical interests run to Julian the Apostate (44) and the Byzantine Empire (65). Yet the Duke keeps coming up in odd contexts: Bonamy has a Wellington nose (84 ff.), Wellington serves as the model of a gentleman (49), a stall keeper exacts praise of the Duke from Jacob (75), and there are other incidental references to him or to his exploits (82, 167). Thus, an obsolete model of the heroic type is introduced into the background of our latter-day hero, partly through his own interests, partly through his cultural surroundings.

he retains his "irresponsible optimism" even after being jilted by Florinda (93); he loves riding and a good country pub—his father's son! (99-100). There is also a touch of the artistic temperament: he is writing on Marlowe—a kindred spirit? (105-6); he is well liked even by bohemians like Helen Askew and Dick Graves (110) and likes them in turn (111); yet he prefers the bourgeois Clara Durrant to the artist's model Fanny Elmer (122). As to taste, he prefers Shake-speare to other writers, including all the French put together (125); he is judicious and inquisitive about painting (126); he is beginning to form general views about such things as history and women (150). Finally we realize that enumeration won't do; the sum is always greater than the list of attributes; every inclusion marks an ex-clusion; the characteristics given in the text in an apparently random or casually selective form are meant to give only a partial view; and we conclude that wholeness of vision is for the gods. But if this is true of man's seeing, it is also true of his being: Jacob is incompletely seen because he is incomplete, and the absurdity of his demise before realizing his potentialities represents an attenuated form of the human condition. In this way, *Jacob's Room* becomes more than a fine character study, more than a sad tale of the hero who dies young: it establishes a general symbol of man's fate.

□

If human life is here envisaged as fragmentary and unfulfilled, there are strains of unity in experience that give rise to local forms, and these generate meanings in passages that appear randomly descriptive. One such strain is the theme of the light that burns over Cambridge. This is made to seem a cliché in the satirical sketch of the three typical dons (38-40), who are amusingly portrayed as nourishing their little lights—"Greek burns here; science there; philosophy on the ground floor" (38). But a more evocative statement of this theme is introduced at the solemn moment of chapel service in one of the world's most beautiful buildings:

They say the sky is the same everywhere. . . . if you are of a mystical tendency, consolation, and even explanation, shower down from the un-broken surface. But above Cambridge—anyhow above the roof of King's College Chapel—there is a difference. Out at sea a great city will cast a brightness into the night. Is it fanciful to suppose the sky, washed into the crevices of King's College Chapel, lighter, thinner, more sparkling than the sky elsewhere? Does Cambridge burn not only into the night, but into the day?

Look, as they pass into service, how airily the gowns blow out, as though nothing dense and corporeal were within. What sculptured faces, what certainty, authority controlled by piety, although great boots march under the gowns. In what orderly procession they advance. Thick wax candles stand upright; young men rise in white gowns. . . . As the sides of a lantern protect the flame so that it burns steady even in the wildest night—burns steady and gravely illumines the tree-trunks—so inside the Chapel all was orderly.

. . . If you stand a lantern under a tree every insect in the forest creeps up to it—a curious assembly, since though they scramble and swing and knock their heads against the glass, they seem to have no purpose—something senseless inspires them. One gets tired of watching them, as they amble round the lantern and blindly tap for admittance, one large toad being the most besotted of any and shouldering his way through the rest. Ah, but what's that? A terrifying volley of pistol-shots rings out—cracks sharply; ripples spread—silence laps smooth over sound. A tree—a tree has fallen, a sort of death in the forest. After that, the wind in the trees sounds melancholy.

But this service in King's College Chapel—why allow women to take part in it? Surely, if the mind wanders (and Jacob looked extraordinarily vacant, his head thrown back, his hymn-book open at the wrong place,). . . . (29–30)

And so on. This seems to be a string of random authorial ideas and metaphors, mixed with elements of the character's stream of consciousness while woolgathering during chapel service, but upon inspection it serves to compose a unified image of many of the fiction's concerns.

a) The opening images of a sky the same everywhere and of cities glowing in the night will be elaborated in the subsequent descriptions of Greece as part of a panoramic view of prewar Europe: "Now one after another lights were extinguished. Now great towns—Paris— Constantinople—London—were black as strewn rocks" (160). Not only Cambridge but all the illuminated centers of Western culture are seen as lights brightening the darkness, then going out in the general debacle.

b) The light of Cambridge burning into the night is also to be associated with Jacob's career of self-cultivation and articulation as an individual, e.g., "The lamps of London uphold the dark as upon the points of burning bayonets. . . . Every face, every shop, bedroom window, public-house, and dark square is a picture feverishly turned— in search of what? . . . What do we seek through millions of pages? . . .—oh, here is Jacob's room" (96).

c) The apparent incorporeality of the students in their flowing gowns (which is immediately belied by the "great boots" underneath) connects them with the image of moths hovering around a flame. The flame is another form of the light of Cambridge: "Thick wax candles stand upright; young men rise in white gowns . . ." (30). The blindness and vanity of their movements toward the light are enlarged by the succeeding image of insects clustering round a lantern in a forest.

d) This image is not merely an imposed narrative metaphor but an extension of the substance of Jacob's daydream, as he remembers an incident of butterfly-collecting and associated experiences: "The tree had fallen the night he caught it. There had been a volley of pistol-shots suddenly in the depths of the wood. . . . The tree had fallen, though it was a windless night, and the lantern, stood upon the ground, had lit up the still green leaves and the dead beech leaves. It was a dry place. A toad was there. And the red underwing had circled round the light and flashed and gone. The red underwing had never come back, though Jacob had waited" (21-22).[5]

e) The meaningless impulse of moths and men toward the light; the tree fallen without obvious cause to the tune of pistol shots; Jacob's sense of a "death in the forest" mingling with the audible organ tones, "buttressing human faith" (30)—these associated ideas not only report the contents of Jacob's mind but render the aspiration and futility of the chapel service and of the students on the verge of their careers. But the scene is relieved of its anxiety not only by the mild humor of Jacob's not keeping up with the service but by the image in Jacob's mind of a toad, "the most besotted of any," shouldering its way toward the light with the more soul-like butterflies.

Woolf returned to the image of insects round a lantern in an essay, "Reading," written shortly after *Jacob's Room*.[6] In the course of recounting her reading at an English country house, she introduces the memory of a youthful butterfly hunt, awkwardly referring to her father (or one of her brothers) as "the leader." Most of the elements of Jacob's butterfly hunt are presented again, but the language even more distinctly suggests traditional images of the psyche or soul:

[5]The novel is, in fact, full of insects: the stag-beetle in John's collection (21); the pale clouded yellows, blues, painted ladies, and peacocks that are found on Dods Hill (22); the death's head moth, the moth "with kidney-shaped spots of a fulvous hue," and the commas in Jacob's collection; the red underwing, the white admiral, and the purple butterfly that he had never caught (21-22); two white butterflies that help draw Jacob into a trance (35); the bumblebee (51-52) and convolvulus moth (55), probably in Mrs. Pascoe's Cornish garden; "the hawk moth, at the mouth of the cavern of mystery" (72)—a metaphor of the impulse to explain Jacob; a medley of hives, insects, spiders, webs, and honey, used first as a metaphor of London and then more specifically in relation to business activity in the City (162); and finally, the moths which link Mrs. Pascoe looking at the sea to the Greek women who are calling to their children to come and have the insects picked from their heads (175).

[6]On the day in which she records finishing the novel, Nov. 15, 1921, Woolf projects writing the essay: (*Diary*, pp. 40-41). For the text, see *Collected Essays*, II, 12-33; the passages quoted below are from pp. 22-25.

The lantern shoved its wedge of light through the dark, as though the air were a fine black snow piling itself up in banks on either side of the yellow beam. The direction of the trees was known to the leader of the party, who walked ahead, and seemed to draw us, unheeding darkness or fear, further and further into the unknown world. Not only has the dark the power to extinguish light, but it also buries under it great part of the human spirit. . . . We waited in a group, and the little circle of forest where we stood became as if we saw it through the lens of a very powerful magnifying glass. Every blade of grass looked larger than by day. . . . Then there emerged here a grasshopper, there a beetle, and here again a daddy-longlegs, awkwardly making his way from blade to blade. Their movements were all so awkward that they made one think of sea creatures crawling on the floor of the sea. . . . We felt we were surrounded by life, innumerable creatures were stirring among the trees. . . . Perhaps it was alarming to have these evidences of unseen lives. . . . And then, standing there with the moth safely in our hands, suddenly a volley of shot rang out, a hollow rattle of sound in the deep silence of the wood which had I know not what of mournful and ominous about it. It waned and spread through the forest: it died away, then another of those deep sighs arose. An enormous silence succeeded. "A tree," we said at last. A tree had fallen.

The interest of this passage is not limited to its amplification of the similar scene in *Jacob's Room*. It leads to one of the central passages in Woolf's work, an account of a type of experience which occurred within the circle of light on certain sleepless nights throughout her life, as well as in the reflective moments of key characters in her fiction:

What is it that happens between the hour of midnight and dawn, the little shock, the queer uneasy moment, as of eyes half open to the light, after which sleep is never so sound again? Is it experience, perhaps—repeated shocks, each unfelt at the time, suddenly loosening the fabric? Only this image suggests collapse and disintegration, whereas the process I have in mind is just the opposite. It is not destructive whatever it may be, one might say that it was rather of a creative character.

Something definitely happens. The garden, the butterflies, the morning sounds, trees, apples, human voices have emerged, stated themselves. As with a rod of light, order has been imposed upon tumult; form upon chaos. Perhaps it would be simpler to say that one wakes, after Heaven knows what internal process, with a sense of mastery. Familiar people approach all sharply outlined in morning light. Through the tremor and vibration of daily custom one discerns bone and form, endurance and permanence. Sorrow will have the power to effect this sudden arrest of the fluidity of life, and joy will have the same power. Or it may come without apparent cause, imperceptibly, much as some bud feels a sudden release in the night and is found in the morning with all its petals shaken free.

It will be recognized that Woolf is here describing not only a phase in her own creative process but the transient intuition of order and the sense of being in tune with that order which come to Clarissa Dalloway, Mrs. Ramsay, Lily Briscoe, Orlando, Bernard, and other masters of life or art in Woolf's work. To relate the autobiographical reminiscences of "Reading" to Jacob's youthful experience is to place him in this company—if not fulfilled in his sense of mastery, at least imaginatively inclined to it.

One further aspect of the intuition of order is to be distinguished in Jacob's experience: the dualism of life and death, which is crystallized in the image of a circle of light in an encompassing darkness. The sure grasp of the reality of things which comes to the butterfly collectors watching the insects emerge and which comes to the sleeper as he wakes to discover the objects in and around his room— this grasp is accompanied by a clear view of the mortality which encumbers them. The atmosphere of an undersea world (which had similarly prefigured Rachel's movement toward death in *The Voyage Out*) and the quickly rejected suggestions of "collapse and disintegration" both add a leaden echo to Woolf's account of her liberating experience. The same note is to be found in Jacob's recollection that the red underwing had eluded him and had never returned; it is the note of unfulfillment that is to go with him through his short life—a note sounded by the shot in the forest that comes in so eerie, and perhaps prophetic, a way.

Beyond these meditations on childhood and Cambridge experiences as matrices for Jacob's vital unfolding, other passages present his cultural education in a more direct and sustained manner. One of these is a metaphoric expansion of an obvious image of high intellectual development:

> There is in the British Museum an enormous mind. Consider that Plato is there cheek by jowl with Aristotle; and Shakespeare with Marlowe. This great mind is hoarded beyond the power of any single mind to possess it. Nevertheless (as they take so long finding one's walking-stick) one can't help thinking how one might come with a note-book, sit at a desk, and read it all through. . . .
>
> . . . Stone lies solid over the British Museum, as bone lies cool over the visions and heat of the brain. Only here the brain is Plato's brain and Shakespeare's; the brain has made pots and statues, great bulls and little jewels, and crossed the river of death this way and that incessantly, seeking some landing, now wrapping the body well for its long sleep; now laying a penny piece on the eyes; now turning the toes scrupulously to the East. . . .
>
> [Jacob] read on. For after all Plato continues imperturbably. And Hamlet utters his soliloquy. And there the Elgin Marbles lie, all night long, old Jones's lantern sometimes recalling Ulysses, or a horse's head. . . .

The *Phaedrus* is very difficult. And so, when at length one reads straight ahead, falling into step, marching on, becoming (so it seems) momentarily part of this rolling, imperturbable energy, which has driven darkness before it since Plato walked the Acropolis, it is impossible to see to the fire.

The dialogue draws to its close. . . . Plato's argument is stowed away in Jacob's mind, and for five minutes Jacob's mind continues alone, onwards, into the darkness. (107-9)

This vision of the British Museum as a personified sum of human thought and creative energy bears some resemblance to Hardy's vision of a cosmic brain in *The Dynasts* and to other then-current notions of a collective mental being more important than the individual mind.[7] But Woolf's account emphasizes equally the process by which individual minds derive from and are differentiated from the collective mind. The perception of this process is dramatized by being ascribed to Jacob himself as he waits to retrieve his walking stick at the check room; we can tell that this is Woolf's intention because the heroes of mind here listed are, with the exception of Aristotle, Jacob's favorites. To support this rumination, an analogy is formed between the stone walls and cultural contents of the museum and the flesh and mind of men like Jacob. A further analogy is developed between Jacob's contribution to Plato's survival by his reading and the bringing of statuary out of the dark by the night watchman's lantern (the word that connects the two acts is "recalling" in its twin senses of remembering and calling back—in this case, from the dark). Finally, the rhythm of reading joins with the rhythm of general intellectual progress so that Jacob becomes part of a metaphoric march of mind, even marching on alone after the end of Plato's text. Yet one characteristic distinguishes the individual from the group mind: its mortality. The cultural brain is capable of crossing and recrossing the Styx, observing a variety of funerary customs, and maintaining its resiliency across the ages. Individuals of many cultures have made part of the brain, then, and Jacob is one of them, but he is only "momentarily" part of its "imperturbable energy"—or "so it seems."[8]

It is no accident that such affinities with classical things are ascribed to Jacob at the same time that his mortality is insisted upon.

---

[7]There is a similar description in *A Room of One's Own* (pp. 39-40): ". . . there one stood under the vast dome, as if one were a thought in the huge bald forehead which is so splendidly encircled by a band of famous names."

[8]The close alliance of youth with the march of mind is emphasized in the 1916 essay, "Hours in a Library" (*Collected Essays*, II, 34-35), a piece which may have focused for Woolf the image of a young man reading. The essay takes its title from that of Leslie Stephen's collected literary essays.

Not only do his "photographs from the Greek" (37), his attention to the Elgin Marbles (107), and his conversations on Virgil and Sophocles indicate that his conventional training in the classics has taken root, but he consciously takes up a classical stance by boasting to Durrant that "probably . . . we are the only people in the world who know what the Greeks meant" (75). Even his social ideals are derived from notions of Greek life, e.g., the *hetaerae* for feminine behavior (75); and he refers to Greek politics for modern problems, though aware that "their solution is no help to us" (149). His trip to Greece is, then, the culmination of a long preparation, and when he climbs a moutain near Olympia, he "enjoyed himself immensely. Probably he had never been so happy in the whole of his life" (143).

The association of Jacob with the "Greek myth" may be made fancifully, as Sandra does when she sees his head "exactly on a level with the head of the Hermes of Praxiteles. The comparison was all in his favour" (144). There are traces of this tendency to interpret the classical subjectively in Jacob himself: he is "extraordinarily moved" by one of the caryatids of the Erechtheum, partly because it reminds him of Sandra (151). Thoughts of Greece are mingled with his developing sense of himself, but he also marks and accepts the distance between the life of the past and his existence in the present: ". . . his meditations were given an extraordinary edge; Greece was over; the Parthenon in ruins; yet there he was" (149).[9]

Having posited that *Jacob's Room* is a fiction in which an individual is shown partially constituted by his transactions with his society, we are now prepared to see that society, in its largest sense, as Western civilization. Indeed, it might be claimed that the underlying subject of the novel is not Jacob but his culture and that the death of one in the first of the world wars marks the demise of the other. Generalizations about civilization are numerous: initially, there are scornful references to modern men as "civilization's triumphs" (95) or as "the height of civilization" (164). The shock of Greece's present "ramshackle condition" and its peasant survivals give him pause: "The whole of civilization was being condemned" (137); on the other hand, he plans to repeat his visits to Greece as "the only chance I can see of protecting oneself from civilization" (145). His development towards thinking "a great deal about the problems of civilization" (149) comes mainly from experiencing the Parthenon, and this

[9]The use of this latter phrase begins with Jacob's discovery of the structures on the Acropolis: "There they are" (147). (In "Reading," Woolf describes the discovery of individual beings as a sudden standing-forward.) The phrase reaches full eminence in the conclusion of *Mrs. Dalloway.*

emerges as the high point of his career, as well as the climax of the action:

The extreme definiteness with which they [the columns] stand, now a brilliant white, again yellow, and in some lights red, imposes ideas of durability, of the emergence through the earth of some spiritual energy elsewhere dissipated in elegant trifles. But this durability exists quite independently of our admiration. Although the beauty is sufficiently humane to weaken us, to stir the deep deposit of mud—memories, abandonments, regrets, sentimental devotions—the Parthenon is separate from all that; and if you consider how it has stood out all night, for centuries, you begin to connect the blaze (at midday the glare is dazzling and the frieze almost invisible) with the idea that perhaps it is beauty alone that is immortal. (147-48)

The idea of the immortality of beauty, independent of our subjective reactions to it, is itself a Greek endowment. It is here set amid a number of classical *topoi* of light and darkness, unity and plurality, the essential and the conditional. Whether or not we consider these notions as implicit in Woolf's esthetics, we can take Jacob's perception to be a high point in his cultivation. It is still ironic, however, that Jacob's grasp of the eternal occurs almost at the point when he succumbs to his mortal condition.[10]

A further consequence of Jacob's vision of the classical ideal is the development of his sense of history. The narrative voice had early made the point that "all history backs our pane of glass" (47) (an image of the mind as a mirror); now Jacob "began, as if inspired by what he had read [obviously a classical text], to write a note upon the importance of history—upon democracy—one of those scribbles upon which the work of a lifetime may be based; or again, it falls out of a book twenty years later, and one can't remember a word of it" (150). And the close of this chapter on his Greek experience crystallizes it in an image of "the bright, inquisitive, armoured, resplendent, summer's day, which has long since vanquished chaos; which has dried the melancholy mediaeval mists; drained the swamp and stood glass and stone upon it; and equipped our brains and bodies with such

---

[10]Woolf's own adherence to the "Greek myth" is recorded in "On Not Knowing Greek," *Collected Essays*, ii, 1-13, esp. p. 11: "Does not the whole of Greece heap itself behind every line of its literature? They admit us to a vision of the earth unravished, the sea unpolluted, the maturity, tried but unbroken, of mankind. Every word is reinforced by a vigor which pours out of olive-tree and temple and the bodies of the young. . . . Back and back we are drawn to steep ourselves in what, perhaps, is only an image of the reality, not the reality itself, a summer day's imagined in the heart of a northern winter. . . . It is the language that has us most in bondage; the desire for that which perpetually lures us back."

an armoury of weapons that merely to see the flash and thrust of limbs engaged in the conduct of daily life is better than the old pageant of armies drawn out in battle array upon the plain" (163)—a sense of spiritual progress gained while the armies gather for war.

We are taken back to the vision of history near the opening of the text, when the Flanders family climbs Dods Hill and Archer and Jacob stand in "the Roman fortress" scanning the bay (15). No sense of history came to the family on climbing that hill, such as will come to Jacob on the Acropolis, but later Mrs. Flanders and the mystical Mrs. Jarvis walk up the hill, thinking of the dead and Mrs. Flanders's lost brooch and the passage of time: "But their voices floated for a little above the camp. The moonlight destroyed nothing. The moor accepted everything. Tom Gage cries aloud so long as his tombstone endures. The Roman skeletons are in safe keeping. Betty Flanders's darning needles are safe too and her garnet brooch. And sometimes at mid-day, in the sunshine, the moor seems to hoard these little treasures, like a nurse" (133).

So history emerges as a great mound or compost of artifacts, lives, deaths, and time, and it is with this accumulation that the individual is ultimately identified: ". . . There remains over something which can never be conveyed to a second person save by Jacob himself. Moreover, part of this is not Jacob but Richard Bonamy—the room; the market carts; the hour; the very moment of history" (71). Yet, though the self is a collection rather than a unity, it nevertheless remains the center of human concern: "The march that the mind keeps beneath the windows of others is queer enough. . . . Now distracted by brown panelling; now by a fern in a pot; . . . yet all the while having for centre, for magnet, a young man alone in his room" (94).

□

Woolf was, while working on *Jacob's Room*, aware that Joyce was writing a work toward the same end of capturing the lived experience and the fragmentariness of life; she also acknowledged that he was probably doing it better.[11] Passages of "stream-of-consciousness" in *Jacob's Room* are few and clumsy, e.g.:

("I'm twenty-two. It's nearly the end of October. Life is thoroughly pleasant. . . .")
"I say, Bonamy, what about Beethoven?"
("Bonamy is an amazing fellow. . . .") (71)

---

[11]*Diary*, p. 28, 26 Sept. 1920; her later distaste for *Ulysses* seems explicable only on the grounds of an ineradicable residue of prudery, although she partly accounts for it by her resistance to T. S. Eliot's elaborate claims for the novel (*Diary*, p. 47, 16 Aug. 1922; pp. 50–51, 26 Sept. 1922).

Or this:

About half-past nine Jacob left the house, his door slamming, other doors slamming, buying his paper, mounting his omnibus, or, weather permitting, walking his road as other people do. Head bent down, a desk, a telephone, books bound in green leather, electric light. . . . "Fresh coals, sir?" . . ."Your tea, sir." . . . Talk about football, the Hotspurs, the Harlequins; six-thirty *Star* brought in by the office boy; the rooks of Gray's Inn passing overhead; branches in the fog thin and brittle; and through the roar of traffic now and again a voice shouting: "Verdict—verdict—winner—winner," while letters accumulate in a basket, Jacob signs them, and each evening finds him, as he takes his coat down, with some muscle of the brain new stretched. (88–89)

Here the succession is not from reported inner speech to reported public speech and back again, as in the first passage quoted, but from omniscient narrative ("Jacob left the house"), to a listing of observed phenomena (the perceiver unspecified but presumably Jacob: "a desk, a telephone . . . 'Fresh coals, sir?' "), and back to omniscient narrative ("Jacob signs them"). The effect of these shifts is to record subjective observations but not to relinquish the omniscient narrator's imposed control of them.

There are also efforts to keep up with Joyce's experiments in conveying the simultaneity of experience by an easy transition from one consciousness to another, e.g.:

He was certainly thinking about Home Rule in Ireland—a very difficult matter. A very cold night.

The snow, which had been falling all night, lay at three o'clock in the afternoon over the fields and the hill. . . . At six o'clock a man's figure carrying a lantern crossed the field. . . . Spaces of complete immobility separated each of these movements. The land seemed to lie dead. . . . The worn voices of clocks repeated the fact of the hour all night long.

Jacob, too, heard them, and raked out the fire. He rose. He stretched himself. He went to bed. (97–98)

The effect of this transition between unrelated actions at roughly coincident times is to elide their moral as well as physical atmospheres. Not only is the discontinuity of movement in the fields carried on in Jacob's discrete movements, conveyed in staccato sentences, but the image of the dead land has something to say about the nation faced with the Home Rule question. Nevertheless, such passages come as set pieces and do not avoid the stigma of the mere technical exercise. Woolf had not yet developed the characteristic style that was to mark her later work, but she was already experimenting with a number of techniques for fusing one character's point of view with another's, the character's with the narrator's, and the narrator's with something larger than any personal perspective.[12]

An innovative means of representing the quality of Jacob's experience lies in shifting from one narrative point of view to another to build up a medium of consciousness, a mental atmosphere in which men like Jacob may be found to exist. (This synthetic consciousness is derived from the multiple relationships which offer a rounded view of a character, as discussed above.) The effect of such composite views is to make Jacob manifest in the absence of a direct view of him. A number of such composites are recorded in accounts of social occasions (e.g., pages 70-71, 138-39), but the most comprehensive is one that forms the entire thirteenth chapter. As Jacob and Bonamy sit in Hyde Park, the movements and thoughts of most of the other characters are sketched in—whether or not they are concerned with Jacob, although most of them are in Hyde Park at about the same time.

The manifestation of Jacob by this synthetic structure is achieved not by filling in his attributes but by juxtaposing images of loss, accident, and failure in such a way as to surround him with negativity, to create him not as a presence but as an absence. Such a claim will require substantiation:

a) "Jacob was silent" (163)—although Bonamy is sarcastically commenting on the social scene ("The height of the season").

b) " 'Jacob! Jacob!' thought Clara," who is walking with "kind Mr. Bowley" and thinking of an occasion when "Jacob had never come" (166).

---

[12]In a ground-breaking article, Ann Banfield employs recent linguistic theory to define the features of the style usually called "stream-of-consciousness." ("Narrative Style and the Grammar of Direct and Indirect Speech," *Foundations of Language*, x [1973], 1-39; quotations are cited parenthetically.) Drawing most of her examples from Virginia Woolf, Banfield distinguishes such passages as the opening of *Mrs. Dalloway* from both direct and indirect discourse on the criteria of absence of embedded speech, replacement of verbs of communication by "verbs of consciousness," and prevalence of pronouns, indicating assumed personal designations by a mind that need not provide names for persons of whom it is aware. Banfield calls such writing (translating the French *style indirect libre*) "the free indirect style. . . . It captures something between speech and thought which can neither be paraphraseable in a propositional form nor cast into an expression with a new first-person referent according to the Direct Speech Conventions. We might say that it articulates the 'stream-of-consciousness' " (p. 29). She goes on to describe the ability of this mode to include not only thoughts but also perceptions, even of overheard speech: "Even when a dialogue is presented in the free indirect style, it is not understood as actual spoken *words*, but as words *heard* or *perceived*, registering on some consciousness. This has a counterpart on the visual plane. Descriptions in this style present scenes viewed from the limited perspective of one character. [E.g.,] Woolf's description of Mrs. Ramsay's reaction to a sentence of direct speech . . ." (pp. 31-32).

c) ". . . a horse galloped past without a rider"—as observed by Julia Eliot, who is on her way to visit a sickbed (167).[13]

d) Florinda, after jilting Jacob, sees a newcomer enter Verrey's and concludes from his stare, " 'He's like Jacob'. . . . She stopped laughing" (168–69)—perhaps from an unfulfilled love for him.

e) Fanny's misery at losing Jacob ("This is life. This is life. . . .") leads her to erect a statuelike image of him more calcified and alien than even Sandra's statuary idealizations: "Fanny's idea of Jacob was more statuesque, noble, and eyeless than ever" (170).

f) "The wires of the Admiralty shivered with some far-away communication" (171); the news of the gathering of forces for the war mingles with accounts of a patriotic march down Whitehall and the sterile deliberations of statesmen—all conspiring to send Jacob to his death.

g) "Jacob rose from his chair in Hyde Park, tore his ticket to pieces, and walked away. . . . The long windows of Kensington Palace flushed fiery rose as Jacob walked away; a flock of wild duck flew over the Serpentine; and the trees were stood against the sky, blackly, magnificently" (173). That is our last direct view of him.

h) Reverend Andrew Floyd (he had earlier been seen proleptically in this act) (20) sees Jacob "but hesitated, and let the moment pass, and lost the opportunity" (173–74).

i) Later that day, Clara, on her way to the opera, "started. She saw Jacob. 'Who?' asked Mrs. Durrant sharply, leaning forward. But she saw no one" (174).

A yet wider vision of the space around Jacob is achieved by releasing the narrative perspective from its usual conventions and allowing it to move freely over the surface of the earth, as only novels like *War and Peace* and poems like *The Dynasts* have been free to do. The panoramic vision begins to operate during Jacob's ascent of the Acropolis by night:

---

[13]The incidence of accident and illness in such a low-keyed novel as this is staggering: on the first page we are told that "accidents were awful things" (5) (Mrs. Flanders must be thinking of her husband's recent death, and this is her explanation of his fatal failure to change his boots after duck-hunting [14]); she tells of a "gunpowder explosion in which poor Mr. Curnow had lost his eye" (8) (is he a relative of "the boy Curnow" who attends Mrs. Durrant in Cornwall?); she assures Archer that a steamer won't sink in the storm raging outdoors (11); her brother Morty is repeatedly recalled as having disappeared in the Far East (13, 36, 136, 175); "The Scilly Isles might well be obliterated by a roller sweeping straight across" (46) (this seems to be Jacob's reflection); the Durrants' father's "death was a tragedy" (58) (this sounds like an accidental death); a post office van on Jacob's street almost runs down a little girl (62); and there are various nonlethal acts of destruction like Florinda's throwing a vase (73).

It was dark now over Athens. . . . At sea the piers stood out, marked by separate dots; the waves being invisible, and promontories and islands were dark humps with a few lights. . . . The mainland of Greece was dark; and somewhere off Euboea a cloud must have touched the waves and spattered them—the dolphins circling deeper and deeper into the sea. . . . In Greece and the uplands of Albania and Turkey, the wind scours the sand and the dust, and sows itself thick with dry particles. . . . Now the agitation of the air uncovered a racing star. Now it was dark. Now one after another lights were extinguished. Now great towns—Paris—Constantinople—London—were black as strewn rocks. . . . [Mrs. Flanders] raising herself slightly on her elbow, sighed like one who realizes, but would fain ward off a little longer—oh, a little longer!—the oppression of eternity.

But to return to Jacob and Sandra.

They had vanished. There was the Acropolis; but had they reached it? The columns and the Temple remain; the emotion of the living breaks fresh on them year after year; and of that what remains?

As for reaching the Acropolis who shall say that we ever do it, or that when Jacob woke next morning he found anything hard and durable to keep for ever? Still, he went with them to Constantinople. . . .

But the wind was rolling the darkness through the streets of Athens, rolling it, one might suppose, with a sort of trampling energy of mood which forbids too close an analysis of the feelings of any single person, or inspection of features. All faces—Greek, Levantine, Turkish, English—would have looked much the same in that darkness. At length the columns and the Temples whiten, yellow, turn rose; and the Pyramids and St. Peter's arise, and at last sluggish St. Paul's looms up. (159-61)

The effects of this passage are multiple:

a) By following the movement of the wind from east to west, the narrative shifts from its eastern European scenes back to London, where the next chapter opens in Hyde Park; it is as if the focus had followed Jacob on his homeward trip from Constantinople.

b) By being framed from the standpoint of the nations of the world rather than from that of individuals, broad questionings of the meaning of life are more deeply grounded—"had they reached it?" and "what remains?" (and Jacob's "what for?" which directly follows) are embodied in the lights going out across the globe and the uniformly darkened faces of many national types.

c) By including in its description of the Greek seas images used earlier in describing Jacob's Scarborough and Cornwall experiences, the narrative fuses disparate times and places into symbols of an individual life; these images include the piers and waves seen from Dods Hill (15; see also pages 5, 9, 47, 51, 56, 140, 175) and the rock mistaken by Jacob for "a large black woman" (8). The sea imagery, which has been copious in a book set partly in Cornwall, the Yorkshire coast, and Greece, comes to a crescendo here at the finale—ominous in its overtones—of Jacob's life.

d) The wind, which effects the transitions between places and covers all with a morbid darkness, has a valence different from the traditional Romantic image, in which wind conveys the interanimation of things by a flow of vital energy.[14] A closely associated image, the web of organic filaments that extends throughout the universe, enters the ensuing forest scene: "So when the wind roams through a forest innumerable twigs stir; hives are brushed; insects sway on grass blades; the spider runs rapidly up a crease in the bark; and the whole air is tremulous with breathing; elastic with filaments" (162). The force of these compounded images of universal pall and organic vitality is to associate Jacob's single life with a vast cosmic process, with its regular fluxions of life and death. For the first time there is a hint that the absolute value of his personal existence may be reduced to an insectlike typicality, if not absurdity.

e) The final implication of this view of Jacob from the perspective of the earth as a whole is that his effort, even his limited accomplishment of making an identity out of the encounter with the world, is doomed to ineffectuality and uncertainty: "There was the Acropolis; but had they reached it? . . . As for reaching the Acropolis who shall say that we ever do it . . .?" Reaching the Acropolis becomes a pursuit of cultural identity, individual fulfillment, and all the higher goals implied by the age-old symbol of the ascent of a hilltop. But the human condition stands in pathetic contrast to the solid and imperious value of the classic stones on their outcropping of rock. Jacob's life is seen here in its ultimate ephemerality, with the classic recognition that such is the fate of men, who call for aid against death in vain.

□

The most famous use of the moth image in Woolf may stand as a summary statement of the theme of *Jacob's Room*:

It was as if someone had taken a tiny bead of pure life and decking it as lightly as possible with down and feathers, had set it dancing and zigzagging to show us the true nature of life. Thus displayed one could not get over the strangeness of it. One is apt to forget all about life. . . .

[14]A naive statement of the pantheist view is Betty Flanders's speculation on her dead husband's fusion with nature (14). It is, however, possible that the wind that raises and lets fall the leaves outside Jacob's windows carries something of him in the final scene (176).

The insignificant little creature now knew death. As I looked at the dead moth, this minute wayside triumph of so great a force over so mean an antagonist filled me with wonder. Just as life had been strange a few minutes before, so death was now as strange. The moth having righted himself now lay most decently and uncomplainingly composed. O yes, he seemed to say, death is stronger than I am.[15]

[15]"The Death of the Moth," Collected Essays, I, 360–61.

mrs. dalloway

"A virgin forest
in each"

Mrs. Dalloway (1925) has been analyzed widely and often well, perhaps because it is the one among Woolf's major works that most closely satisfies the traditional view of what a novel should be. Despite its manifest oddness and systematic technical innovation, this is in the first instance a novel, by virtue of its thorough absorption in social life and its close character study. There are, to be sure, passages of essay inserted in the text (especially the disquisition on Proportion and Conversion), but these may be regarded not as an attempt at a mixture of genres but rather as passionate intrusions by the author, based on personal experience. Indeed, the comparative absence here of the mixture of genres which was to enrich her later fiction requires that we look beneath the novelistic surface to grasp the work's uniqueness among portraits of high-society life.

As a series of experiments with the emergent techniques of perspectival narration, temporal discontinuity, and rhythmic juxtaposition of elements, *Mrs. Dalloway* may be considered the first important work of the literary period initiated by *Ulysses*—although hardly an advance upon it. Several critics have noted the resemblance between Mrs. Dalloway's walk and encounters on a single day in London and Leopold Bloom's equally busy June day in

Dublin, but the extent of the resemblance has not been appreciated.[1] The date of the former is as precise as the latter—a Wednesday (19) in June (6), 1923 (80) (the Wednesday falling in mid-June, 1923, was the thirteenth). The day apparently begins at ten, as Clarissa leaves her house to the sound of Big Ben striking the hour (6), for the next hour struck is 11 A.M. (24), during the skywriting scene, when Clarissa is returning home (and the Smiths are sitting in Regent's Park awaiting their consultation with Sir William Bradshaw). Time moves to 11:30 as Peter Walsh leaves the Dalloway house (53-55); to 11:45 as Walsh passes the Smiths in Regent's Park (79) (but this is problematic, as Roll-Hansen has shown, for Peter has not only walked to the park from Westminster in a quarter-hour but has had his nap and dream too); to noon, the hour of the Smiths' appointment, and also the moment when Clarissa lays her green party dress on the bed (104); to 1:30 P.M., as the Smiths leave Sir William's (113), near the time of Lady Bruton's lunch for Hugh Whitbread and Richard Dalloway (113-15); to three, as Dalloway returns home (129-30), arriving about 3:30, in the middle of Clarissa's nap (140); to six, when Rezia hears the clocks after her husband's suicide (165); to shortly after six, as Walsh reads Clarissa's letter (171). The day ends after three the following morning, as Clarissa ruminates on Smith's suicide (204), before returning to the end of her party. Time is a matter of concern to the characters, who write odes to it, as does Smith (78, 162), personify it—or its church bells—as does Clarissa (141), and approvingly connect it with British institutions like Greenwich, as does Whitbread (113). It should be noted, however, that all times given are not Greenwich mean time but daylight saving time, as instituted by "the great revolution of Mr. Willett's summer time" (178).

The homely particularity of these time indications implies a concept of time as a series of "life junctures" rather than an impersonal scheme. These life junctures are established by the presence of certain sensory phenomena in different contexts, for example, the sound of Big Ben; by common perceptions among unrelated observers, for example, those of the Prime Minister's car or of a skywriting plane; and by convergences at occasions of group activity, for example, Mrs. Dalloway's party. Time is *relativistic* here, in the sense that it depends on the systems of measurement, the state of

---

[1]Some of the raw data has been collected in Diderik Roll-Hansen, "Peter Walsh's Seven-League Boots: A Note on *Mrs. Dalloway*," *English Studies*, L (1968), 301-4. Other reflections on the choice of setting in a modern metropolis are given in Miroslav Beker, "London as a Principle of Structure in *Mrs. Dalloway*," *Modern Fiction Studies*, XVIII (1972), 375-85.

motion of the bodies involved, and the degree of simultaneity or divergence involved in the recording of disparate events. But Woolf also entertained the current notions of time as *relative*, subjective, and even personal. In a number of canceled passages—whose deletion from the finished work does not diminish their interest—Woolf mused on the personality that may be ascribed to various clocks, developing the notion of the personal life-time which they represent:

In Westminster, where temples, meeting houses, conventicles & steeples of all kinds are congregated together, there is at all hours and halfhours, a round of bells, correcting each other, asseverating that time has come a little earlier, or stayed a little later, here or there. . . .

It might have been the seat of time itself, this island of Westminster, the forge where the hours were made, & sent out, in various tones and tempers, to glide into the lives of the foot passengers, of studious workmen [,] desultory women within doors, who coming to the window looked up at the sky as the clock struck, as if to say, What? or Why? They had their choice of answers; from the different sounds or [for "now"?] colliding, or running side by side, melting into each other, forming, for the moment, a trellis work of sound which, as it faced away, was suddenly renewed from some other steeple; St. Margarets, for example, saying two minutes after Big Ben how now, really & indeed, it was half past eleven. Yes, it was half past eleven, St. Margarets said, in her sad voice, upon hearing which, [it] was necessary to make haste, or again to loiter; or to attempt some kind of comparison, or to think how not merely that time differed but that the tone of it was possessed of the strangest power; now militant & masculine; now curtly prosaic, & now in the voice of St. Margarets *flower in the mind*, & had the power, like some breeze which visits a garden at dawn, to brush every flower and leaf in the minds territory, lifting, stirring, strangely, very strangely.[2]

These passages suggest that both clock-time—which had "come a little earlier, or stayed a little later"—and the men who live by it— "they had their choice of answers"—can endow temporality with the significance and even the personified appearance of human living. And this shaping process does not contest the claim that "now, really & indeed, it was half past eleven"; it merely records the fact with a note of amusement. There is in the final clauses, moreover, another dimension or intuition of time, at which Woolf could only hint and into which it is impossible to delve.

Equally precise and equally individual is the treatment of space in this novel. *Mrs. Dalloway* outdoes *Ulysses* in following its main

[2]MS. in the British Museum, Vol. i, 5, 10. [Hereafter cited as B.M.] These passages correspond to pp. 6 and 55–56 of the text, respectively (the latter passage's focus on St. Margaret's is also picked up on p. 141).

characters' perambulations through the city, so that London becomes as powerfully charged a system of space as it is for more
overtly urban novelists. Clarissa's route is best known: she crosses
Victoria Street (6), passes Buckingham Palace to enter St.
James's Park (9), crosses Piccadilly (10) on the way to Bond Street (11), and
proceeds as far as Brook Street (20) before returning to Westminster. Her husband makes almost the same tour in reverse, starting at Lady Bruton's in Brook Street (124), walking with Hugh
Whitbread down Conduit Street (124, 127), crossing Piccadilly and
the Green Park (128), and passing through Dean's Yard (129) to his
home. Their daughter strikes out at right angles to this Westminster-
Mayfair axis, taking a bus eastward to the City (149) after tea with
Miss Kilman in Victoria Street (138, 142); she pays an extra penny
to proceed up the Strand (150), gets off at Chancery Lane (150) to
explore the Temple (151), and then retreats via the Strand and a
Westminster bus (153).

Peter Walsh's is the most extensive exploration, as befitting a
Londoner just returned from India: on leaving Clarissa he crosses
Victoria Street (54) but strikes out through the middle of the city,
passing up Whitehall (56) and Trafalgar Square (58); he follows a
girl up Cockspur Street (59), across Piccadilly, up Regent Street,
past Oxford and Great Portland Streets, and down a side street
(60), where he loses her; he then goes on to Regent's Park (61),
where he encounters the Smiths and has his dream, and back to
Regent's Park tube station (91), where he takes a taxi to his solicitors'
in Lincoln's Inn (52). He emerges from his divorce consultation,
walks north past the British Museum (167) to his hotel in Bloomsbury (173), dines and dresses for the party, and walks down "Bed-
ford Place leading into Russell Sq." (179) then on to Westminster
by way of Whitehall (180). The Smiths follow a simpler route: from
Regent's Park to Harley Street for their consultation and home to
lodgings off the Tottenham Court Road (98). Thus each of the main
characters traces a circle around himself, extending himself into
space, moving through his characteristic part of London for personal
services or on social rounds, and returning home for life or death—all
except Walsh, the odd man out, who has not returned to his hotel by
the end of the text, ending where we first saw him, at Clarissa's.

We may summarize these movements in space and time by indicating the narrative divisions so conspicuously *not* provided by the
author in her effort to maintain the flow of living experience. *Mrs.
Dalloway* may be divided into twenty-one sections, averaging ten
pages each in length, as follows:

Section	Pages	Character-focus and situation	Time
I	5-16	Clarissa's shopping trip	10:00-11 A.M.
II	16-25 (30-33)	Londoners (including the Smiths and Clarissa) observing Prime Minister's car and skywriting	10:00-11 A.M.
III	25-30	Septimus in Regent's Park—fantasies	10:00-11 A.M.
IV	33-45	Clarissa at home	11:00 A.M.
V	45-54	Peter's visit to Clarissa	after 11:00 A.M.
VI	54-63	Peter's walk to the Park	after 11:30 A.M.
VII	63-72	Peter's dream and memories of Bourton	± 11:30 A.M.
VIII	72-79	Septimus and Rezia in Park—fantasies	± 11:30 A.M.
IX	79-92	Peter's memories of Bourton, etc.	after 11:45 A.M.
X	92-104	Smiths leaving Park—summary of Septimus's career	just before noon
XI	104-13	The Bradshaw consultation	12 noon-1:30 P.M.
XII	113-25	Lady Bruton's luncheon	1:30-3 P.M.
XIII	125-32	Richard's return home	arriving at 3 P.M.
XIV	132-41	Clarissa on Miss Kilman	before 3:30 P.M.
XV	141-48	Miss Kilman at tea and at church	after 3:30 P.M.
XVI	148-53	Elizabeth's bus ride	after 3:30 P.M.
XVII	153-66	Septimus's suicide	6:00 P.M.
XVIII	166-81	Peter's preparations for the party	after 6:00 P.M.
XIX	181-201	The party—shifting points of view	?-3:00 A.M.
XX	201-5	Clarissa's withdrawal and return	?-3:00 A.M.
XXI	205-13	Conversation of Peter and Sally	?-3:00 A.M.

This specificity of time and place has another effect beyond that of capturing the quality of life in an English upper-middle class setting. *Mrs. Dalloway*, like *Jacob's Room* and *To the Lighthouse*, is intimately tied to the England of the postwar years, not only recording the human losses and the moral atmosphere but probing at its basic institutions. It is no accident that this fiction is about the wife of a member of Parliament, and was originally conceived as a short story to be called "The Prime Minister," for *Mrs. Dalloway* may be considered in part a political novel in the modern mode—updating Trollope's milieu, in effect.

Clarissa is the offspring of the Parrys, who were "courtiers once in the time of the Georges" (7) but who were not "very well off" (67) in Clarissa's time. They have seen their home, Bourton, descend to a distant relation, one Herbert, so that Clarissa sadly says, "I never go there now" (48). The family's social energies are summed up in Uncle William: "He had turned on his bed one morning in the middle of the War. He had said, 'I have had enough'" (13). Clarissa admires the grand ladies who carry on in heroic fashion after learning of the death of their sons (7, 12), rather scorns those like Miss Kilman who have been socially injured by the war (14), and remains ignorant of the war's influence on Smith's suicide, with which she does sympathize. She was a sentimental Radical in youth (169) but now concludes that "the most dejected of miseries sitting on doorsteps (drink their downfall) . . . can't be dealt with, she felt positive, by Acts of Parliament for that very reason: they love life" (6). Her husband is a Tory (planning to write Lady Bruton's family history if he becomes unemployed in the event of a Labour victory [122]), mildly progressive ("having championed the downtrodden and followed his instincts in the House of Commons" [127]), and in a position to tell Walsh what the "conservative duffers" meant "to do about India" (177). All have been numbed by the war's horror: Lucrezia Smith shrugs off her husband's loss of his friend Evans by thinking, "Every one has friends who were killed in the War" (74); a Mr. Bowley, who resides at the Albany, is moved at the sight of "poor women, nice little children, orphans, widows, the War—tut-tut" (23); and the narrator comments, "This late age of [the] world's experience had bred in them all, all men and women, a well of tears" (12).

Social class lines are, however, still well drawn: the crowds still respond to the symbols of authority and tradition, as a policeman responds to "something white, magical, circular, in the footman's hand, a disc inscribed with [the Prime Minister's] name" (20); "a Colonial insulted the House of Windsor" and meets with hostility in a pub (21); the men at White's "seemed ready to attend their Sovereign, if need be, to the cannon's mouth, as their ancestors had done before them" (21); and Hugh Whitbread is still "afloat on the cream of English society" (114). Lady Bruton pursues her favorite scheme of emigration (a social safety valve of long standing) and is favored with a *tête-à-tête* with the Prime Minister at Clarissa's party. But there have been profound changes that are only superficially apparent: ". . . something happened which threw out many of [Smith's employer's] calculations, took away his ablest young fellows, and eventually, so prying and insidious were the fingers of the European War, smashed a plaster cast of Ceres, ploughed a hole in the geranium beds, and utterly ruined the cook's nerves at Mr. Brewer's establishment at Muswell Hill" (95). For a recent arrival like Walsh, this subtle change can only be guessed at: "more than suspecting from the words of a girl, from a housemaid's laughter—intangible things you couldn't lay your hands on—that shift in the whole pyramidal accumulation which in his youth had seemed immovable" (178).

The consistently political ambience of *Mrs. Dalloway* is focused in the figure of the Prime Minister, which moves through the text from beginning to end. At the outset his car appears in Mayfair as Clarissa is doing her shopping, causing a stir of interest from many perspectives which anticipates the interest given to the skywriting airplane (16-22).[3] At the close the Prime Minister's visit helps knit together Clarissa's struggling party, providing a lift for the servants (181) as well as for the guests (189). This political symbol has long been associated with Clarissa, for early in life Walsh has berated her with it: "She would marry a Prime Minister and stand at the top of the staircase; the perfect hostess he called her . . ." (9). In the closing pages we see the prophecy partially fulfilled as the perfect hostess stands at the top of the stairs, and as for marrying the Prime Minister, her husband's career is not yet over. Smith's fate, too, is sketched with reference to this symbol of political eminence: he believes that his new religion must be conveyed urgently to the Prime Minister (75, 162).[4]

Even more powerful as a symbol of the state of society envisaged in this fiction is that of illness. All are ill: Clarissa, turned white-haired since her bout of influenza (6), Evelyn Whitbread, chronically ill of an unspecified internal ailment (8), Smith, with his war psychosis, Ellie Henderson, subject to chills (185), and even the shamming Lady Lexham, who excuses herself from the party by pretending a cold (184). Attitudes toward sickness range from Dr. Holmes's policy of benign neglect to Elizabeth Dalloway's preference for the ill (150), with Sir William Bradshaw's Harley Street manner falling somewhere between. The most corrosive ailment in this society seems to be disease of the heart, and the condition takes on the symbolic proportions it had acquired in Ford's *The Good Soldier*: Clarissa's heart has been affected by her illness (6), and Walsh has always accused her of having no heart (10); he also declares this of Whitbread (9). Yet the unconventional Sally Seton, now Lady Rosseter, can reduce the symbol to a cliché—"What does the brain matter . . . compared with the heart?" (213)—and Clarissa acknowledges that her daughter's affection for the objectionable Miss Kilman "proves she has a heart" (149). These sentimental pieties hint at the prevailing scarcity of the real thing in a society sick at heart.

□

[3] That this is the Prime Minister's car and not the Queen's or the Prince of Wales's (as is supposed on p. 17) is suggested by the facts that its occupant is a male (17) and that it passes without stopping at St. James's Palace, the residence of the Prince (22).
[4] The only other reference to the office is a joking one: Lady Bruton calls the obsequious Whitbread, "My Prime Minister" (122); the joke, of course, is that she is a travesty of a queen.

The cumulative effect of such repeated notations and images is to establish a systematic network of social elements—human time, city space, personal relationships, professional and institutional activities, publicly shared symbols, political issues—so as to arrive at a vision of modern life on a national scale. This collective existence is not to be apprehended externally, as it would be by a social scientist or a naturalist novelist, but internally, as it is experienced by its participants. To this end, the internal monologues of the characters express their sense of relation to various social entities together with their sense of themselves as individuals distinct from these entities. Woolf's own notions of collective existence were highly developed,[5] but what is of most interest in *Mrs. Dalloway* is the form that such beliefs take in characters of different kinds, responding to situations that arise directly from the action.

Septimus Warren Smith maintains the most radical form of belief in a collective existence, joining not only people but also objects and even sensory phenomena in an organic unity:

But they beckoned; leaves were alive; trees were alive. And the leaves being connected by millions of fibres with his own body, there on the seat, fanned it up and down; when the branch stretched he, too, made that statement. The sparrows fluttering, rising, and falling in jagged fountains were part of the pattern; the white and blue, barred with black branches. Sounds made harmonies with premeditation; the spaces between them were as significant as the sounds. A child cried. Rightly far way a horn sounded. All taken together meant the birth of a new religion——(26)

The character of this religion is soon fleshed out with honored elements of mystical, pantheist, and antinomian creeds: "Men must not cut down trees. There is a God. . . . Change the world. No one kills from hatred . . . there is no crime . . . there is no death" (28).

Even more dramatic a consequence of Smith's religion is the relationship to society it entails:

Look, the unseen bade him, the voice which now communicated with him who was the greatest of mankind, Septimus, lately taken from life to death, the Lord who had come to renew society, . . . suffering forever, the scapegoat, the eternal sufferer, but he did not want it, he moaned, putting from him with a wave of his hand that eternal suffering, that eternal loneliness. (29)

---

[5]See my article, "Woolf and McTaggart," ELH, XXXVI (1969), 719-38; and J. Hillis Miller, "Virginia Woolf's All Souls' Day," in *The Shaken Realist: Essays in Modern Literature in Honor of F. J. Hoffman*, ed. O. B. Hardison, Jr., *et al.* (Baton Rouge, 1970), pp. 10-27.

The ascription of these beliefs to Smith is remarkable less as an instance of psychological insight than as an application of modern anthropological knowledge of primitive religion and society.[6] Woolf deepens her portrait of the outsider by relating him to the archetype of the scapegoat, which has traditionally accompanied the communal ideal. By the exclusion, sacrifice, or crucifixion of one of its members the group establishes or reaffirms its own organic ties. The image is first signaled when Rezia calls Septimus's attention to "a few sheep" grazing in the park (29). The role of Christ figure or lamb of God comes to him not merely out of religious hysteria or personal megalomania but from his sense of himself as a sacrificial object who affirms the collective existence by separating or sacrificing himself. Septimus thinks of himself as "this last relic straying on the edge of the world, this outcast, who gazed back at the inhabited regions . . ." (103). Thus his suicide is not the cowardly escape that Dr. Holmes names it (164) but is conceived as an act of martyrdom: impaling himself on the spikes below, he cries to the world at large, "I'll give it you!" (164)—yielding his own life for mankind.[7]

In contrast to Smith, Peter Walsh espouses a humanist doctrine that connects him with people, not things: "I prefer men to cauliflowers" (5); ". . . he did not like cabbages; he preferred human beings" (211-12). But Walsh shares with Smith the warped personality and the status of the outcast: on his return, Clarissa finds in him "the same queer look; . . . a little out of the straight his face is" (46); "I know what I'm up against, he thought, running his finger

[6]A rather idiosyncratic application; see, e.g. Jacqueline E. M. Latham, "Thessaly and the Colossal Figure in *Mrs. Dalloway*," *Notes and Queries*, xvi, (1969), 263: " 'Heaven was known to the ancients as Thessaly,' says a character in Virginia Woolf's short story, 'Kew Gardens,' first published in 1919. And in *Mrs. Dalloway* Septimus Warren Smith, sitting in Regent's Park, believes his friend Evans has returned to life from Thessaly. Although Thessaly was never used by the Greeks to mean heaven, it seems clear that it had this connotation for Virginia Woolf."

[7]The primitive christological significance of the sacrifice is enhanced in a typescript passage: "He would kill himself. He would give his body to the starving Austrians" ("The Prime Minister," MS. of a story in the Berg Collection of the New York Public Library, p. 13). Cf. the notebook passage: "The whole world was clamouring Kill yourself, kill yourself, for our sake" (dated 22 Nov. 1924, Berg Collection, p. 25). In addition, Smith acquires properties of the drowned sailor in *The Waste Land*, who has a similar provenance in the *pharmakos* tradition: ". . . he himself remained high on his rock, like a drowned sailor on a rock" (77); he "lay like a drowned sailor, on the shore of the world" (103); "the most exalted of mankind; the criminal who faced his judges; the victim exposed on the heights; the fugitive; the drowned sailor; the poet of the immortal ode; the Lord who had gone from life to death" (107). These terms associate Smith not only with the main themes of Eliot's poem but also with Leopold Bloom as persecuted savior (in his "Circe" fantasy) and eternal scapegoat (under the Cyclops's anti-Semitic attack).

along the blade of his knife" (52); ". . . he could not come up to the scratch, being always apt to see round things" (174-75). But Peter plays the social game, however badly and unwillingly: he becomes an imperial administrator in India, despite his youthful socialist beliefs (56); he is an easy mark for women, for "nobody of course was more dependent upon others . . .; it had been his undoing" (174); and he decides to go to Clarissa's party despite his distaste for it.

For Clarissa Dalloway, unlike the principal males, the commitment to social unity conflicts with a vigorous sense of individuality, and in this tension lies her chief interest as the titular heroine. On the one hand, she believes in something like Smith's organic universe: ". . . somehow in the streets of London, on the ebb and flow of things, here, there, she survived, Peter survived, lived in each other, she being part, she was positive, of the trees at home; of the house there, ugly, rambling all to bits and pieces as it was; part of people she had never met; being laid out like a mist between the people she knew best, who lifted her on their branches as she had seen the trees lift the mist, but it spread ever so far, her life, herself" (11-12). This belief is of long standing, having been expressed to Peter during their youth, and it still retains some of the intimations of immortality which it then carried:

. . . she felt herself everywhere; not "here, here, here"; and she tapped the back of the seat; but everywhere. She waved her hand, going up Shaftesbury Avenue. She was all that. So that to know her, or any one, one must seek out the people who completed them; even the places. . . . It ended in a transcendental theory which, with her horror of death, allowed her to believe, or say that she believed (for all her scepticism), that since our apparitions, the part of us which appears, are so momentary compared with the other, the unseen part of us, which spreads wide, the unseen might survive, be recovered somehow attached to this person or that, or even haunting certain places, after death. Perhaps—perhaps. (168)

These fumblings for a belief in survival, amid images of the self's mixing with the people and places of one's life, bears a close resemblance to a number of meditative passages scattered through *A Writer's Diary*. Despite Clarissa's previous appearance as a superficial social butterfly in *The Voyage Out*, Woolf has been able to invest her with a depth that carries something of the author's own temper. It is a temper that leans toward a doctrine of collective existence, a fusion of selves in a community of love, an infusion of the marks of identity into the people one knows and into the earth, which endures.

But Woolf's self-projection has another side. Clarissa is an apostle of individuality, has a strong instinct of withdrawal from others, and is presented in the course of the narrative as vigorously preserving her sense of identity. Images of cloistral isolation and virginal inviolability attach to her (33, 35, 36, 45).[8] She admires the woman in the window across the way as a model of her own privacy:

. . . she watched out of the window the old lady opposite climbing upstairs. Let her climb upstairs if she wanted to; let her stop; then let her, as Clarissa had often seen her, gain her bedroom, part her curtains, and disappear again into the background. Somehow one respected that—that old woman looking out of the window, quite unconscious that she was being watched. There was something solemn in it—but love and religion would destroy that, whatever it was, the privacy of the soul. (139-40)

The negative side of this individualism is recognized by Clarissa herself as egotism, expressed in her jealousy at Peter's new love affair and later at Lady Bruton's luncheon invitation to her husband: "But the indomitable egotism which for ever rides down the hosts opposed to it, the river which says on, on, on; even though, it admits, there may be no goal for us whatever, still on, on; this indomitable egotism charged her cheeks with colour . . ." (50-51). At its worst, egotism leads her to social conformity, strongly tinged by sexual prudery, as when in youth she had been horrified by gossip about a neighbor's adultery: ". . . it was her manner that annoyed [Peter]; timid; hard; arrogant; prudish. 'The death of the soul' " (66). At its best, egotism defines her as a unique being, an ultimate reality, as Peter sees her revealed at the close: "It is Clarissa. . . . For there she was" (213).[9]

[8]This urge to chastity is accompanied by homosexual feelings, e.g., toward Sally Seton: ". . . she could not resist sometimes yielding to the charm of a woman. . . . she did undoubtedly then feel what men felt. . . . this falling in love with women" (36, 37).
[9]One of the most curious but as yet unexplained aspects of the text is its *dédoublement* of one of the classic English novels, *Clarissa Harlowe*. Like the title figure of Richardson's work, Woolf's title figure is a lady of good family, "mistress of all the Accomplishments, natural and acquired, that adorn the Sex" but virginal, prudish, tending toward the frigid. Beyond the analogy of the heroines, there is a marked similarity between the two plots; in each, the heroine's family opposes her marriage to an ardent suitor, partly on mercenary, partly on personal, grounds—in the one case, because Lovelace is perhaps too fashionable, in the other, because Walsh is not fashionable enough. Here the parallel ends: Woolf's Clarissa does not allow herself to be carried off, does not suffer a crisis of conscience (although she has to keep on convincing herself that a marriage to Peter wouldn't have worked), and does not rise to tragic martyrdom. The relationship seems to have occurred to Woolf during the writing of *Mrs. Dalloway*: "And should I demolish Richardson? whom I've never read. Yes, I'll run through the rain into the house and see if *Clarissa* is there. But that's a block out of my day and a long long novel" (*Diary*, p. 64; 3 Aug. 1924). The fact that this comes almost as an after thought—and the suspicion that Woolf failed to follow up her impulse to read *Clarissa*—need not rule out the novel's relevance here. Certainly Woolf had some familiarity with *Clarissa* by 1922, when she wrote "On Re-reading Novels": Henry James "surmounts in *The Ambassadors* problems which

Despite its grounding in social and political life, then, *Mrs. Dalloway* is designed as the fictional biography of a single character. Woolf's often-quoted introduction to the Modern Library edition has somewhat misled criticism into focusing on Clarissa and Septimus as a twin center, to the detriment of the novel's compelling unity. The work proceeds by a series of juxtapositions of the central figure and those who surround her: Peter Walsh, Sally Seton, Miss Kilman, and others besides Septimus. Its form suggests the model of a center with radial links to a number of points on the circumference rather than the polar opposition described in some readings.[10] Even a center/circumference model falsifies the dynamics of the work: Mrs. Dalloway is traced forward from morning to night on a given day and simultaneously back from the present into her past so as to fill in a potential biography. By catching up the entire course of a life still ongoing and directed toward the future, the narrative treatment parallels the deepening meditation of the heroine herself, so that her final acknowledgment of Septimus's relationship to her sheltered life is but the fulfillment of a gathering insight. Not only does the tale move toward Clarissa's enlightenment and imaginative expansion in the closing moments, but the elaboration of certain motifs and images throughout the work leads to a growing sense of the protagonist's permeation of the text. The experimentalism of *Mrs. Dalloway* is perhaps most unique in this: it uses the conventions of the English social novel toward a metaphysical aim—the dawn of an individual's conviction of her own reality and the simultaneous evocation of that sense in the reader. In reaching toward the epiphany of a human subject rather than of a god, the fiction represents a "displacement" of previous literary modes, a transformation of myth into modern mythos, and a secularization of traditional religious concerns. This can be shown in the working of theme and action as the text moves from Peter's "It is Clarissa herself . . ." (56), through his sustained remembrance of her—". . . there she was,

baffled Richardson in *Clarissa*" (*Collected Essays*, II, 128). But she remained relatively indifferent to Richardson; e.g., in the retrospective essay, "Phases of Fiction" (1929), she admits that it contains "little reference or none to Fielding, Richardson, or Thackeray" (*Collected Essays*, II, 56).
[10]A considerable literature has been built up on the varieties of polar significance to be accorded these characters: thus, for Keith Hollingworth, in *Studies in Honor of John Wilcox*, ed. A. D. Wallace and W. D. Ross (Detroit, 1958), p. 242, Septimus is the "incarnation of the death-instincts, Clarissa Dalloway of the instincts of life." For Alex Page, "A Dangerous Day: Mrs. Dalloway Discovers Her Double," *Modern Fiction Studies*, VII (1961-62), 123, "he is the id to her ego." And for Francis L. Mollach, "Thematic and Structural Unity in *Mrs. Dalloway*," *Thoth*, V (1964), 62-73, her development is from repression to semiliberation at the close.

however; there she was" (85)—to the manifestation of her at the close: "For there she was" (213).

□

The dialectic of communion and individuation that occurs in the narrative provides the justification for the fiction's elaborate experimentation with point of view. Although Woolf's use of the technique has been studied in detail by Richter and has been given philosophical depth by Auerbach, it has not generally been seen as an extension of the text's thematic concerns. The transition between Clarissa and Lucrezia by way of their perception of the Prime Minister's car (16, 18); between the London crowd and the Smiths by way of the skywriting airplane (23-25); between Peter and Lucrezia through their efforts to comfort a child, Elise Mitchell (72-73) (they later see each other directly, when the Smiths seem to be arguing [79]); between Walsh and Lucrezia again by way of the street singer (91-92); these carefully constructed perspectival situations are less exhibitions of experimental technique or epistemological theory than substantiations of the characters' personal experience. From these passing encounters and conjoint perceptions, human life is constituted.

The clearest indication that multiple points of view make up an underlying structure of experience—if not a group mind or unity of consciousness—are the instances of eerie coincidence. After Septimus's plunge from the window, Lucrezia dreams of passing through a window into a garden: "It seemed to her as she drank the sweet stuff that she was opening long windows, stepping out into some garden. But where?" (165). The movement of stepping from or leaping through a window into a garden, together with the hills and nearby sea of the surrounding landscape, place the dream at Bourton, where Clarissa had similarly "plunged" (5) (Bourton is set amid hills near the Severn [169]). Similarly, Clarissa's echoing of the motto "Fear no more" while taking her midday nap (45) is echoed by Septimus during his trancelike state before suicide (154).

The most extended and impressive example of a shared system of symbols in *Mrs. Dalloway* is the specter of an old woman. Early in the text, Clarissa thinks of Miss Kilman with distaste: "For it was not her one hated but the idea of her, which undoubtedly had gathered into itself a great deal that was not Miss Kilman; had become one of those spectres with which one battles in the night; one of those spectres who stand astride us and suck up half our life-blood, dominators and tyrants ..." (14-15). Later, Clarissa and Peter share an unspoken image of a preternatural presence:

"I am in love," he said, not to her however, but to some one raised up in the dark so that you could not touch her but must lay your garland down

81

on the grass in the dark. . . . He had deposited his garland. Clarissa could make what she would of it.

"In love!" she said. That he at his age should be sucked under in his little bow-tie by that monster! (50)

The ambiguity of this specter is emphasized not only by the varying reactions of Peter and Clarissa to its presidency over love but also by Clarissa's association of it with her image of a spiritual vampire like Miss Kilman.

The benign aspects of this figure are expanded soon after in Peter's dream:

The grey nurse resumed her knitting as Peter Walsh, on the hot seat beside her, began snoring. In her grey dress, moving her hands indefatigably yet quietly, she seemed like the champion of the rights of sleepers, like one of those spectral presences which rise in twilight in woods made of sky and branches. The solitary traveller, haunter of lanes, disturber of ferns, and devastator of great hemlock plants, looking up suddenly, sees the giant figure at the end of the ride. (63)

The position of the figure in a forest, its statuelike aspect, its protective yet vaguely threatening influence mark this as an archetypal elaboration of the metaphoric images that had previously appeared in Peter's and Clarissa's minds.

A manuscript draft of these paragraphs employs phrases which further emphasize the psychological projection of a feminine archetype:

And then a great brush swept smooth across his mind. . . . Again the great & benignant power took him into its keeping. (B.M., I, 24)

In her white dress, moving her hands indefatigably yet quietly, she seemed like the champion of the rights of sleepers; like one of those spectral presences which, rise up in twilight, in woods, made of sky & branches yet endowed with a vast personality, *with benignity,* yet extremely aloof, & yet lure the solitary traveller to their arms by some promise of understanding— with a sense of power. An [word illegible], a voyager, to confide his suffering to them, to say, as he advances down the grassy ride, how they alone understand his immense weariness, which ceases to be weariness on the spot, & becomes luminous with the silver light of the sky between the branches, & deep, & romantic, & refreshing, as the leaves rustle & shake in the twilight wind. (B.M., I, 25)

This figure in the sky is only a state of mind. She is my embodiment of an instinct. *She has no external existence.* She blesses my extreme weariness, & consents to take me up into her arms. . . . For if I can conceive of her, then, in some sense she exists. Thus guarding himself as well as he can, from ridicule, he is astonished, to find himself advancing towards the sky & leaves, as if they were the complement of his own person; as if they conspired [?] against an existence otherwise incomplete. (B.M., I, 26)

This was to be thought of, then, as a "great & benignant power," "a vast personality," who "blesses [man's] extreme weariness," a being endowed with divine afflatus and archetypal generality. It is also recognized not merely as a "state of mind" (as in G. E. Moore's philosophy) but as the "embodiment of an instinct," the Jungian projection of a universal impulse— in this case, toward completion and security with the feminine aspect of oneself, "the complement of his own person." Although these phrases are omitted in the published text, enough of their meaning is carried on in the specification of a "giant figure," emanating its "womanhood" and proffering "great cornucopias full of fruit" (63, 64).[11]

The crystallization of Peter's benign dream vision into the image of a nurturant female brings with it a new figure, which commands equal attention: the solitary traveler. Among the attributes ascribed to him—atheism (63), subjective idealism (63-64), tendencies toward withdrawal and extinction (64)—there is one that probably marks him as Peter himself: ". . . he is elderly, past fifty now" (64) (Peter is fifty-three [83]). Walsh as solitary traveler passes in his dream to a house where "coming to the door with shaded eyes, possibly to look for his return, with hands raised, with white apron blowing, is an elderly woman who seems (so powerful is this infirmity) to seek, over the desert, a lost son; to search for a rider destroyed; to be the figure of the mother whose sons have been killed in the battles of the world" (65). This apparition combines elements of Peter's imagination—the figure at the door, a landlady named Mrs. Turner (64), who serves him at his return (65)—with elements of Clarissa's—the bereaved Lady Bexborough and Mrs. Foxcroft, "eating her heart out because that nice boy was killed" (6-7). Peter wakes and associates his dream with a scene at Bourton at the time of his broken romance with Clarissa (65); moreover, he recalls "an old nurse, old Moody, old Goody, some such name they called her, whom one was taken to visit in a little room with lots of photographs, lots of bird-cages" (67). This old nurse is still going strong, doing service at the party: ". . . old Ellen Barnet, who had been with the family for forty years, . . . and remembered mothers when they were girls. . . . And they could not help feeling, Lady Lovejoy and Miss Alice, that some

---

[11]Reuben A. Brower, in *The Fields of Light: An Experiment in Critical Reading* (New York, 1951), p. 135, sees this as Peter's "vision of the consolatory woman who gives the kind of understanding which Peter had attributed to the girl [he follows on his walk] and which he had not found in Clarissa."

little privilege in the matter of brush and comb was awarded them having known Mrs. Barnet—'thirty years, milady,' Mrs. Barnet supplied her. . . . The dear old body, . . . Clarissa's old nurse" (183).

This configuration of images in Peter's and Clarissa's minds has obvious relations with the archetypes of the eternal feminine or *magna mater*, but it need not be pursued outside the text to reveal its powerful local significance. The solitary traveler is soon to be associated not only with Peter but also with Septimus: "He saw things too—he had seen an old woman's head in the middle of a fern" (74). Smith is even identified with the specter itself: "Septimus cried, . . . raising his hand like some colossal figure who has lamented the fate of man for ages in the desert alone . . ." (78). The old woman as repository of eternal loving is then elaborated in a street singer: ". . . the battered woman—for she wore a skirt—with her right hand exposed, her left clutching at her side, stood singing of love—love which has lasted a million years, she sang, love which prevails, and millions of years ago her lover, who had been dead these centuries, had walked, she crooned, with her in May . . ." (90).[12] A similar figure penetrates the awareness of Dalloway as he crosses the park, but he consigns her to his mental lumber room of social problems: "But what could be done for female vagrants like that poor creature, stretched on her elbow (as if she had flung herself on the earth, rid of all ties, to observe curiously, to speculate boldly, to consider the whys and the wherefores, impudent, loose-lipped, humorous), he did not know" (128). Finally, this old woman appears as the tutelary spirit who reveals Clarissa to herself:

Oh, but how surprising!—in the room opposite the old lady stared straight at her! . . . It was fascinating to watch her, moving about, that old lady, crossing the room, coming to the window. Could she see her? It was fascinating, with people still laughing and shouting in the drawing-room, to watch that old woman, quite quietly, going to bed alone. (204)

□

Not only are the characters' imaginations stocked with collective images, drawn from a larger community of mind, but the narrative employs these images to further characterize them. In the most outstanding instance, the underlying affinity between Clarissa and Septimus is expressed by their persistent likening to birds. Both have noses "beaked like a bird's" (13) or are "beak-nosed" (17); both are

[12]No further discussion of the song is necessary now that it has been identified and thematically related by Miller in *The Shaken Realist*, pp. 114-15, except to note that it remarkably reappears in Malcolm Lowry's *Under the Volcano* in the context of that work's setting on All Souls' Day.

attentive to the flight of birds, as seen in Clarissa's memory of "the rooks rising, falling" (5), and in Septimus's interest in "swallows swooping, swerving, flinging themselves in and out, round and round, yet always with perfect control . . ." (77); both are associated with birds in the minds of others, e.g., Scrope Purvis sees Clarissa with a "touch of the bird about her, of the jay, blue-green, light, vivacious" (6), and Septimus makes Rezia think of a "young hawk" (161). On the same page Septimus sees Rezia similarly: ". . . he could feel her mind, like a bird, falling from branch to branch, and always alighting, quite rightly." This image of the characters assumes more than metaphoric significance, however, as the bird becomes a complex symbol through repeated and diverse uses. It is a means of communication with the universe: "A sparrow perched on the railing opposite chirped Septimus, Septimus, four or five times over and went on, drawing its notes out, to sing freshly and piercingly in Greek words how there is no crime and, joined by another sparrow, they sang in voices prolonged and piercing in Greek words, from trees in the meadow of life beyond a river where the dead walk, how there is no death" (28).[13] The bird also is identified with the street singer (adding to her connections with an ancient spring and with the great mother archetype): ". . . with the bird-like freshness of the very aged, she still twittered 'give me your hand and let me press it gently' " (91). At Clarissa's moment of epiphany, she is marked by a renewed identification with the fragility and the creativity of birds: ". . . there was in the depths of her heart an awful fear. Even now, quite often if Richard had not been there reading the *Times*, so that she could crouch like a bird and gradually revive, send roaring up that immeasurable delight, rubbing stick to stick, one thing with another, she must have perished" (203).

Finally, the bird appears in a mythical guise but only to be rejected as too fanciful an intrusion into the direct contact of men and women at Clarissa's party: "The curtain with its flight of birds of Paradise blew out again. And Clarissa saw—she saw Ralph Lyon beat it back, and go on talking. So it wasn't a failure after all! it was going to be all right now—her party. . . . something now, not nothing, since Ralph Lyon had beat back the curtain" (187). The birds of Paradise, who can never come down to earth because they lack feet,[14] perhaps connote the imaginative designs which some of Woolf's

---

[13]The further use of the motif of birds speaking Greek will be discussed in connection with *The Years*. It is by now well known that the motif is drawn from Woolf's own hallucinations during her manic periods.

[14]The *locus classicus* for the poetic use of this bit of "natural history" is Coleridge's "The Eolian Harp," ll. 20-25.

characters entertain: beautiful, decorative, perhaps necessary illusions, they must be firmly beaten back for individuals to emerge and social life to proceed.

Another collective phenomenon that figures strongly in *Mrs. Dalloway* is the image of Shakespeare—although it does not have the central position that it takes in *Night and Day*. Clarissa alternates between quotations from *Cymbeline* and *Othello* to express her attitudes toward life and death: "Fear no more the heat o' the sun" (*Cymbeline*, act 4, scene 2); "If it were now to die,/'Twere now to be most happy" (*Othello*, act 2, scene 1). Septimus, on the other hand, has been imaginatively formed by "the intoxication of language—*Antony and Cleopatra*" (98; see also 94, 95, 99, 101). Even in his dying moments, this inspiration persists: "He was not afraid. At every moment Nature signified . . . standing close up to breathe through her hollowed hands Shakespeare's words, her meaning" (154). By the same token characters are to be judged negatively to the degree to which they dislike or misread the poet: "Richard Dalloway got on his hind legs and said that no decent man ought to read Shakespeare's sonnets because it was like listening at keyholes (besides, the relationship was not one that he approved)" (84); in Septimus's room, Dr. Holmes "opened Shakespeare—*Antony and Cleopatra*; pushed Shakespeare aside" (101); Lady Bruton "never spoke of England, but this isle of men, this dear, dear land, was in her blood (without reading Shakespeare)" (198).[15]

Clarissa's repeated quotation of the dirge from *Cymbeline*—"Fear no more the heat of the sun"—has generally been taken as her self-encouragement to face life and the demands of the social world, in contrast to Septimus's escape from his fear by suicide. It will be recalled, however, that the dirge contains a biting ambiguity, which makes its way into the fiction: the singers are congratulating the (supposed) departed for escaping the rigors of nature, history, age—of life itself.[16] Thus Clarissa's affinity for the refrain may be taken as a mark of her strong propensity for death, which she indulges in

---

[15]This use of the Bard as a symbolic criterion and focus of value is similar to that pursued by Mrs. Hilbery in *Night and Day*; it therefore comes as no surprise that Mrs. Hilbery not only appears in *Mrs. Dalloway* at a crucial point, toward the end of the party (209-10), but is also endowed with some of the *mana* ascribed to her in the earlier work: "And up came that wandering will-o'-the-wisp, that vagous phosphorescence, old Mrs. Hilbery, stretching her hands to the blaze of [Sir Harry's] laughter . . . which, as [Clarissa] heard it across the room, seemed to reassure her on a point which sometimes bothered her . . . : how it is certain we must die" (193). Mrs. Hilbery is also mentioned on p. 135.

[16]For additional implications of the quotation, see Maud Bodkin, *Archetypal Patterns in Poetry: Psychological Studies of Imagination* (London, 1963 [1934]), pp. 87-88.

imagination throughout the work: on her morning walk (12), during her midday activity (45), and on her withdrawal from the party (202-4). A passage from the manuscript version makes her drift toward death even clearer by ringing in another line of the dirge: "Thou thy worldly task hast done, Mrs. Dalloway read. Tears unshed, tears deep, salt, still, stood about her for all deaths and sorrows . . ." (B.M., II, 128). We can sense from this that Clarissa's tendency toward virginal coldness and withdrawal into chaste isolation is an expression of the universal reversion to the security of effortless stasis. And her temptation by death is furthered by her anxiety in face of the dangers of living. Summing up a number of marks of this fear, in a canceled passage, Clarissa is seen "thinking of her childhood all the time; the oddest ideas coming to her; fragments of poetry; & a sense of being out out far to sea, & alone; & blown on, very dangerously, for she never lost her sense that it is dangerous, living even one day. A rope walker, & beneath death; so she thought most people felt . . ." (B.M., II, 125).

It is at the end of this prolonged transaction with death that Clarissa chooses life, and her affirmation must be seen as the temporary resolution of a continuing ambivalence in the heroine—and in her creator. The extent of Clarissa's response to the authority of Septimus's act is suggested by another canceled passage: "She felt no pity for the young man who had killed himself; not for his wife; nor for herself; nothing but pride; nothing but joy; for to hear Big Ben strike Three, Four, Five, Six, seven, was profound & tremendous. . . . She must go back; she must breast her enemy; she must take her rose; Never would she submit—never, never!" (B.M., III, 99). Given this power of affirmation, a figure of satire in Woolf's earlier conception becomes in the course of the narrative a protagonist of life: she "forced herself with her indomitable vitality to put all that aside, there being in her a thread of life which for toughness, endurance, power to overcome obstacles and carry her triumphantly through he had never known the like of" (171).

□

From this standpoint, the contrast between the life-affirming Clarissa and the death-seeking Septimus may seem absolute, but the ambiguity in Clarissa's imagination—and her self-identification with the suicide—serves to align the two characters, even to blunt the distinction between life affirmation and death wish. The two main actions of the plot—suicide and party—are parallel in intention and effect despite their gross disparity in social acceptability. Both are designed as self-sacrifice for others—although both Clarissa and Septimus have an abiding bitterness about social life. Not only

Septimus thinks of himself as making an act of sacrifice—Clarissa responds to her husband's, and her former lover's, criticism of her parties (133) with the impressive claim: ". . . it was an offering; to combine, to create; but to whom? An offering for the sake of offering, perhaps. Anyhow, it was her gift" (135).[17] This vision of a social ritual as creative and self-justifying elevates Clarissa above the stature of the social butterfly and endows her with some of the ironic qualities of the *pharmakos* that adhere to Septimus.

Clarissa's coming to consciousness in her contemplation of Septimus's self-sacrifice has long been acknowledged as the climax of the work and one of the great scenes of modern literature. In order to grasp its wider significance, we may recall a remark of Frye's: "An extraordinary number of comic stories, both in drama and fiction, seem to approach a potentially tragic crisis near the end, a feature that I may call the 'point of ritual death'. . . . In *Mrs. Dalloway* the actual suicide of Septimus becomes a point of ritual death for the heroine in the middle of her party."[18] While Frye describes the structure of the scene in generic terms—taking the work as a comedy, which entails a meeting with and release from the threat of death—it remains to be seen what role this potentially tragic interlude plays in the work's larger mythos.[19] In recent studies of myth and archetype, such movements of the hero are called patterns of "withdrawal and return"—a temporary removal from the active role, a pause for meditation and inspiration, and a rededication to the social group and its destiny. This pattern has less in common with the death and rebirth of the hero as sacred king or divine incarnation than it does with the role of the hero as prophet or social leader. We may say, then, that there is a division of function within the conjoint protagonist of *Mrs. Dalloway*: while Septimus plays the role of sacrificial object—scapegoat or dying god—Clarissa plays the role of the

---

[17]Clarissa's indelible attribute of party-giving is well summarized in Frank Baldanza, "Clarissa Dalloway's 'Party Consciousness,' " *Modern Fiction Studies*, II (1956-57), 24-30, which draws on the short stories where she functions similarly. Seven of these, including two hitherto unpublished, are collected in *Mrs. Dalloway's Party* (London, 1973).

[18]*Anatomy of Criticism: Four Essays* (New York, 1968 [1957]), p. 179. For a number of suggestions on the myth and ritual motifs in this work, including its "rapprochement avec les rîtes religieux de 'purification,' 'libération du mal,' [et] rituel mystique," see Bernard Blanc, "La Quête de Mrs. Dalloway," *Le Paillon* (Nice), no. 3 (Dec.-Jan. 1972), pp. 10-13.

[19]Another indication that the fiction was conceived in terms of classical genres is Woolf's plan for a continuing chorus of observers among the incidental characters, an idea developed in connection with her reading of the *Choephoroi* of Aeschylus; see Harvena Richter, *Virginia Woolf: The Inward Voyage* (Princeton, 1970), p. 139, for quotations from Woolf's notebook.

social leader who temporarily withdraws for insight into the true significance of a leader's role and for rededication to it. Septimus as the outcast whose death reinvigorates his society is matched by Clarissa as social organizer who raises her activity from mindless social climbing to principled life affirmation.

The dramatic pattern of Septimus's sacrificial leap and Clarissa's meditative withdrawal and return parallels that of works manifesting the concept of a saving grace or way of redemption. If the joint protagonists are on the same side in the process of regaining health for their sick and perhaps moribund society, dramatic tension must be introduced in another opposition. It is not the hero of death and the heroine of life who are at odds but they, the healers, and others whom we may call the "forcers." Each is allotted his personal forcer, and for Clarissa it is Miss Kilman: "If only she could make [Mrs. Dalloway] weep; could ruin her; humiliate her; bring her to her knees crying, You are right. . . . It was to be a religious victory" (138). Similarly, the mordant portrayal of Septimus's forcer, Sir William Bradshaw, represents not merely a personal expression of the author's experience of psychiatrists[20] but an effort to exorcise a demonic power. Although the portrait is often wittily satirical, it is connected with the deepest themes of the work by being posed in mythic terms.

Sir William is seen not only by Septimus but by Clarissa, during her withdrawal and return, as a diabolic figure, a malevolent magus: "Suppose [Septimus] had had that passion, and had gone to Sir William Bradshaw, a great doctor, yet to her obscurely evil, without sex or lust, extremely polite to women, but capable of some indescribable outrage—forcing your soul, that was it—if this young man had gone to him, and Sir William had impressed him, like that, with his power, might he not then have said (indeed she felt it now), Life is made intolerable; they make life intolerable, men like that?" (203). The afflatus of these terms—"obscurely evil," "indescribable outrage," "his power" to make life intolerable—derives from something more than the immediate situation or from Clarissa's empathic leap to Septimus's point of view. They suggest a figure of some permanence in the human imagination, a figure which can inspire anxiety by its symbolic connection with bewitchment, hypnotism, and other ritual practices which depend on the surrender of the victim's will. Although these practices are often designed for medical

---

[20]Leonard Woolf has movingly described his wife's pathological fear of and hostility to psychiatrists and has given one instance of a doctor resembling Bradshaw in insensitivity and humbug: *Beginning Again: An Autobiography of the Years 1911–1918* (London, 1963), p. 82.

ends, there is a tradition of rituals and superstitions involving control by a manipulative power who represents not a god but a demon—or, to put it in psychoanalytic terms, not the paternal ideal but the father in his threatening and coercive aspect. We are to regard Sir William, in common with Clarissa and Septimus, not merely as an authoritarian bully but as a shaman.[21] He is described as "the ghostly helper, the priest of science" (104) and as the executioner assigned to implement the ritual sacrifice of Septimus—who is reciprocally seen as "the criminal who faced his judges, the victim exposed on the heights" (107).

Of course, there is a humorous element in this identification, for Sir William is also a comic figure: the pedantic doctor who believes in the efficacy of his restoratives, his science, and his mealy-mouthed persuasion. Comedy is also conveyed through a satire of psychiatry and its banal vision of social improvement: "Worshipping proportion, Sir William not only prospered himself but made England prosper, secluded her lunatics, forbade childbirth, penalized despair, made it impossible for the unfit to propagate their views until they, too, shared his sense of proportion . . ." (110). The benevolence comes through finally as a pose; his real mode of operation is politically familiar: ". . . he had to support him police and the good of society, which, he remarked very quietly, would take care, [at a sanitarium] in Surrey, that these unsocial impulses . . . were held in control" (113). In sum, his domineering and sterilizing powers acquire the force of a blight on the land, rendering men infertile and enforcing the illness he is presumed to be curing. His medicine for England's feeble state is prosperity, in a modern rather than ancient sense of the term; its distance from true benevolence may be gauged from Elizabeth's idea of becoming a doctor because "she liked people who were ill" (150).

In contrast to Bradshaw's sterile influence, Septimus represents a potential force for revitalization. His name itself means "seventh"—an obvious reference to the seventh son of folklore, always lucky or gifted, often with occult powers, and with an instinctive knowledge of restorative powers that makes him a good doctor.[22] When the normal Clarissa is related to an abnormal Septimus, the one is too readily seen as queenly and socially competent (49), the

[21]This version of the magus or shaman lacks the anthropological sophistication of the later fictional use of the type by John Fowles in *The Magus*. Both novels are considerably adumbrated by E. M. Butler, *The Myth of the Magus* (Cambridge and New York, 1948).
[22]See Funk and Wagnall's *Standard Dictionary of Folklore, Mythology and Legend*, s.v. "seventh son."

other as "the eternal sufferer" (29), a social reject. Despite this sharp contrast, Septimus is not more deluded in thinking himself "lord of men" (75) than is Clarissa in finding it her vocation to "assemble" (205). The main difference between them is that he feels himself "in Hell" (69), while she repeatedly adverts to Heaven (6, 46, 52, etc.). Notwithstanding their very different points of view, they share certain essential attitudes, even using the same phrases: her formula for self-encouragement is "Fear no more the heat o' the sun" (12, 34, 204), and he takes up the refrain: "Fear no more, says the heart in the body; fear no more" (154). Clarissa finds a love of life in others (6), in the London air (9), in precious moments of the day (33), and in herself: "What she liked was simply life" (134). But Septimus, too, is aware of life in leaves and trees (26) and even at his death affirms, "Life was good. The sun hot" (164) (repeating his earlier view on page 103).[23]

Thus the exhortation to "fear no more the heat o' the sun" becomes an identification with the source of vitality central to mythologies from the primitive and classical to the scientific. Modern readers have little difficulty in acknowledging the heroine, who first appears with a promise to bear flowers and who stages her social triumph dressed in green, as a Flora figure. We are inclined to reject the hero's claim to be Jesus Christ, "lately taken from life to death, the Lord who had come to renew society" (29), but skepticism must deal more subtly with his claim to control the power of the sun. When the Prime Minister's car blocks traffic early in the text, Septimus relates all events to himself: "The world wavered and quivered and threatened to burst into flames. It is I who am blocking the way, he thought. Was he not being looked at and pointed at; was he not weighted there, rooted to the pavement, for a purpose?" (18). The suggestion of Septimus's powers is complex, for it carries the threat that the world will burst into flame—that his is not an infusion of divine energy but of "some horror . . . come almost to the surface" (18). Confirming part of his claim, it is stated that "the sun became extraordinarily hot because the motor car had stopped . . ." (17). It is, to be sure, a June day, "the sun was hot" (72) in Regent's Park and the newspaper reports that "there was a heat wave" (159).

[23]Others share the view: Walsh finds it "absorbing, mysterious, of infinite richness, this life" (180); and even Bradshaw answers his despondent patients: "Why live? they demanded. Sir William replied that life was good" (112). But Clarissa is aware that "life is made intolerable; they make life intolerable, men like that" (203). These and other general statements are given concrete associations in Marilyn S. Samuels, "The Symbolic Function of the Sun in *Mrs. Dalloway*," *Modern Fiction Studies*, xviii (1972), 387-99.

But are we to dismiss Septimus's claims to threaten the earth with fire or to bring vital warmth as mere delusions of grandeur?

No final answer can be given, but it seems established that the tendency of this fiction is to assimilate its protagonists from their initially realistic mode to archetypal stature. The process is cumulative and cannot be hinged on any single detail, but on certain occasions there is a breakthrough from one stylistic level to the other. The most obvious example of this *Aufhebung* is the transformation of the street singer into "the voice of an ancient spring spouting from the earth" (90), singing in the words of a Strauss *Lied* the eternal tale of man and woman, life and death, earth and the cosmos: ". . . she laid her hoary and immensely aged head on the earth, now become a mere cinder of ice, she implored the Gods to lay by her side a bunch of purple heather, there on her high burial place which the last rays of the last sun caressed; for then the pageant of the universe would be over" (90–91).[24] This is the final vision of reality in *Mrs. Dalloway*: the world has become a "mere cinder of ice," the eternal feminine has lost love, youth, and now life ("her high burial place"), and the sun has not only departed but may never come again. Such a world needs a savior, some return of vital force, some medicine for its illness or resurrection from its death. The official doctors, Holmes and Bradshaw, cannot help; Miss Kilman's assuagements by the balms of Christianity do not generally appeal.[25]

[24]The enormous importance of this figure here, and later in *The Years*, can be gathered from Woolf's description of a street encounter: "An old beggarwoman, blind, sat against a stone wall in Kingsway holding a brown mongrel in her arms and sang aloud. There was a recklessness about her; much in the spirit of London. Defiant—almost gay, clasping her dog as if for warmth. How many Junes had she sat there, in the heart of London? How she came to be there, what scenes she can go through, I can't imagine. O damn it all, I say, why can't I know all that too? Perhaps it was the song at night that seemed strange; she was singing shrilly, but for her own amusement, not begging." Quoted in Bell, *Virginia Woolf: A Biography* (London, 1971), II, 74, from the unpublished diaries in the Berg Collection, 8 June 1920.
[25]In an essay published in the same year as *Mrs. Dalloway*, Woolf wrote: ". . . it is to the Greeks that we turn when we are sick of the vagueness, of the confusion, of the Christianity and its consolations, of our own age" (*Essays*, I, 13). This statement gives some inkling of a contributory motivation for Woolf's enterprise: it proceeds in part from her antipathy to Christianity and her high valuation of a healthier, classical culture. It is a judgment consistent with the marked strain of atheism running through *Mrs. Dalloway*: "Those ruffians, the Gods, shan't have it all their own way—her notion being that the Gods, who never lost a chance of hurting, thwarting and spoiling human lives, were seriously put out if, all the same, you behaved like a lady. . . . Later she wasn't so positive, perhaps; she thought there were no Gods; no one was to blame; and so she evolved this atheist's religion of doing good for the sake of goodness" (87). There is some distance here between the author and her character's naive humanism, but their forms of rejecting conventional Christian solace are similar: "Why creeds and prayers and mackintoshes? [Miss Kilman's habitual garb] when, thought Clarissa, that's the miracle, that's the mystery; that old lady, she meant . . ." (140–41).

The world does not receive its savior but Clarissa Dalloway does. The personification of Woolf's suicidism joins with the personification of her social self in a dramatic scene which we may take to be the manifestation of the artist in her text. That this scene—so often described in critical terms ranging from withdrawal and return to encountering the *Doppelgänger*—should bear all these and one more attribution is a mark of its symbolic universality. The one further model to be adduced is that of revelation, *anagnorisis*, or epiphany— the showing forth of the god and awed recognition of him by participants in the action or the audience. In her meditation in "the little room" (201)—like the prayer closet of devotional tradition—the heroine learns the identity, power, and value of a life thrown away for life itself.

The scene opens formally: "She went on, into the little room where the Prime Minister had gone with Lady Bruton. . . . There was nobody."

a) Her first associations are with the crucifixion, theologically vague but corporeally vivid: "Always her body went through it, when she was told, first, suddenly, of an accident; her dress flamed, her body burnt. He had thrown himself from a window. Up had flashed the ground; through him, blundering, bruising, went the rusty spikes." Since the authenticity of the hero's restorative act is so closely linked with physical suffering and death, it is necessary for the communicant to witness and empathize with those events.

b) "A thing there was that mattered; a thing, wreathed about with chatter, defaced, obscured in her own life, let drop every day in corruption, lies, chatter. This he had preserved." The "thing . . . that mattered" is here connected with a shilling once thrown in the Serpentine, which Clarissa had recalled on page 11 and now associates with Septimus's flinging away of his life. We remain unable to specify the object of sacrifice; what is emphasized is the contrast between the freedom of the sacrificial act and the "corruption" of daily life surrounding it.

c) "Death was defiance. Death was an attempt to communicate, people feeling the impossibility of reaching the centre which, mystically, evaded them; closeness drew apart; rapture faded; one was alone. There was an embrace in death." Despite the modern terminology—"an attempt to communicate," "reaching the centre," "one was alone"—these perceptions of death stand in a long tradition of mystical asceticism marked by the renunciation of worldly goods and human contacts, the movement toward death as release from the world and entry into a blessed state, the metaphoric substitution of a new order of being for earthly loves—"there was an embrace in death."

d) "Somehow it was her disaster—her disgrace. It was her punishment to see sink and disappear here a man, there a woman, in this profound darkness, and she forced to stand here in her evening dress." The next stage of religious experience is contrition—not only for her own life ("to stand here in her evening dress"), but for those of others ("here a man, there a woman")—and personal identification with the expiatory act of the one who takes on the world's faults: "Somehow it was her disaster—her disgrace."

e) "No pleasure could equal, she thought, straightening the chairs, pushing in one book on the shelf, this having done with the triumphs of youth, lost herself in the process of living, to find it, with a shock of delight, as the sun rose, as the day sank." The usually precise grammar of even Woolf's most difficult sentences fails at this point, and the text may be imperfect, but the impression is clear: the next sensation of the sequence is pleasure—indeed, "no pleasure could equal" it. Clarissa is referring to other experiences of sudden illumination and joy, and she goes on to recall some at Bourton and London; most significant is her inclusion of the present moment among the shocks of delight upon discovering what has all along been there.

f) Clarissa passes through a number of additional perceptions—of the old woman going to bed in her chaste isolation, of "the clock striking the hour, one, two, three," of the refrain "Fear no more the heat o' the sun" (and "If it were now to die, 'twere now to be most happy" on pages 202-3)—and now comes to her conclusion: "She felt somehow very like him—the young man who had killed himself. She felt glad that he had done it; thrown it away while they went on living." Her overt selfishness in feeling "glad that he had done it" is quickly evaporated by the ironies of the dying and reviving god motif (of which the scapegoat is a special case): he has "thrown it away while they went on living"—and their living on is linked to his leap of faith. At the spectacle of his heroism, she can identify herself with him, if not emulate him: "She felt somehow very like him. . . ."

g) "The clock was striking. The leaden circles dissolved in the air. But she must go back. She must assemble. . . . And she came in from the little room." The sounds of time passing serve to return her to the temporal world to which she is bound. But she can affirm her vocation within it: "She must assemble"—plan assemblies, bring people together, act for social cohesion. The scene ends as formally as it began: ". . . she came in from the little room."

□

The fiction expresses an opposition between two views of life that Woolf alternately entertained; these views are explicit in two essays of the period, couched in language closely related to the images of *Mrs. Dalloway*:

[Montaigne's] essays are an attempt to communicate a soul. . . . Communication is health; communication is truth; communication is happiness.[26]

That illusion of a world so shaped that it echoes every groan, of human beings so tied together by common needs and fears that a twitch at one wrist jerks another, where however strange your experience other people have had it too, where however far you travel in your own mind someone has been there before you—is all an illusion. We do not know our own souls, let alone the souls of others. Human beings do not go hand in hand the whole stretch of the way. There is a virgin forest in each; a snowfield where even the print of birds' feet is unknown. Here we go alone, and like it better so. Always to have sympathy, always to be accompanied, always to be understood would be intolerable. But in health the genial pretence must be kept up and the effort renewed—to communicate, to civilize, to share, to cultivate the desert, educate the native, to work together by day and by night to sport. In illness this make-believe ceases.[27]

Neither of these ultimate points of view is uppermost in Woolf; she entertained both, sometimes at the same time. We might dismiss them as the extremes of a manic-depressive psychosis; we had better regard them as pulses of a rhythm of response to reality—perhaps in tune with the rhythm of reality itself—one that will generate the structure and style of *To the Lighthouse* and *The Waves*.

[26]"Montaigne," *Collected Essays*, iii, 23-24; first published in 1924. These equations are given in *Mrs. Dalloway* on pp. 103-4.
[27]"On Being Ill," *Collected Essays*, iv, 196; first published in 1926.

to the lighthouse

"A central
line down the
middle"

To the Lighthouse (1927) is divided into three parts containing, respectively, nineteen, ten, and thirteen sections (marked by arabic numerals). Part II is markedly shorter than the others, the relative lengths of the parts approximating a ratio of 6:1:3. The narrative point of view, a subject treated exhaustively by Leaska,[1] is dominated by one character (Mrs. Ramsay) in thirteen of the sections of part I; by an "omniscient author" in eight of the sections of II; and by another character (Lily Briscoe) in eight of the sections of III. As Leaska observes, there is within each section frequent shifting from one point of view to another, with some occasional ambiguity as to the correct designation, but one or another character usually emerges as the focal point, assimilating the sensibilities of those around him. We may summarize the shift of perspective as moving from an older, maternal figure to a younger, virginal one by way of an intermediate consciousness of indeterminate characteristics and comprehensive vision.

The action is set on the Isle of Skye in western Scotland (17).[2] The time in part I is mid-September (35), shortly before World War I (al-

[1]Mitchell A. Leaska, *Virginia Woolf's Lighthouse: A Study in Critical Method* (London, 1970).
[2]There is no cause for several critics' uncertainty about locale, after this explicit statement in the text; doubts about the consistency of Woolf's Scottish geography may

though no explicit designation of the war is made in the text). Action begins after 6 P.M. (35) with discussion of plans for a family outing, continues till just after 7 P.M. (107) when the lateness of some of the children and guests is noted, advances to almost 11 P.M. (176) when Mrs. Ramsay finds her children awake after dinner, and concludes after midnight (198) when the last light in the house is extinguished. Part II spans ten years, (228–229), but events are only vaguely correlated with the calendar; three deaths in the family are recorded by bracketed statements but are not dated (except to say that Andrew Ramsay dies in the war). The temporal movement in this section is distinguished instead by its rhythm of diurnal and seasonal cycles. These cycles will be discussed below; it is enough to observe here that this part ends in September (219) with the return of the family and some of the original guests after a ten-year absence (at least for Lily Briscoe). The return to the original season is matched by a return at evening; after arriving, Lily sleeps and is awakened by the sun as part II ends. Part III takes place on the morning of her first day on Skye (225), beginning before eight with the family outing (delayed for ten years) and extending until lunchtime just before arrival at the Lighthouse. (There is reason to believe that the final scene on the lawn occurs simultaneously.)

The characters include a professional philosopher named Ramsay, specializing in epistemology and metaphysics (according to his son's account: [40]), aged over sixty in part I (111) and seventy-one in part III (315); his wife (both their given names are unspecified), aged fifty (16); and their eight children: sons Andrew (apparently the eldest), Roger, Jasper (ages unspecified), and James (aged six in I [11], sixteen in III [230]); and daughters Prue (the first to marry), Rose, Nancy (ages unspecified), and Cam, the youngest (38) (aged seven and later seventeen "perhaps" [230]). In part I the Ramsays' guests include William Bankes, botanist, a widower past sixty (77); Augustus Carmichael (age unspecified), poet, an elderly widower; Charles Tansley, doctoral candidate in philosophy under Ramsay, later reported to be married (302); Paul Rayley (age unspecified), who becomes engaged to Minta Doyle in part I and is described when married as having two sons; Lily Briscoe, amateur painter, unmarried, aged thirty-three (84) and later forty-four (232); and Minta Doyle, aged twenty-four (96), who becomes engaged to Rayley in part I and is later reported to be unhappily married to him (267–68). In part III,

be resolved if Paul Rayley's expression of willingness to go to Edinburgh to replace his fiancée's lost brooch (122) is to be regarded as a lover's hyperbole. Atmospheric resemblances to the Stephens' summer home in Cornwall are, of course, insufficient to place it there.

Bankes, the Rayleys, and Tansley do not reappear; a new guest, Mrs. Beckwith, is repeatedly mentioned but does not enter the action; she is described as elderly, good-natured, and a sketcher (e.g., 236).

In addition to the family and guests, there are a number of servants who figure in the action, although not as motivating or even speaking characters (with one exception). The house staff consists of Mildred, the cook (88), whose "masterpiece" is the boeuf en daube (125) served at dinner in part I; Ellen, the parlormaid (88), who also serves at dinner (149); Marie, the Swiss chambermaid, who cries for her dying father (19), misses her beloved mountains (48), and serves the boeuf en daube (154)—although she is called Marthe (155) at the time—Kennedy, the gardener, repeatedly described as being unsatisfactory (104, 218, 274); and Mrs. Maggie McNab (217), who is pictured eating milk soup in the kitchen (88, 211, 213), is employed occasionally to wash up after dinner (217) (does this include the dinner central to part I?), and after occasional cleanups during the war years, is engaged to make the house ready for reinhabitation—receiving assistance from a Mrs. Bast (217). Before the house acquires symbolic and dramatic values, then, it is equipped with a minimal body of servants who themselves acquire symbolic force—especially Mrs. McNab, as shall be seen.

□

The first element of the prose fiction to achieve symbolic dimension is the house. The term "lighthouse" refers not only to the "stark tower on a bare rock" (311-12) which is the goal of a family journey but also to the house itself, shining in the darkness. (It even acts as a beacon to Minta, Paul, Andrew, and Nancy returning from the beach [123].) The house is continually threatened by physical decay (47), not only when left neglected in the war years, but even when occupied. Yet it is preeminently a place of plenitude and vitality: "The house seemed full of children sleeping and Mrs. Ramsay listening; of shaded lights and regular breathing" (80). After the climactic dinner, during which the house's light stands out amid the darkness that is soon to engulf it, Mrs. Ramsay feels that the others will "come back to this night; this moon, this wind; this house: and to her too" (175); and after a period of emptiness, in which it is inhabited only by the "little airs" of the wind, the house becomes full again (219). The final views of the house are almost all external: to Lily painting on the lawn it is silent and undisturbed (250, 294) except for one moment of activity which leads her to a quasi-mystical experience; to the Ramsays on their boat going to the Lighthouse their home is "the little house," distant and strange (256), so that Cam, after her father points it out, stares "where no house was" (258). The house achieves its measure of immortality, however, by its place in Lily's painting—to the extent, of course, that the latter is immortal.

The house contains an unspecified number of rooms, including a drawing room with a window looking out on a terrace and lawn, a dining room with a window facing the bay, a staircase with a window, family bedrooms, servants' rooms in the attic, and service rooms. Certain elements of the house receive special attention. There are the doors, which Mrs. Ramsay believes should be kept shut in order to prevent decay from dampness (80) but which are not consistently shut (47); their locks begin to fail in the period of decline (212). Doors are often slammed shut, either by the wind (212), in anger (226, 305-6), or with "finality" (218)—so that the action becomes metaphoric for Lily (a question "opened doors in one's mind that went banging and swinging to and fro" [226]). Floors are less often observed in descriptions of the house, but they readily serve as bases of significant activity: the sunlight on the floor which Lily would not willingly disturb (78), the airs following the light across the floors through the house (197), the shadows of birds on the bedroom floor (201), and the straw scattered over the floors during the war years' decadence (213). The floors, like the walls, are display settings for natural phenomena, the house reflecting its environment on its broad surfaces, like paintings. By an easy extension, the floor can figure as the space of Cam's mind (88) and of Mrs. Ramsay's mind (102 and 104)—mingling with her memory of the Lighthouse light crossing her bedroom floor (103)—in addition to being a more generalized space of restful unconsciousness ("the floor of the sea" [131]).

A number of articles of furniture attain comparable interest on both the literal and metaphoric planes—particularly the table. A kitchen table is Andrew's example of an object under philosophical examination, and Lily is sufficiently stimulated by this to imagine a "phantom kitchen table" in amusing detail (40-41) (the image returns to her on 240-41). It is a dining table that structures relationships in the major scene of part I; in part III, Lily returns to "her old place at the breakfast table" (225)—apparently the same as the dining table, since she has a similar view out the window (226). The table, like the floors, functions as a flat plane on which the mind can arrange its contents: Lily uses elements of the tablecloth pattern and table setting to experiment with the composition of her painting. Beyond these functions in mental activity, tables play a role in people's imaginings of others: Mrs. Ramsay moves "like a ghost among the chairs and tables" of the old friends who come to mind (136); the furnishings of the house are themselves "crazy ghosts of chairs and tables" salvaged from the Ramsays' London home (46). Finally, like the

Lighthouse or any other object humanized by thought and activity, the table is simply a table after all and is perceived as such by Lily: "to feel simply that's a chair, that's a table, and yet at the same time, It's a miracle, it's an ecstasy" (310).

Of all the elements of the house, windows are most prominent and evocative. Part i, "The Window," is a series of enactments at the drawing room window where Mrs. Ramsay is pictured with James (e.g., 32), the dining room window where the Ramsays and their guests see the fluid chaos of darkness outside their structured realm of sociability, the staircase window in which Mrs. Ramsay sees the moon (179) (Lily sees it herself on page 231), and the window in the "other room" (doubtless the drawing room) through which she sees the Lighthouse again and concludes, "Nothing on earth can equal this happiness" (191). Mrs. Ramsay makes it a principle that windows should be open, as doors should be shut (47), an arrangement combining vision and protection, illumination and security. The windows of the house perform their habitual functions of admitting light and allowing vision, as Tansley and Ramsay observe the weather; of framing scenes and figures like paintings, as Ramsay sees his wife and is seen by her; of permitting movement from inner to outer spaces, as Ramsay tickles his disappointed son's leg across the window sill; and of giving out light to the external world, as the house does incidentally and as the Lighthouse does by design. Windows are not an unmitigated advantage, and Mrs. Ramsay closes the children's window a bit in the night (178) despite her principle of open windows and closed doors. Moreover, windows may be threatened by outside forces: the invading airs nose and rub the window on the staircase (197), and the weeds growing up around the house beat against the windows (213). But with the return of daylit life the windows transmit "the voice of the beauty of the world" (219) and are put in play again as people see, are seen by, and hide from others (227, 228). Finally, the window becomes a pictorial area in which the artist attempts to adjust her vision of reality: Lily catches a movement of the air at the window (prepared for on page 300), compares it with the shadow on the steps where she had once painted Mrs. Ramsay, and thus reaches her moment of recovery of her dead friend (309-10). At the same time, the windows of the Lighthouse are seen clearly, even to the dab of white on one of them (311), which aligns them with the "wave of white [that] went over the window pane" as Lily paints.

Beside the house, an adjunct to its domesticity, is the garden. Throughout the first two-thirds of the narrative, the garden is largely a place for conventional activity: walks by Ramsay and by Bankes and Lily, games by Jasper and Nancy, etc. In the final movement the garden is an imaginative setting for remembrances of Mrs. Ramsay: by Mrs. McNab (210-11), by James (285), and by Lily (304). The garden consists mainly of trees—including elms, which help to stabilize Mrs. Ramsay (174), and pears, in which Lily visualizes the unseen kitchen table of Andrew's metaphysics (41 ff.) (One of these trees also provides the solution to Lily's compositional problem.) There are, of course, flowers, including red-hot pokers, which the Ramsays pass on their promenade, and geraniums, planted in two urns between which Ramsay moves while pacing the terrace. There is also a hedge through which Lily and Bankes pass on their walk (35, 44) and which figures prominently in Lily's painting of the garden. There are birds, too; they roost in the trees and add their images of domesticity: starlings in the elms (44), two rooks nicknamed Joseph and Mary (126), swallows which invade the house (213), and gulls, detached from the seascape (e.g., 72, 205, 293). Although pools and fountains are important metaphors of personal experience throughout, there seem to be no bodies of water in the garden.[3] Finally, the lawn assumes the aspect of a world for Lily: "The lawn was the world . . ." (298). This is the literal structure of the garden; of its symbolic and mythical implications, more shall be said. But the literary associations convened by this catalogue are those of the classical and biblical *topos* of the *locus amoenus* or pleasance, transferred from its erotic pastoral context and domesticated to the ethos of English family life.

□

Although most of the action is centered on the house and garden, significant events take place on the sea between them and the Lighthouse, so that another cluster of elements becomes evident. House and Lighthouse are perched on islands; these islands are surrounded by waters and waves, crossed by winds which carry storm and calm, further articulated by dunes and rocks, and populated by fishermen— some of whom become castaways. This version of the Isle of Skye— a "poor little place" according to Ramsay (110)—contains the town of Finlay (92), a harbor with dunes stretching out from it, a rocky beach, and a bay with the Lighthouse on a rock. Skye is here well vegetated, shaped like a leaf (at least to Cam, from her point of view in the bay [289]), and associated with other islands of peace and fruitfulness: "The sigh of all the seas breaking in measure round the isles" (220), the "blessed island of good boots" (238), and the tropical

[3]Further, there is a greenhouse (a term—and a structure—mediating between the garden and the house) which is under repair (104-5), at a price which Mrs. Ramsay fears to tell her husband. This is an indication, among others, of their attitudes toward flowers: Mrs. Ramsay is perpetually seen among them, while Ramsay is indifferent (106, 111, 112).

island in Lily's sexual fantasy of Paul Rayley (271-72). But the island is vulnerable to the accidents of existence that pervade this fictional world: from the perspective of the Lighthouse the island looks "like the top of a rock which some big wave would cover" (313). By the same token, life at the Lighthouse is much like ordinary life: the lighthouse-keepers have their creaturely concerns (the tuberculous hip of the keeper's boy [13]), they take part in the system of family ties, like Tansley's lighthouse-keeper uncle (144), and their washing can be seen spread on the rocks to dry (286).

Living on the island, if only during summers, provides abundant material for the imagining of ideal realms. The dunes seem to Mrs. Ramsay "to be running away into some moon country, uninhabited of men" (25); in the meditation of Bankes, they are the realm where his past friendship with Ramsay, "in its acuteness and reality [is] laid up across the bay among the sandhills" (37-38); for Ramsay, "That was the country he liked best, over there; those sandhills dwindling away into darkness" (109). But the soft sands and misty expanse of the dunes is set against the abrupt presence of the rocks: Minta loses her brooch among the beach rocks in a moment of exhilaration at Rayley's proposal (120), James sees the bare Lighthouse starkly on its rock (the noun is used five times on pages 311-12) and concludes, ". . . It's like that" (312), and Ramsay reaches the Lighthouse by leaping defiantly and "lightly like a young man . . . on to the rock" (318). It is perhaps not premature to conclude that the rock that forms the substructure of both island and Lighthouse is set up as an unchangeable and irreducible existence, in contrast with the destructive fluidity of the waters and the idyllic visions inspired by the dunes. Part of the action will effect an accord between the close-up view of the rock, representing the here-and-now when James finally reaches the Lighthouse, and the distant view of the dunes, which has early been defined as a vision of eternity: Lily and Bankes "looked at the dunes far away, and instead of merriment felt come over them some sadness—because the thing was completed partly, and partly because distant views seem to outlast by a million years (Lily thought) the gazer and to be communing already with a sky which beholds an earth entirely at rest" (36-37).

The other large constituent of the island setting is the sea. Among the normal references to the sea in scenic descriptions, two terms call attention to themselves: "waves" and "waters."[4] Considering the author's elaboration of the waves into an image of human life in a

[4]Some of this imagery has been collected in Irène Simon, "Some Aspects of Virginia Woolf's Imagery," *English Studies*, XLI (1960), 192-94; reprinted in Jacqueline E. M. Latham, ed., *Critics on Virginia Woolf* (London, 1970), pp. 79-81.

fiction shortly afterward, it is not surprising that it is here one of the most frequent significant terms. From the opening pages, when Mrs. Ramsay imagines the waves breaking on the Lighthouse rocks (14), to the closing pages, in which the arrival of the Ramsays at the Lighthouse is accompanied by the dashing of waves against the rocks, the waves are a constant presence. Elaborations of the term occur when Mrs. Ramsay's meditation is accompanied by ambivalent interpretations of the waves' meaning:

> . . . the monotonous fall of the waves on the beach, which for the most part beat a measured and soothing tattoo to her thoughts and seemed consolingly to repeat over and over again as she sat with the children the words of some old cradle song, murmured by nature, 'I am guarding you—I am your support', but at other times suddenly and unexpectedly . . . had no such kindly meaning, but like a ghostly roll of drums remorselessly beat the measure of life, made one think of the destruction of the island and its engulfment in the sea. . . . (29-30)

Mrs. Ramsay hears the sound again while thinking of the imperfections of her marriage, which ideally is a harmony of "two different notes" (64); the sound of the waves "heard dully, ominously" (65) in the background makes the harmony "die on her ear now with a dismal flatness" (65). The beating of the waves against the land also provides an image of resistance to the destructive element for both the Ramsays: for her in the metaphor of her husband as a channel stake "upon which the gulls perch and the waves beat" (72) and for him in "the sight of human ignorance and human fate and the sea eating the ground we stand on" (73), which calls for his heroic resistance.

For Lily, the other main perspective of the work, the wave is an image of the rhythm of domestic happiness but with a peculiar final stroke that conveys her own anxieties: ". . . she felt, too, as she saw Mr. Ramsay bearing down and retreating, and Mrs. Ramsay sitting with James in the window and the cloud moving and the tree bending, how life, from being made up of little separate incidents which one lived one by one, became curled and whole like a wave which bore one up with it and threw one down with it, there, with a dash on the beach" (76) (this pattern of rhythmic flow and final dissolution is to predominate in *The Waves*). For Mrs. Ramsay, on the contrary, the breaking of the waves becomes softened to form an image of personal experience: the Lighthouse light "silvered the rough waves a little more brightly, as daylight faded, and the blue went out of the sea and it rolled in waves of pure lemon which curved and swelled and broke upon the beach and the ecstasy burst in her eyes and waves of pure delight raced over the floor of her mind" (103-4). Waves can be eluded, observed, or even toyed with, as Nancy escapes the advancing tide (120), as the children go out after dinner to "watch the waves" (180), and as Lily and Tansley play ducks and drakes (247).

But the waves' abiding presence infects even the firm land, for stable things waver as if under water, e.g., the guests (173), elms (174), shadows (202), candles (231). This wavering quality, like the waves' movement, is no mere accident of perception; it is connected with the rhythm of reality itself by its normative position in other images. From the boat in the bay Cam sees her house and garden as "unreal," while "this was real; the boat and the sail with its patch; Macalister with his earrings; the noise of the waves—all this was real" (257-58). And Lily asks herself about Mrs. Ramsay's experience of this reality: "What did the hedge mean to her, what did the garden mean to her, what did it mean to her when a wave broke? (Lily looked up, as she had seen Mrs. Ramsay look up; she too heard a wave falling on the beach)" (304).

Lily is specially favored in comprehending the wavelike nature of reality, since she approaches it through art (and through a type of subjectivity to be discussed below): ". . . the whole wave and whisper of the garden became like curves and arabesques flourishing round a centre of complete emptiness" (275). Her final vision of Mrs. Ramsay in a shadow thrown on the steps is accomplished by an esthetic perception (and expressed in an alliterative formula): "Some wave of white went over the window pane" (310). For Lily can grasp the perspectival variability of objects and enter into the rhythmic flow of existence, both of which are associated with the waves: "All that in idea seemed simple became in practice immediately complex; as the waves shape themselves symmetrically from the cliff top, but to the swimmer among them are divided by steep gulfs, and foaming crests. . . . And so pausing and so flickering, she attained a dancing rhythmical movement, as if the pauses were one part of the rhythm and the strokes another, and all were related. . . . Down in the hollow of one wave she saw the next wave towering higher and higher above her" (244). The action of painting, then, requiring the perspectives of both cliff top and water level (from which the Lighthouse is seen in part III), allows Lily imaginatively to extend herself to water level perspective to complement her cliff top view. Moreover, it allows her to enter into the rhythm of the waves themselves, with their crests and troughs—a rhythm, it will be observed, akin to the light-dark-light of the Lighthouse and therefore suggesting pulsation, flow, and alternation in a wavelike picture of reality akin to that of modern physics.

The waters surrounding the island are, then, not simply an image of annihilation or "transition,"[5] in contrast with the stability of the land, but a sum of reality constituted by but extending beyond the men who experience it. Lily perceives the totality of the beings in this world as circumambient water: "She seemed to be standing up to the lips in some substance, to move and float and sink in it, yes, for these waters were unfathomably deep. Into them had spilled so many lives. The Ramsays'; the children's; and all sorts of waifs and strays of things besides. A washerwoman with her basket; a rook; a red-hot poker; the purples and grey-greens of flowers: some common feeling which held the whole together" (295). Into this fluid medium of environing life which they have partly generated, men make their way by imagination and in boats. Venturing out into the stuff that surrounds them involves both a thrill of conquest and a threat of destruction for the mind and for the body. This complex of action and image provides the plot of part III, in which members of the family travel to the Lighthouse while the painter's eye and mind travel to the lost friend. Throughout the three parts, however, there are ample evidences of the human enterprise of sailing for food, communication, and adventure—as well as ample evidence of the dangers of all such enterprises.

Although early in the narrative a sailboat is seen in the bay (36), most of the images of navigation in part I are metaphoric: Mrs. Ramsay starts herself going again after a moment of lethargy at dinner "as a sailor not without weariness sees the wind fill his sail" (131); Lily sees that "when she turned to William Bankes, smiling, it was as if the ship had turned and the sun had struck its sails again" (132); Mrs. Ramsay silently communicates her fear that if the conversation continues so badly "life will run upon the rocks" (143); Lily feels herself left out of Rayley's newly formed engagement: ". . . he, bound for adventure; she, moored to the shore. . . . Lily wanted to . . . be included among the sailors and adventurers" (158); when the men withdraw, "they had gone up on to the bridge of the ship and were taking their bearings" (174). A more complicated relationship between metaphysical and maritime navigation develops in part II: the little airs which traverse the house are directed by ships' lights (197); ships hoot in the silence although there is no one to hear them (201); fishing boats are seen by hypothetical sleepers who walk the beach—an "ashen-coloured ship for

---

[5]Cf. Norman Friedman, "The Waters of Annihilation: Double Vision in *To the Lighthouse*," *ELH*, XXII (1955); reprinted in Morris Beja, ed., *Virginia Woolf: To the Lighthouse* (London, 1970), pp. 149-68. Other positions taken in this article have the requisite complexity.

instance, come, gone" (207)—after Andrew dies. In part III the images are mainly literal, although not always visible: three ships sunk in a storm and eight others that survived are reported (254); the "thought of the storm and the dark night and the fishermen striving there" (254) stirs Ramsay; "the cliffs looked as if they were conscious of the ships, and the ships looked as if they were conscious of the cliffs" (280), while a steamer draws a "great scroll of smoke" which is later described in progressive stages of disintegration. The closing pages bring a return of the metaphoric mode, so that the boat becomes an image of the self: "One glided, one shook one's sails (there was a good deal of movement in the bay, boats were starting off) between things, beyond things" (295). Finally, when Lily achieves her vision of Mrs. Ramsay and looks out to find the Ramsays' boat in the bay, her question "Where was that boat now?" (310) rings with more than local significance.

For James's steering is seen as the achievement of a quest and, capped by his father's acknowledgment of his success, as an integration of personality and attainment of manhood—his venturing over the waters having brought him not only to a confrontation with the stark reality of the Lighthouse but also to a fulfillment of the life project typified by sailing. That, at least, is the force of the poem Mrs. Ramsay reads in her anthology, William Browne's "The Syrens' Song": "Steer, hither steer your winged pines, all beaten Mariners" (184) ("beaten" is to be taken as storm-lashed, not defeated). Like her husband, with his grandiose self-images of mariner and castaway, Mrs. Ramsay is an enthusiastic voyager in life, and the entire plot hangs on her promise to James (178) one day to journey to the Lighthouse despite Ramsay's experienced recognition of the threat of storm. When James finally accomplishes the journey he is initiated into manhood under the archetype of all voyagers by sea.

Given an island like Skye and such thematic elements as these, it is to be expected that fishermen should populate the work. There is a full set of topical responses to the environment, from the dinner table discussions of the fishing industry and the fishermen's economic problems (141, 146, 148) to the slices of conversation between Ramsay and Macalister as the latter sails the Ramsays to the Lighthouse. One of the most poignant moments in this awareness of the fishermen comes as Ramsay reads in Scott's *The Antiquary* of the death of the fisherman Steenie and of his father Mucklebackit's grief (184–85).[6] Not only does Ramsay "relish" the elemental con-

---

[6] It is striking that Woolf herself felt the same way. In an essay on *The Antiquary* written in 1924 (*Collected Essays*, I, 139–43), even her language is similar—"their

frontation of man and nature in the storm (254), but he enjoys the fishermen's sports (283) and is "happy, eating bread and cheese" with them (314). This is not an intellectual's affectation but a streak of simple humanity in Ramsay, which is one of his more attractive characteristics. It also represents a heroic side of his mentality, for he makes an unsentimental recognition of the human effort to front the difficulties of life: "Naturally men are drowned in a storm, but it is a perfectly straightforward affair, and the depths of the sea (he sprinkled the crumbs from his sandwich paper over them) are only water after all" (316). It comes as no surprise, then, that he is often depicted as a leader of a heroic enterprise, like a captain controlling his ship in a storm (315).

For entailed by the maritime setting and by the emphasis of the narrative images is the threat of storms. The elementary action—the postponed trip to the Lighthouse completed by the same characters ten years later—hinges on this threat. Without dilating on the implications of human enterprise checked by nature's indifference, of the encroachment of death on life, and of the peace of the house broken by the war of elements without, we can see in the storms one of the central symbols of this fiction. For storms not only defeat the faring forth of fishermen—and all men's imaginative voyages on the waves that constitute the rhythm of life—but also create the prevalent condition of body and spirit described as "castaway."

Storms are reported throughout the work: in part I, adverse winds that foil the outing, and later Tansley's report of similar buffetings at his uncle's lighthouse; in part II, a cosmic chaos that is unleashed in the night (and is symbolically expanded into the upheaval of World War I); and in part III, the reminders of the storm of the previous Christmas, with its sunken ships and drowned sailors. The transitions between these storms are perhaps less obvious. As part I closes, Mrs. Ramsay observes increasing winds (175) and takes protective action by closing her children's windows (178); in contrast, as the universal uproar dies down in part II, we find indications of "peace" (219), and the last movement begins on a "beautiful still day" (227). But the most important impact of the storm is on men's minds and particularly on their sense of themselves. Ramsay sees himself as a heroic leader guiding his followers through a storm (57–59) (not a maritime but a mountain storm, to be sure); he also sees himself on a promontory eaten away by the sea (71–72) (cf. his wife's image of him as a stake marking a channel). Lily imagines

---

astonishing freshness, their perennial vitality" (p. 141)—and the scene of the fisherman's death is equally valued (p. 142).

herself on a "windy pinnacle and exposed without protection to all the blasts of doubt" (245); Cam invents a story about "making for safety in a great storm after a shipwreck" (314) and finds her father a fit leader in the fable (255). Yet storm, or at least wind, is necessary for vital movement: Ramsay is irritated when his boat is becalmed (at the point closest to absolute rest in the book) and is pleased when the wind allows the family to continue its progress toward the Lighthouse (288) (but the same wind blows the smoke of the steamer about and thus spoils the composition of Lily's painting [296]).

Perhaps the most general statement of man's vision of himself amid the storm is provided by Mrs. Ramsay's reading of the Grimm fable of the Fisherman and His Wife. The immediate response in the tale to the wife's increasing demands is the blowing up of a preternatural storm that includes elements of the cosmic chaos to be found elsewhere in this fiction: "But outside a great storm was raging and blowing so hard that [the fisherman] could scarcely keep his feet; houses and trees toppled over, the mountains trembled, rocks rolled into the sea, the sky was pitch black and it thundered and lightened, and the sea came in with black waves . . ." (97). Although some critics have identified Mrs. Ramsay with the fisherman's wife in her inordinate desire (purportedly, to manipulate other people's marriages), we may see her as one who can still the sea's upsurges so that "barbarity was tamed, the reign of chaos subdued" (77). It may be anticipated that some of the workings of this fiction will revolve around the partial assuagement of the destructive element and the inevitable failure of the heroine finally to still it.

The human lot under the threat of storms is repeatedly crystallized in images of shipwreck and men cast adrift. The most prominent reminder of such disaster comes from Cowper's "The Castaway," which Ramsay uses as a refrain for his own condition (and which his children pick up in part iii): ". . . we perished, each alone." The image runs throughout the book: in Ramsay's thoughts of his life as "the passage to that fabled land where our brightest hopes are extinguished, our frail barks founder in darkness" (13); in Mrs. Ramsay's reading of the Browne poem about the "beaten Mariners"; in the reports of the drowned fishermen; and in Cam's make-believe of their own boat foundering. A summary of these strands is made by Cam, reconciled as she is to the journey, the threat of shipwreck, and the state of being cast adrift: "Waves were all round them, tossing and sinking, with a log wallowing down one wave; a gull riding on another. About here, she thought, dabbling her fingers in the water, a ship had sunk, and she murmured, dreamily, half asleep, how we perished, each alone" (293). Storms, shipwreck, death itself, it seems, can be assimilated into the vision of human experience assembled in this work.

□

Having said this much about Ramsay's self-image in relation to the structural images of the narrative, we may enlarge the portrait of him presented by the two strains of imagery together. As a philosopher, Ramsay is up against the fundamental Socratic imperative for philosophical knowledge: Know thyself! He is a man unable to say, "This is what I like—this is what I am" (73). His traversal of the speculative steps represented by the alphabet stops at R, his own initial. He cannot reach R because his thought is so tied up with his self-images as heroic leader, lonely castaway, and victim of man's transient fame that he is interrupted in his philosophical speculations: "He turned from the sight of human ignorance and human fate and the sea eating the ground we stand on, which, had he been able to contemplate it fixedly might have led to something; and found consolation in trifles so slight compared with the august theme just now before him . . ." (73). Critical attempts to assess Ramsay's character in positive or negative sums usually lack the double attitude of Lily: ". . . how strangely he was venerable and laughable at one and the same time" (74). For this double sense, perhaps the best image generated in the text is that of a seal, which Mrs. Ramsay mentally sees diving backward into an aquarium tank and which Lily metaphorically approximates: ". . . he would have flung himself tragically backwards into the biting waters of despair" (230). But, Lily continues, "He looked like a king in exile." The mythological implications of this royal exile will be discussed in their place and will confirm the presence of a regal bearing in this *paterfamilias*. Part of this afflatus derives from his aura of apostasy, his standing up to the superior force of the universe and even to its ruling powers—he jumps off the boat to the Lighthouse with the expression of a man declaring "There is no God" (318).

Of Mrs. Ramsay's queenly stature there can be even less doubt: she is portrayed as a queen "raising from the mud a beggar's dirty foot and washing it" (16-17) and later is seen in close conjunction with a picture of Victoria (27); as Helen of Troy (46); as having "royalty of form" (51). She is decidedly classical in beauty (and, as shall be seen, in archetypal associations): William Bankes sees her as "Greek, blue-eyed, straight-nosed. . . . The Graces assembling seemed to have joined hands in meadows of asphodel to compose that face" (50). There is an element of banter in her acknowledgment of the role when she jokes with the children that dinner should not be delayed: " 'Not for the Queen of England,' said Mrs. Ramsay emphatically. 'Not for the Empress of Mexico' " (124-25). But she makes her appearance at dinner in full state, "like some queen who, finding her people gathered in the hall, looks down upon them, and descends among them, and acknowledges their tributes silently, and accepts their devotion and their prostration before her" (128-29). At the same time, there is something disturbing, even sinister, about her powers, which later will be found to resemble those not only of earthly queens but also of deities: "There was something frightening about her. She was irresistible. Always she got her own way in the end. . . . led her victims, Lily felt, to the altar" (157). The threatening aspect of the goddess is remarked when she serves the boeuf en daube to consummate the dinner (which becomes symbolically a marriage festival): she "hovered like a hawk suspended . . . peered into the depths of the earthenware pot" (162-63). After her death, the images of Mrs. Ramsay are considerably less commanding and emphasize her ghostliness, her ineffectuality, though still with mythological associations: for Mrs. McNab she is (four times repeated) the lady in the grey cloak hovering in her garden (210-11); for Lily remembering her on the beach, she is "so short-sighted that she could not see" (247). Even the final vision of her, roaming in fields with a basket of flowers, has a tentative note: "Mrs. Ramsay walking rather fast in front, as if she expected to meet some one round the corner" (309).[7]

Mrs. Ramsay's concern not only for other people but for her garden and greenhouse is reflected in the consciousness of her as a master not only of social ties and personal love but also of natural fruition. Tansley thinks of her, "with stars in her eyes and veils in her hair, with cyclamen and wild violets. . . . stepping through fields of flowers and taking to her breast buds that had broken and lambs that had fallen" (27); Mrs. McNab remembers her as "a lady in a grey cloak, stooping over her flowers" (211). Lily has visions of her "stepping with her usual quickness across fields among whose folds, purplish and soft, among whose flowers, hyacinths or lilies, she vanished . . ."; of her "going unquestioningly with her companion, a shadow, across the fields . . . ," which are named "the fields of death" (279). James's memory of his father's interruption of his childhood bliss focuses this image of his mother: ". . . in what garden did all this happen? For one

[7]This hesitancy in the image of the mother-figure as a saving grace initiates a broad tendency in Woolf's later fiction; see Jean O. Love, *Worlds in Consciousness: Mythopoetic Thought in the Novels of Virginia Woolf* (Berkeley, Los Angeles, and London, 1970), pp. 178-79, on the decline of the *magna mater* character—and also of the resolution by way of art—after *To the Lighthouse*.

to the lighthouse

had settings for these scenes; trees that grew there; flowers; a certain light; a few figures. Everything tended to set itself in a garden.
. . . he could see through it a figure stooping, hear, coming close,
going away, some dress rustling, some chain tinkling" (285). With
all this there can be little doubt that we have here a Flora figure,
carrying with it the symbolic burden of the fruitfulness of earth, the
spring of the year, the happiness of an earlier age (whether of childhood or before the Fall), i.e., the archetype of the mother.

An important article by Joseph Blotner has brought together much
of the textual evidence, along with supporting information from
psychology and mythology, to establish the Demeter and Persephone
story at the heart of the fiction.[8] What must be emphasized in making
this ascription is neither the learned or classical character of this
work (although Woolf's method in some ways resembles Lawrence's
and Joyce's, among modern fictional masters of mythology) nor the
psychoanalytic or anthropological authenticity of this recurrence of
an age-old myth but the fictional enactment of the mythic associations. Thus the final vision of Mrs. Ramsay in "the fields of death"
is significant chiefly because of its influence on Lily's art, coming
directly before the visionary recovery of the dead in the shadow on
the steps which helps the artist to achieve the finished painting:
"She had let the flowers fall from her basket, Lily thought, screwing
up her eyes and standing back as if to look at her picture . . ." (308).[9]
The myth underscores the relevance of this scene to the overriding
themes of marriage, death, and imaginative recovery of the dead:
". . . her mother now would seem to be making it up to her [Prue];
assuring her that everything was well; promising her that one of
these days that same happiness [of marriage] would be hers" (308).
For the artistic observer the encounter with death is imbued with
images of rocks and waves, with the elements of the fiction recast so
as to resemble the landscape of the myth: "Down fields, across
valleys, white, flower-strewn—that was how she would have painted
it. The hills were austere. It was rocky, it was steep. The waves

[8]Joseph L. Blotner, "Mythic Patterns in *To the Lighthouse*," *PMLA*, LXXI (1956),
547–62; reprinted in the Beja anthology, *Virginia Woolf*, on pp. 169–88. Unfortunately,
the article tries to do too much, adding the family's Oedipal situation and Mrs.
Ramsay's secondary associations with Rhea to its central theme. For a review of the
Demeter figure's appearances among the writings of Woolf's contemporaries, see Lil-
lian Feder, *Ancient Myth in Modern Poetry* (Princeton, 1971), pp. 13 ff.
[9]The shift in antecedents of the pronouns "she" and "her" furthers the identification
of Lily herself with Mrs. Ramsay and with the third figure in the scene, the dead
daughter Prue, in accordance with traditional identifications of Demeter and Persephone adduced by Blotner (nn. 12, 15). Also note his reminder that Persephone
dropped her gathered flowers at her abduction, quite as Mrs. Ramsay does in this
vision of her death.

sounded hoarse on the stones beneath. They went, the three of them together, Mrs. Ramsay walking rather fast in front, as if she expected to meet someone round the corner" (309). It is some deathly figure— perhaps Dis himself—that Mrs. Ramsay meets, and it is at this point in her vision that Lily sees the shadow on the step, enabling her to complete her painting and her esthetic "vision."

There is a negative element in Mrs. Ramsay as well as outside her, "some demon in her" (66), something "willful" and "commanding" (79). It is evident in her tutelary role of encouraging marriage, not only for the Rayleys and for Prue, but more aggressively for Lily. She visits the latter by night and parodies the male guests: "All this she would adroitly shape; even maliciously twist; and, moving over to the window, in pretence that she must go,—it was dawn, she could see the sun rising,—half turn back, more intimately, but still always laughing, insist that she must, Minta must, they all must marry . . ." (80). This procreative imperative is not enough to overcome the virginal streak in Lily, with which her esthetic vocation is associated (81); Lily chooses to direct her attention to her painting when overlooked by Rayley, but she acknowledges that she is urging "her own exemption from the universal law" (81). Moreover, although she chafes at the domineering impulse in Mrs. Ramsay, she is able to paint her and her child together as an abstract composition and to teach Bankes that "Mother and child then—objects of universal veneration . . . might be reduced . . . to a purple shadow without irreverence" (85) (the association of Mrs. Ramsay with a shadow will be discussed below).

Mrs. Ramsay's imagination is capable of "drifting into that strange no-man's land where to follow people is impossible and yet their going inflicts such a chill on those who watch them" (131-32). This no man's land is seen as the floor of the sea and is part of Mrs. Ramsay's occasional death vision (131). But her desire to remove herself to it, away from the affairs of men, is thwarted by her beneficent tendencies: ". . . the life in her, her resolve to live again, had been stirred by pity" (132). In keeping with this ambivalence, Mrs. Ramsay's ordering of the festive dish at dinner (of which, more later) is accompanied by "two emotions . . . , one profound—for what could be more serious than the love of man for woman, what more commanding, more impressive, bearing in its bosom the seeds of death; at the same time these lovers, these people entering into illusion glittering eyed, must be danced round with mockery, decorated with garlands" (156). The universal interdependence of love and death is here acknowledged—as it is in the Demeter and Persephone myth—

even in the act of celebrating marriage.[10] But there is also a strong resistance toward entering into marriage at all.

Mrs. Ramsay guards the bowl of fruit at the center of the table, presiding over it as a center of the festive scene but wishing to keep it inviolate and composed, like a work of art which she knowledgeably inspects: ". . . she had been keeping guard over the dish of fruit (without realising it) jealously, hoping that nobody would touch it. Her eyes had been going in and out among the curves and shadows of the fruit, among the rich purples of the low-land grapes, then over the horny ridge of the shell, putting a yellow against a purple, a curved shape against a round shape . . ." (168). The values on display here include both fruition and a state prior to fruition—ripeness without realization, marriage and virginity combined.

This ambiguity in Mrs. Ramsay's attitude to life is reflected in other phases of the action which involve the underlying myth. In part ii, the change of atmosphere from fall to winter is expanded into a seasonal cycle; the course of a year (or of several years) is run through and is ended by death: "The spring without a leaf to toss, bare and bright like a virgin fierce in her chastity, scornful in her purity, was laid out on fields. . . . [Prue Ramsay, leaning on her father's arm, was given in marriage that May.] . . . [Prue Ramsay died that summer in some illness connected with childbirth, which was indeed a tragedy, people said]" (204-5). The "tragedy" involved here, the passage from spring through summer toward winter, and from youthful innocence to marriage (and childbearing) and thus on to death, corresponds to the rhythm of tragedy as it derives from Greek myth and ritual. But the peculiar form of such myths is their cyclic repetition, winter giving way to spring and new growth—to resurrection, if not for the individual, at least for the tribe or race— and this peculiarity makes possible a regenerative note in the work's treatment of death (as will be seen in analyzing its tripartite structure).

Just as Mrs. Ramsay is enlarged by attributes of goddess and queen, her husband is given some of the powers of a presiding deity or king. More precisely, Ramsay is identified as a Dis-like demon-king: ". . . an enormous need urged him . . . to approach any woman, to force them, he did not care how, his need was so great, to give him what he wanted: sympathy" (233). To him is assigned the role of

[10]For the psychological implications of the Demeter and Persephone myth, see C. G. Jung and C. Kerényi, *Essays on a Science of Mythology: The Myth of the Divine Child and the Mysteries of Eleusis*, trans. R. F. C. Hull (Princeton, 1969 [1949]), *passim*; also Erich Neumann's numerous studies of the Great Mother archetype.

leading the family party to the Lighthouse as a "procession . . . , a little company bound together and strangely impressive" (240; see also 242, 250); but this ceremony is a funeral remembrance, and the children resist taking part "in those rites he went through for his own pleasure in memory of dead people" (255). This funereal streak in Ramsay is raised beyond a mere character trait by tantalizing references to his "fiery unworldliness" (43); and there is a reverberation in Mrs. Ramsay's awareness that "her husband required sacrifices" (30). But in him, as in nature, the Dis-like element can be assuaged, and the personified night is found to be at peace toward the close of part II: "They would see then night flowing down in purple; his head crowned; his sceptre jewelled; and how in his eyes a child might look" (220).

Although the Ramsays are the only characters to present a consistent set of mythological associations, Augustus Carmichael, too, has a role in the work's play with the Demeter and Persephone mythos. He is early seen "basking," but this animal aspect is associated only with his "yellow cat's eyes" (21). At the end of the narrative he is still basking but has been transformed to suggest a much larger animal, "basking like a creature gorged with existence" (274)— a "sea monster" (294) (there may be a reminiscence here of Wordsworth's leech gatherer in "Resolution and Independence"). As a poet he combines the mixed receptivity and detachment of the artist, the faintly satirized traits of the esthete, and the deep feeling of the lover of virile youth (he writes a widely-read elegy for Andrew Ramsay). Finally, he takes on the aspect of a priest officiating at a ritual (171), as he closes the dinner by holding his napkin like a "long white robe" (172), chanting a rhythmic lyric of celebration and fecundity, and doing faintly ironic homage to Mrs. Ramsay—from whom he alone in the company withholds complete sympathy (67). "He wanted nothing" (21, 300), and yet "embraced them all" (21); he has no need of words (21, 319), and yet knows Persian or Hindustanee (22) and presumably some of the wisdom of the East; he appears entirely self-absorbed, and yet seems also to take in everything, so that he provides the echo of Lily's thought at the climax: "They will have landed" (319)—his only directly quoted speech (apart from the lyric) in the text.

This mélange of sea beast, poet, priest, and presiding deity marks Carmichael as another version of the shamanistic figure seen in its negative side in *Mrs. Dalloway*. Here the magus who knows all and forgives all is brought into the action as an efficacious force for the continuity of life. When Lily experiences her moment of recovering Mrs. Ramsay—at the same time that the family reaches the Lighthouse—he emerges from his sea beast's basking as a priest or god sanctifying the epiphany of the risen dead, strewing flowers appropriate to the underworld, and pointing its message to man: "He stood there spreading his hands over all the weakness and suffering of mankind; she thought he was surveying, tolerantly, compassionately, their final destiny. Now he has crowned the occasion, she thought, when his hand slowly fell, as if she had seen him let fall from his great height a wreath of violets and asphodels which, fluttering slowly, lay at length upon the earth" (319). Carmichael's role is not limited, however, to his "crowning the occasion" of Mrs. Ramsay's imaginative recovery through ritual and art. The words recall those used of the chief dish in the dinner scene—"This will celebrate the occasion . . . celebrating a festival" (156)—and we must return to this, the longest action in the book, for a crystallization of the mythic implications with which we have been occupied.

□

Before the ritual action of the dinner can be followed, the scene must be set—employing the literal statements scattered through the text. The dining room has a door at one end and a window at the side; the table is "long" and set for fourteen, i.e., with six down the long sides (130); there is a fruit bowl in the center and eight candles along it (150). Mrs. Ramsay sits at the end farthest from the door (173) (she walks the length of the table in leaving); Ramsay is at the other end (130), with Minta on one side (152, 159) and Jasper, Rose, Prue, and Andrew in a row at his other hand (169); at her end of the table, Mrs. Ramsay seats Bankes (130) and Rayley (155); Lily is opposite Bankes (162), therefore next to Rayley; Tansley is opposite her (133), therefore next to Bankes; as Lily can see Minta at the other end of the table, they would be on opposite sides; the stated presence of only two characters (Lily and Rayley) on one side leaves room for the group of four children; the presence of three characters on the other side allows us to deduce the position of Carmichael, Roger, and Nancy between Minta and Tansley; Lily's row faces the window, to which Tansley has his back (133); the two remaining members of the family, Cam and James, are abed (176).[11] Dinner is called by a gong (129), accompanied by a silent prayer by Mrs. Ramsay that the pièce de résistance be not overcooked; there is a delay in assembling (the children are mentioned only at page 149); Minta and Rayley (and presumably Nancy and Andrew) enter only as the main course is served (152); the atmosphere is

[11]A similar arrangement is set out in David L. Higdon, "Mrs. Ramsay's First Name," *Virginia Woolf Quarterly*, i, No. 2 (1973), 46–47.

disturbed during the soup course, partly by Ramsay's resentment against Carmichael's taking a second plate of soup, partly by a withholding of Mrs. Ramsay's social efforts.

The first hint of festivity occurs when the fruit bowl is described as a cornucopia, symbol of plenty from the ancients to Yeats; it makes Mrs. Ramsay "think of a trophy fetched from the bottom of the sea, of Neptune's banquet, of the bunch that hangs with vine leaves over the shoulder of Bacchus (in some picture)" (151) (possibly one of Caravaggio's). The festive mood and its classical symbols are enlarged by the entry of the newly engaged couple, simultaneous with the serving of the boeuf en daube: Mrs. Ramsay

peered into the dish, with its shiny walls and its confusion of savoury brown and yellow meats, and its bay leaves and its wine, and thought, This will celebrate the occasion—a curious sense rising in her, at once freakish and tender, of celebrating a festival, as if two emotions were called up in her, one profound—for what could be more serious than the love of man for woman, what more commanding, more impressive, bearing in its bosom the seeds of death; at the same time these lovers, these people entering into illusion glittering eyed, must be danced round with mockery, decorated with garlands. (155-56)

The Demeter-like aspect of Mrs. Ramsay as she presides over this occasion is clear, but hers is not the only divine force invoked by the scene and its potent stew: the laurel (bay) of Apollo and the wine of Dionysus are domesticated into elements of the family's subsistence. For Mrs. Ramsay the laurel is incidental to marriage: ". . . they all must marry, since . . . whatever laurels might be tossed to her . . . an unmarried woman has missed the best of life" (80); for Lily the erotic associations of wine are expanded in her vision of a savage rite, with "some winy smell," in conjunction with her feeling for Rayley (270). But there is a reminder that fruition is accompanied by a compact with death, for the similar compact which required Persephone's return to Hades is alluded to by the metaphor of the "seeds of death" (perhaps with a submerged image of the pomegranate which hindered Persephone's return from Hades). The mingling of erotic revelry and a Dionysian, tragic undertone makes "celebrating a festival" more than a metaphor, if not quite a myth.

Further afflatus is added to the family dinner by Mrs. Ramsay's reflections on its psychological and metaphysical influence:

It partook, she felt, carefully helping Mr. Bankes to a specially tender piece, of eternity; . . . there is a coherence in things, a stability; something, she meant, is immune from change, and shines out (she glanced at the window with its ripple of reflected lights) in the face of the flowing, the fleeting,

116

the spectral, like a ruby; so that again to-night she had the feeling she had had once to-day already, of peace, of rest. Of such moments, she thought, the thing is made that remains for ever after. This would remain. (163)

This intimation of immortality is pathetically denied by the impending deaths in the family and the coming of the dark time of night, war, and winter in part ii—already observable at the dinner but still excluded by window pane, candlelight, and sociability. But this is not to deny the persistence of the scene as a "moment" in the memory of some participants, who can use it, as Lily does, in their efforts to recall the dead and recapture the past. "It is a triumph," says Bankes when the dish is served (156), and although he may intend no more than a triumph over English cookery and its destruction of nutritive values, the significance is generalized when Mrs. Ramsay agrees that it is a "perfect triumph" (163).

For Ramsay and Carmichael, too, the dinner is sanctified, and their way of expressing that sense is to chant a poem, "Luriana, Lurilee," by Charles Elton,[12] which appears trivial but carries considerable implication in both its quoted and its unquoted lines:

> Come out and climb the garden path
>   Luriana Lurilee,
> The China rose is all abloom
> And buzzing with the yellow bee.
> We'll swing you on a cedar bough,
>   Luriana Lurilee.
>
> I wonder if it seems to you
>   Luriana Lurilee,
> That all the lives we ever lived
> And all the lives to be
> Are full of trees and changing leaves,
>   Luriana Lurilee.
>
> How long it seems since you and I,
>   Luriana Lurilee,
> Roamed in the forest where our kind
> Had just begun to be,
> And laughed and chattered in the flowers,
>   Luriana Lurilee.

---

[12]Elizabeth F. Boyd, "Luriana, Lurilee," *Notes and Queries*, x (1963), 380–81, identifies the poem, describes the Woolfs' relationship to Elton, and cites the posthumous publication of the poem in V. Sackville-West and Harold Nicolson, eds., *Another World than This* (London, 1945).

> How long since you and I went out,
>   Luriana Lurilee,
> To see the kings go riding by
> Over lawn and daisy lea,
> With their palm leaves and their cedar sheaves,
>   Luriana Lurilee.
>
> Swing, swing, swing on a bough,
>   Luriana Lurilee,
> Till you sleep in a humble heap
> Or under a gloomy churchyard tree,
> And then fly back to swing on a bough,
>   Luriana Lurilee.

The obvious deficiencies of the verse actually help to make this an effective closing of the dinner in a mindless chant of satisfaction and a rhythmic recessional movement. The poem also participates in the symbolic texture of the scene by invoking the garden, prominent throughout, by identifying it with Eden in the third stanza, and by inviting the girl addressed (associated with Mrs. Ramsay by Carmichael's gesture [172]) into this garden. Moreover, in the second stanza the poem raises questions about the nature of personal existence, in the fourth introduces a memory of "kings" with palm leaves and cedar sheaves, which carry connotations of Christ's entry into Jerusalem and other traditional notes of resurrection,[13] and in the final stanza addresses itself to the fact of death and the desire for the beloved's return. The recessional movement becomes, then, more than a set of playful gestures: "Augustus Carmichael had risen and, holding his table napkin so that it looked like a long white robe he stood chanting: . . . and as she passed him he turned slightly towards her repeating the last words: Luriana, Lurilee, and bowed to her as if he did her homage. Without knowing why, she felt that he liked her better than he had ever done before; and with a feeling of relief and gratitude she returned his bow and passed through the door which he held open for her" (172). Carmichael, in transforming himself into a priestlike figure and in chanting these apparently nonsensical lines (with their burden of redemptive concerns), has raised Mrs. Ramsay to a level of glory which completes her symbolic dimension.

□

If the mythological references expand the action by associating it with marriage and harvest ceremonies which are the ritual equiva-

---

[13]See Robert Graves, *The White Goddess: A Historical Grammar of Poetic Myth* (London, 1962 [1948]), pp. 190 and 412, for the Near Eastern association of the palm with the phoenix as a symbol of resurrection, and pp. 338–39, for the connection of cedar with the Old Testament version of earlier fertility rites.

lents of the myth of Demeter and Persephone, we would expect to find other narrative reflections of myth and ritual interests. Although Woolf does not parade learned quotations, we find repeated mention of "triumph" and "tribute" (80, 85, 115, 129, 156, 163, 191, 213, 271); of oracles and puzzles of various kinds, including Carmichael's interminable acrostics (69), Ramsay's thoughts like scraps of scribbled paper (70), and Mrs. Ramsay's treasury of "tablets bearing sacred inscriptions, which if one could spell them out would teach one everything" (82); of urns, namely, the two geranium urns between which Ramsay paces on the terrace (56-60, 70, 209, 256-58); of judgments; among them James's severity at the outset (12; see also 39, 260), Mrs. Ramsay's ideal "tribunal" of judges of things (174), Ramsay's gesture of raising "his right hand mysteriously high in the air" (288), and Carmichael's final survey of man's destiny (319); of demons and beasts, including the pig's skull (176-78)—first covered by Mrs. Ramsay's shawl in a kind of sympathetic magic but emerging as the shawl works loose in the chaos of part II (202, 206, 213)[14]—the skulls of birds in the attic (19), the demons that invest the children (93) and that inspire the Ramsays' actions at times (66), and perhaps the leopards of Bacchus associated with the fruit bowl trophy (151).

Readers who are inclined to credit the assumptions of archetypal criticism will be inclined to see works dominated, as this one is, by symbols of fertility, death, and resurrection as displaced versions of the mythos of romance. Given this context, it is less important to link individual images and situations with specific myths and rituals than it is to establish the fictive forms in which the work's meanings reside. Part I creates, for all its local embellishments and antithetical strands, a consistent picture of what Frye has called "the green world"[15] of love (in this case, marital love) and beauty (here largely psychic rather than physical beauty) in an appropriate natural setting (though on a North Atlantic, not Mediterranean, isle). There follows an invasion of this fertile realm by forces of destruction—seasonal, historical, and metaphysical—expressed in an atmosphere of night and winter. This raising of universal antagonists achieves symbolic crys-

---

[14]The shawl's prior career is also sketched in: Mrs. Ramsay first has it hung over a picture frame, perhaps to hide decay (47); this arrangement of the shawl then frames her own head when she sits before the picture (51); she later removes it and wears it in the garden (104-14); dressing for dinner, she allows the children to choose a shawl to go with her black dress (128); and with this (green?) emblem she attempts to hide the emblem of death (178).

[15]See Northrop Frye's discussion of romance as "the mythos of summer" in *Anatomy of Criticism: Four Essays* (New York, 1968 [1957]), pp. 186-206. For convenience, specific points in this section will be cited parenthetically in the text.

tallization in that all-purpose beast of romance, leviathan (*Anatomy*, page 189): ". . . the winds and waves disported themselves like the amorphous bulks of leviathans whose brows are pierced by no light of reason, and mounted one on top of another, and lunged and plunged in the darkness or the daylight . . ." (208-9). Finally, fulfilling the romance tendency to have things in triads (*Anatomy*, page 187), there is a movement of return to the green world through the psychic efforts of the characters to recover the prewar family happiness, in keeping with the return of fertility and order to the landscape. These psychic efforts are organized by the physical activity of a journey in quest—typically, in the romance tradition, a passage by water. This quest-journey has for its goal a fortresslike tower set on a rock, which acts as a source of illumination to the surrounding world amid the onset of night and storm. We may follow Frye in regarding the Lighthouse as the "point of epiphany": ". . . the symbolic presentation of the point at which the undisplaced apocalyptic world and the cyclical world of nature come into alignment" (*Anatomy*, page 203). (Frye mentions *To the Lighthouse* in this context on page 206.) From this standpoint, the discovery that the Lighthouse is only a lighthouse—as well as being all the dreams men have had of it—is akin to the discovery in ironic works of "the point of demonic epiphany, the dark tower and prison of endless pain, the city of dreadful night in the desert, or, with a more erudite irony, the *tour abolie*, the goal of the quest that isn't there" (*Anatomy*, pages 238-39).

To complicate this romance structure, the plot is not a sustained heroic quest, although the work includes elements of conflict, death, and discovery. Instead, in accord with the historical tendency to displace heroic stature from the superhuman to the average or even subhuman level (*Anatomy*, pages 33-34), the heroic action here is largely drawn from the patterns of comedy rather than from those of romance. The close conjunction of the two *mythoi*, with their common roots in rituals and myths of death and rebirth, puts this work in a tradition stretching back through Shakespeare's late romances to ancient New Comedy. The "argument of comedy," as Frye has described it (with variations in his later essays), involves a "movement from one kind of society to another. At the beginning of the play the obstructing characters are in charge of the play's society, and the audience recognizes that they are usurpers. At the end of the play the device in the plot that brings hero and heroine together causes a new society to crystallize around the hero . . ." (*Anatomy*, page 163). From this definition, it will be obvious that *To the Lighthouse* lacks the revolutionary movement that overthrows the established, usually elder, generation and reorders the world. But there are definite signs in part III of a renewal of the family by the younger generation, overcoming the loss of the original green world and its presiding matriarch. Moreover, this change is brought about through a conflict of father and son that resembles the comic juxtaposition of *senex iratus* and hangdog *eiron* more than it does the tragic conflict suggested by Oedipal rivalry.[16]

Ramsay, despite his absurd self-pity and grotesque posturing, speaks the truth when he thwarts his son's hopes for an immediate expedition to the Lighthouse. It does rain the following day and the trip must be postponed—there are storms in nature, dark times in history, and destructive forces in the universe that shatter youthful hopes and social enterprises. On the other hand, there is a comic resolution to this conflict: as the group finally reaches the Lighthouse, the father approves the son's coming of age (particularly his steering, a function which Ramsay, the leader of expeditions, is handing on to James), and the son comes to recognize the stark truths implicit in the more experienced generation's dour attitude to life. Thus the romance theme of a quest to restore a lost garden is played out in a comic conflict which leads not to a simple replacement of one generation or society by another but to a resolution of complementary truths—a restoration of family unity in the absence of the cohesive force of the mother.

A powerful synthesizing tendency unites the romance quest for a "victory of fertility over the waste land" (*Anatomy*, page 193) and this comic effort to reestablish a healthy society. In keeping with Woolf's experimental method in thematic construction and psychological expansion, the synthetic form here takes in the novelistic elements of man in society, the romance themes presented above, and—if the autobiographical sources of the work are put in evidence—the confessional mode (*Anatomy*, page 308). (It is doubtful that Frye's fourth type of prose fiction, Menippean satire, can be found here, though it is much in evidence in *Orlando* and *Between the Acts*.) *To the Lighthouse* comes closer to the encompassing status of encyclopedic form than any modern work besides Joyce's. Aside from its inclusiveness of genres and *mythoi*, this form is distinguished by its comprehensiveness in presenting an image of human life. Although *To the Lighthouse* does not follow the individual's career from birth

---

[16]We do not take seriously the images of slaying the father by knife or ax (12, etc.) which come to James's mind (although they are elaborated in the broad stream of imagery of mutilation and destruction which runs through the text); neither do we miss the serious note in the frequent metaphors of Ramsay as a blade, beaked bird, or other dismembering figure.

to death, as does *The Waves*, it is as universal a symbol of family life as we possess, ranging from courtship and marriage, through child-raising and children's life at various stages, to the deaths of parents and children and the readjustment of family relations in their wake. In English literature, at least, it is hard to think of a more systematic ordering of the patterns of the generations, with the possible exception of D. H. Lawrence's *The Rainbow*.

□

To the Lighthouse, for all its genteel atmosphere and artful style, presents as intense a vision of human suffering as do much more obviously realistic works. Part of this vividness derives from the work's placement in history: although not entering into affairs of state, it tells with great immediacy what it feels like to be alive before, during, and after a catacylsmic event like World War I. But it is not its value as a document of British response to the enormous loss of young men's lives (mingled with Woolf's own feelings about the prewar death of her brother, Thoby) that makes this a work of high historical seriousness. The war is seen only as an instance of a pattern of historical experience in a vision of cosmic destruction that bears comparison with Tolstoy's or Hardy's. Part ii, "Time Passes," raises the specter of a world undone by natural forces like night, winter, and death, or what we call chaos, and also by human enemies of civilization which join the former in the universal impulse we may call barbarism.

These powers are introduced, oddly enough, not as the antithesis of love but as its attribute—"the most barbaric of human passions" (159). (This idea is developed in Lily's vision of love as savage ritual [270–71].) But in part ii they become associated with nature's dark side and with war, as a regression to animality: ". . . only gigantic chaos streaked with lightning could have been heard tumbling and tossing, as the winds and waves disported themselves like the amorphous bulks of leviathans whose brows are pierced by no light of reason, and mounted one on top of another, and lunged and plunged in the darkness or the daylight (for night and day, month and year ran shapelessly together) in idiot games, until it seemed as if the universe were battling and tumbling, in brute confusion and wanton lust aimlessly by itself" (208–9). There is no evil—original or otherwise—in Woolf's ethics, but this vision of horror is her closest approximation of it. It is compensated by the emergence of counterbalancing forces, which lead to the cyclic return of "peace" in its several senses: "Then indeed peace had come. Messages of peace breathed from the sea to the shore. . . . Through the open window the voice of the beauty of the world came murmuring . . ." (219). Yet chaos persists in human relations and in personal responses to life: Lily feels it in Ramsay's overbearing demand for sympathy (229) and in her own inability to integrate experience except by art (232).

Nevertheless, the tripartite rhythm of *To the Lighthouse* catches up the sequence peace-war-peace among its formal alternations; the work is "fashioned like an hourglass"[17] on the scale of not only diurnal but also historical time. The hourglass figure is, however, a critical ascription of form; the image of a threefold movement of time provided by the text is the Lighthouse beam: ". . . coming regularly across the waves first two quick strokes and then one long steady stroke" (98). This rhythm will be found to operate in the characters' imaginations in various ways, but in one of its aspects it marks the passage of time. The Lighthouse, then, is the embodiment of temporal being in the work: itself immobile and sempiternal, it operates dynamically to mark off the moments of human life.

Temporality exists concretely in *To the Lighthouse* in the form of images of day and night which enter into almost all the work's several levels of action. The donnée of a voyage to the Lighthouse is presented as "a night's darkness and a day's sail" (11); the gradual darkening of the scene as part I progresses is counterpointed by the turning of day into night in the tale of the Fisherman and His Wife (97); the suffusion of part II in universal darkness is accomplished by a merging of successive nights into one ("But what after all is one night? A short space, especially when the darkness dims so soon. . . . Night, however, succeeds to night" [198]), so that day and night run together (209) and "the long night seemed to have set in" (212); the return to peace and the rehabitation of the house are set precisely at the dawn of a new day, as Lily wakes at the end of part II (221); and the concluding trip to the Lighthouse follows the advancing hours of the new day, reaching its goal at about noon, the height of day.

While the characters follow the sun in their social life, organizing their ceremonies and projects in accordance with the appropriate times of day, they respond more acutely to the Lighthouse beam in their private, imaginative life, using it to order their own life rhythms and even to shape their innermost sense of identity. Ramsay thinks of himself, in his philosophical enterprise and heroic leadership, as taking the position of a lighthouse: ". . . he would find some crag of rock, and there, his eyes fixed on the storm, trying to the end to pierce the darkness, he would die standing" (58-59). But he anticipates that "his own little light would shine, not very brightly, for a year or two,

---

[17]James S. Wilson, "Time and Virginia Woolf," *Virginia Quarterly Review*, XVIII (1942), 270.

and would then be merged in some bigger light, and that in a bigger still" (59) (Tansley uses the same metaphor, without its Lighthouse connotations, however: a fellow scholar had "buried his light temporarily" before his philosophical work "saw the light of day" [17]). The most articulate and extended identification with the Lighthouse is Mrs. Ramsay's:

> . . . she looked out to meet that stroke of the Lighthouse, the long steady stroke, the last of the three, which was her stroke, for watching them in this mood always at this hour one could not help attaching oneself to one thing especially of the things one saw; and this thing, the long steady stroke, was her stroke. Often she found herself sitting and looking, sitting and looking, with her work in her hands until she became the thing she looked at—that light for example. (100-101)

She goes further in associating herself with the Lighthouse rhythm by echoing it in three-word phrases ("Children don't forget," "It will end" [101]), although this proves a falsification of her thoughts, and by allowing the light sweeping over her to remind her of its past nighttime visitations, thereby experiencing an esthetic and sexually charged "ecstasy" (103). James, too, is deeply stirred by the light, which acts even more literally as a reflection of himself by appearing mirrored in his eyes: his mother "saw in his eyes, as the interest of the story died away in them, something else take its place; something wondering, pale, like the reflection of a light, which at once made him gaze and marvel" (98). The reflection in James's eyes reminds him of his wish to reach its source, providing an intimation that there is an affinity of the Lighthouse and the imagining self, a longing as instinctive as the eye's desire for light.

The close involvement of light and vision, which is the primary form of experience in Woolf, is extended to a metaphysical plane when the little airs that trek through the house by night—and in the long night of the family's absence—are shown responsive to light: "So some random light directing them from an uncovered star, or wandering ship, or the Lighthouse even, with its pale footfall upon stair and mat, the little airs mounted the staircase and nosed round bedroom doors. . . . Here one might say to those sliding lights, those fumbling airs, that breathe and bend over the bed itself, here you can neither touch nor destroy" (197). They bring a kind of other-worldly existence into the domestic scene, acting as both pure consciousness divorced from any particular character's point of view and as the force of time blanching the flowers and decaying the house. The light, in guiding the airs, makes brave efforts to compensate for darkness, time, and death: "When darkness fell, the stroke of the Lighthouse, which had laid itself with such authority upon the carpet in the darkness, tracing its pattern, came now in the softer light of spring mixed with moonlight gliding gently as if it laid its caress and lingered stealthily and looked and came lovingly again. But in the very lull of this loving caress, as the long stroke leant upon the bed, the rock was rent asunder . . ." (205-6). The polarization of light and dark into a Manichean warfare of benign and baleful powers is accompanied by a recognition that their relation is dialectical, that the destructive moment (the rending of the Lighthouse's own rock?) is built into the rhythm of the light—that the Lighthouse's action is compounded of light and dark in a definite sequence, not of pure light alone. Indeed, the Lighthouse is established as a perspective which is wider than the little airs' view of the house, for it can include the totality of life and death: "Only the Lighthouse beam entered the rooms for a moment, sent its sudden stare over bed and wall in the darkness of winter, looked with equanimity at the thistle and the swallow, the rat and the straw" (213-14).[18]

This equanimity is achieved in human consciousness only with difficulty, and it may be said to be the office of art and the specific function of *To the Lighthouse* to encourage it. For painting, which is the active exemplar of art in this work, is a formalized relationship of light and dark, a means of relating one to the other: ". . . if there, in that corner, it was bright, here, in this, [Lily] felt the need of darkness. . . . There were other senses, too, in which one might reverence them. By a shadow here and a light there, for instance. Her tribute took that form, if, as she vaguely supposed, a picture must be a tribute. A mother and child might be reduced to a shadow without irreverence. A light here required a shadow there" (85). As she paints her second picture Lily remembers this account of her formal purpose and method and reemphasizes the obligation of art to treat even death as a shadow, with esthetic detachment: "Even [Mrs. Ramsay's] shadow at the window with James was full of authority. . . . a light there needed a shadow there" (271).

The equanimity of art in treating light and shade is matched by the Lighthouse as it creates its rhythm of illumination and obscurity. In response to the Lighthouse, James has an insight into the doubleness of reality—an ambiguity that structure maintains with serene indifference: "The Lighthouse was then a silvery, misty-looking tower

---

[18]The difficulty of defining the "little airs" as an impersonal perspective is partly removed and partly complicated by the alternative terms used in the manuscript (Berg Collection of the New York Public Library): "ghostly confidantes," "nameless comforters" (pp. 151-52), "the grey airs of midnight" (p. 155).

with a yellow eye that opened suddenly and softly in the evening. Now—James looked at the Lighthouse. He could see the white-washed rocks; the tower, stark and straight. . . . So that was the Lighthouse, was it? No, the other was also the Lighthouse. For nothing was simply one thing. . . . In the evening one looked up and saw the eye opening and shutting and the light seemed to reach them in that airy sunny garden where they sat" (286). The humanizing metaphor of the Lighthouse as an eye relates it to the human activities of seeing, knowing, and art-making, all of which are similarly double in their incorporation of light and dark in response to the polarities of day and night, life and death, peace and war.

Finally, the growing awareness of this doubleness, not only in the reader, but also in James and Lily, leads to an enactment of the power of art through its attention to light and dark. As Lily paints out her desire for Mrs. Ramsay:

Suddenly the window at which she was looking was whitened by some light stuff behind it . . . so as to throw an odd-shaped triangular shadow over the step. It altered the composition of the picture a little. It was interesting. It might be useful. . . . One must keep on looking without for a second relaxing the intensity of emotion, the determination not to be put off, not to be bamboozled. One must hold the scene—so—. . . . Some wave of white went over the window pane. . . . Mrs. Ramsay—it was part of her perfect goodness to Lily—sat there quite simply, in the chair, flicked her needles to and fro, knitted her reddish-brown stocking, cast her shadow on the step. (309–10)

When the artist holds the scene suspended in a formal relation of light and dark, the action of the "light stuff" and the "wave of white" produces a useful and interesting shadow, and in this esthetic transaction Mrs. Ramsay appears—less as a mystical vision than as an accessible esthetic phenomenon, a shadow, compound of light and dark.[19]

There are further implications of this formalization of experience into design: experience has not only a temporal rhythm but a spatial pattern of light and dark. The shadow cast from the window is triangular; it can assume the role of Mrs. Ramsay in the picture because it takes the form of the "triangular purple shape" in Lily's first painting which was to represent "Mrs. Ramsay reading to James" (84). Moreover, the triangular dark shape is not simply a

[19]The formal transmutation of the dead into the stuff of art is a process that occurs not only within but also by the action of the work as a whole. By her own account, *To the Lighthouse* transmutes Woolf's memories of her parents: "I used to think of [father] and mother daily; but writing the *Lighthouse* laid them in my mind. And now he comes back sometimes, but differently. . . . He comes back now more as a contemporary" (*Diary*, p. 138, 28 Nov. 1928).

stipulative visual substitute or conventional geometric sign; it has an inherent relation to Mrs. Ramsay's sense of herself, for it is her metaphor of her own identity: ". . . one shrunk, with a sense of solemnity, to being oneself, a wedge-shaped core of darkness, something invisible to others. . . . This core of darkness could go anywhere, for no one saw it. . . . Not as oneself did one find rest ever, in her experience . . . but as a wedge of darkness" (99-100). This triangular core is intuited by the artist as she searches for an appropriate visual shape and position to represent the absent personality.

Mrs. Ramsay's is also an individual core which differs from others' dark cores, e.g., Tansley's, in Lily's vision of him "as in an X-ray photograph, the ribs and thigh bones of the young man's desire to impress himself lying dark in the mist of his flesh" (141). Moreover, it is different from other triangular shapes, being designated as "an odd-shaped triangular shadow" (309); but it would seem to have some structural relation to the triads of which the book is composed: the triple moments of the Lighthouse beam and the tripartite structure of the narrative, based on natural time, history, and family life. External reality, personal identity, and esthetic form are thus elided in a common formal order, so that the work demonstrates by its symbolic action the principles of art and life which it envisions.

The shadow itself conveys this interpenetration of life and death, generated as it is in a relation of light and dark. Some shadows are signs of presence, like the one cast by Carmichael on Mrs. Ramsay's page (66). Others are threatening, as in the traditional iconography of death; the pig's skull in the children's room is not only laden with the folklore of the black pig (although Mrs. Ramsay tries to represent it as "a nice black pig like the pigs at the farm" [177]), but it casts a shadow of monstrous proportions: "She could see the horns, Cam said, all over the room. It was true. Wherever they put the light (and James could not sleep without a light) there was always a shadow somewhere" (176-77). Mrs. Ramsay covers the skull with her shawl not to conceal the pig but to transform the shadow, acting in the manner of an artist and critical interpreter as she tries to soothe James: ". . . it was like a bird's nest; it was like a beautiful mountain such as she had seen abroad, with valleys and flowers and bells ringing and birds singing" (177)—i.e., like a green world, the condition in which life has been represented throughout part I. But the children's ambivalent feeling toward the shadow remains.

A literary allusion to the shadow develops the burden of death that lies on all worldly experience.[20] Browsing through a poetry anthology

---

[20]Only Ruby Cohn, "Art in *To the Lighthouse*," *Modern Fiction Studies*, VIII (1962-63), 127-36, takes the trouble to examine this and other allusions.

(in which she also finds Browne's "Syrens' Song"), Mrs. Ramsay turns to Shakespeare's sonnet 98. After quoting the mellifluous tenth line (186) to her somewhat contemptuous husband (187) (he had previously denigrated Shakespeare, largely because of anxieties about his own immortality [70-71]), she moves on to the couplet (which is rendered clearer by fuller citation):

> They [lily and rose] were but sweet, but figures of delight,
> Drawn after you, you pattern of all those.
> Yet seem'd it winter still, and, you away,
> As with your shadow I with these did play.

These lines ultimately derive from the Neoplatonic *topos* of the natural object as a "shadow" of the ideal and ultimately real. This poem explains some of the metaphors with which *To the Lighthouse* is occupied: the beloved as having an esthetic "pattern" of which other lovely objects like flowers are mere "figures" (patterns of the pattern); the correlation of winter with the absence of the beloved, this stage of the year being seen as one of dearth and negation, along with its burden of death and promise of renewal; the "play" of artistic imagination on visible objects ("shadow") in the absence of the beloved. This playing with visible substitutes, reaching through shadow toward substance, becomes a form of esthetic recapture of the beloved—whether successfully recalling the living spirit is not clear. The shadowy ambiguity of all symbolism—itself a compound of presence and absence, of substitution and identity—is one of the central paradoxes of the Western imagination, and it adds further significance to the dual structures of light and dark, art and reality, in the world of this fiction.

The Shakespearian crux comes toward the close of part I. From this point on, the image of the shadow becomes a presence constant but ambiguous: "For the shadow, the thing folding them in was beginning, [Mrs. Ramsay] felt, to close round her again" (188-89); "she could feel [Ramsay's] mind like a raised hand shadowing her mind" (189). In the empty house of part II, "Only the shadows of the trees, flourishing in the wind, made obeisance on the wall, and for a moment darkened the pool in which light reflected itself . . ." (200-201); "Then again peace descended; and the shadow wavered; light bent to its own image in admiration . . ." (202); "In those mirrors, the minds of men, in those pools of uneasy water, in which clouds for ever turn and shadows form, dreams persisted . . ." (204-5); ". . . among passing shadows and flights of small rain [the spring] seemed to have taken upon her a knowledge of the sorrows of mankind" (205). The connections of the shadow are first with troubled and obscure interpersonal relations, then with the disturbance and degeneration in the empty house, and finally with the ephemerality of the seasons and the return of a shadowy peace. The final appearance of the shadow is as a personification of Ramsay, seen again as the Hades figure in the underlying myth: Lily's vision of the dying Mrs. Ramsay shows her "putting her wreath to her forehead and going unquestioningly with her companion, a shadow, across the fields" (279). For, in death as in life, Ramsay is the companion, the shadow of his wife: "She could feel his mind like a raised hand shadowing her mind" (189).

□

The role of art—and particularly, pictorial art—ranges in this work from the mundane to the sublime. From the opening scene, in which Mrs. Ramsay directs James's cutouts from a store catalog (11), to the adverse judgment of Tansley's tie while visiting art galleries (18), to the typical picture of Queen Victoria in the home Mrs. Ramsay visits (27), to the heirloom painting which is jokingly called "the authenticated masterpiece by Michael Angelo" (51), to the large picture of cherry trees Bankes keeps in his drawing room (85)—visual representations are omnipresent in the daily life of men. More consciously esthetic concerns enter with the account of the Paunceforte school of local landscape painters (26), Mrs. Ramsay's grandmother's friends' color techniques (26), Bankes's and Lily's discussions of art and comparing of notes on the great Continental museums (113), the analogy of Raphael's madonnas and children to Lily's painting (271-72), and the nervous reiteration of Tansley's disparaging remarks about lady painters and art appreciation in general. Indeed, everyone seems to be making pictures, more or less consciously: Bankes's mental picture of Mrs. Ramsay, compounded of Greek models and the building activity before his eyes (50-51); Lily's x-ray picture of Tansley (141); Nancy's imaginative transformation of the rock pool into a microcosm of the universe (118-19); Lily's memory of Tansley, which stays in the mind "almost like a work of art" (249). (But in response to this appeal of art, the "little airs" "tried the picture on the easel" [197].) The people of this world have their opinions about art, not only Tansley's and Bankes's limited comprehension, but Ramsay's notions of art as undemocratic (70). Even Mrs. Ramsay has an ideal of the artist and sees James not only as a judge but as "a great artist; and why should he not? He had a splendid forehead" (52). Moreover, the characters are repeatedly seen, and sometimes willingly pose, as esthetic objects: Mrs. Ramsay is aware that she must sit still for Lily's painting (31), and she is posed within the surrounding offered by the gilt frame (51).

The imperative of art-making is developed to its fullest in the creation of Lily's painting.[21] As a painter, Lily's beginning and end is space, but hers is a special sort of space; like Mrs. Ramsay (and Cézanne), she aspires to "the still space that lies about the heart of things, where one could move or rest" (163). She must also find a way of relating outer space to her forms, so that her immediate problem is to find a way of bridging the space between the elements of her design. The two major structures are the house, Mrs. Ramsay's domain, on the one side and the hedge, by which Ramsay measures his pacing, on the other ("that hedge which had over and over again rounded some pause" [69-70; see also 59, 71]). Her provisional solution in her first painting is to "put the tree further in the middle; then I shall avoid that awkward space" (132). When she resumes painting in part III, however, she has learned to regard space itself as one of the elements of her enterprise: "The grey-green light on the wall opposite. The empty places. Such were some of the parts, but how bring them together? she asked" (228). The awkward space in the middle now becomes associated with Mrs. Ramsay: ". . . the step where she used to sit was empty" (232); it is a personal emptiness as well as visual space that must be filled or accommodated by the imagination. Tackling this problem consciously makes space crucial to life in general and to her painting in particular: "Heaven be praised for it, the problem of space remained, she thought, taking up her brush again. It glared at her. The whole mass of the picture was poised upon that weight" (264).

Space becomes a problem not merely of design but of expression: "For how could one express in words these emotions of the body? express that emptiness there? (She was looking at the drawing-room steps; they looked extraordinarily empty). . . . Suddenly, the empty drawing-room steps, the frill of the chair inside, the puppy tumbling on the terrace, the whole wave and whisper of the garden became like curves and arabesques flourishing round a centre of complete emptiness" (274-75). Lily is learning to approach the emptiness as a realm of feeling to be discovered within herself and an essential part of the mortal world she must live in. But she slips

[21]For a close tracing of this process from another standpoint, see Ralph Freedman, *The Lyrical Novel: Studies in Hermann Hesse, Andre Gide and Virginia Woolf* (Princeton, 1966 [1963]), pp. 237 ff. A series of moments in Lily's inspiration is given in Morris Beja, "Matches Struck in the Dark: Virginia Woolf's Moments of Vision," in Beja, ed., *Virginia Woolf*, pp. 226-27 (the essay is included in Beja's *Epiphany in the Modern Novel: Revelation as Art* [Seattle, 1971]). For a careful, but in my reading mistaken, description of the painting and the "line in the centre," see Sharon Kaehele and Howard German, "*To the Lighthouse:* Symbol and Vision," *Bucknell Review*, x (1962), collected in Beja, ed., *Virginia Woolf*, pp. 189-209.

back into thinking of it simply as a loss to be filled up: "For one moment she felt that if they [she and Carmichael] both got up, here, now on the lawn, and demanded an explanation . . . beauty would roll itself up; the space would fill; those empty flourishes would form into shape; if they shouted loud enough Mrs. Ramsay would return" (277). Instead, "nothing happened" after Lily's mute (?) cry of Mrs. Ramsay's name (278), and she returns to her painting. But now it is seen as an object that "must be perpetually remade" out of her memories of the past, mythic dreams, and the scene before her: ". . . she looked at the bay beneath her, making hillocks of the blue bars of the waves, and stony fields of the purpler spaces. Again she was roused as usual by something incongruous. There was a brown spot in the middle of the bay. It was a boat" (279-80).

The space in the middle of the painting is formed largely by the blue bay, and the problem of bridging the empty space between the house and the garden hedge is now answered by a boat—presumably the Ramsays' boat as it heads for the Lighthouse. The family boating activity now becomes part of the subject matter of painting, expanding its range beyond the domestic scene, just as the family itself is in the process of expansion. It is not only the empty steps, specifically the place where Mrs. Ramsay had sat, that must be filled but the larger opening in this picture of the family and its life space. Thus, when the shadow is cast on the steps (filling the emptiness with another emptiness) Lily can with esthetic detachment regard her unfulfilled desire as part of the fulfillment of her picture: " 'Mrs. Ramsay! Mrs. Ramsay!' she cried, feeling the old horror come back— to want and want and not to have. Could she inflict that still? And then, quietly, as if she refrained, that too became part of ordinary experience, was on a level with the chair, with the table" (310). Space is filled by space, desire fulfilled by desire itself—not in an abstract paradox but by a recognition that empty places are as necessary to a painting as filled ones, shadow as necessary as light, death as life, desire as fulfillment. Lily's final gesture brings all these dualities into conjunction: "She looked at the steps; they were empty; she looked at her canvas; it was blurred. With a sudden intensity, as if she saw it clear for a second, she drew a line there, in the centre. It was done; it was finished" (320).

The line does not fill the space on the steps, which is accepted as filled by the shadow. What, then, is the line that completes the painting, the vision, and the prose narrative? It is not, clearly, a representation of any of the objects that have occupied the artist's eye at various stages of the painting—neither tree, nor boat, nor Mrs. Ramsay. To solve this charming and revelatory puzzle, we must again adopt a literalistic assemblage of evidence in order to sketch out what the painting looks like.

Lily's first painting is described sketchily as "that vision which she had seen clearly once and must now grope for among hedges and houses and mothers and children—her picture. It was a question, she remembered, how to connect this mass on the right hand with that on the left. She might do it by bringing the line of the branch across so; or break the vacancy in the foreground by an object (James perhaps) so. But the danger was that by doing that the unity of the whole might be broken" (86). From this we deduce that the house and hedge are the two masses at the sides, that Mrs. Ramsay and James are shown on the steps toward the center of the picture (so it would be possible to move James closer to the foreground to "break the vacancy"), and that the stretching of a tree branch across the middle (as in some Cézannes) is an appealing possibility.

Lily's mental solution at dinner is to move the tree itself closer to the middle, but this is not pursued when she paints again in part III. Further details are added: "Yes, it must have been precisely here that she had stood ten years ago. There was the wall; the hedge; the tree. The question was of some relation between those masses" (229); "There was something . . . she remembered in the relations of those lines cutting across, slicing down, and in the mass of the hedge with its green cave of blues and browns, which had stayed in her mind . . ." (243); "It must have altered the design a good deal when [Mrs. Ramsay] was sitting on the step with James. There must have been a shadow" (248). From this we can detect two other elements of the first painting that might be brought into the center: the garden wall and the shadow of mother and child. None of these is satisfactory; the wall is not mentioned in this role, and Lily's discovery of a shadow on the steps does not lead her to paint it. But a new range of vision is added: "Now again, moved as she was by some instinctive need of distance and blue, she looked at the bay beneath her, making hillocks of the blue bars of the waves, and stony fields of the purpler spaces" (279). We may conclude that the bay is seen beyond the garden wall, occupying the upper center of the canvas, and that in it such objects as the Ramsay boat and the Lighthouse may be placed: "For sometimes quite close to the shore, the Lighthouse looked this morning in the haze an enormous distance away. . . . The boat was in the middle of the bay" (280-81).

Lily's ideas about painting are developing in tandem with her feelings about people, and a new idea is introduced, the notion of perspective. Bankes has been explaining some points about perspective to Lily on their trips to Hampton Court (272), and she is led to extend them more widely: "So much depends then, thought Lily Briscoe, looking at the sea which had scarcely a stain on it, which was so soft that the sails and the clouds seemed set in its blue, so much depends, she thought, upon distance: whether people are near us or far from us; for her feeling for Mr. Ramsay changed as he sailed further and further across the bay. It seemed to be elongated, stretched out; he seemed to become more and more remote. He and his children seemed to be swallowed up in that blue, that distance . . ." (293–94). There is at work here an extended metaphor of optical and emotional perspective, so that remoteness in sight matches remoteness of attitude. What is most relevant to painting, however, is that Lily's interest in following the Ramsays and their boat on their reintegrative journey is carried out in the perceptual effort of distinguishing the sail and lighthouse amid the sea and sky. When, finally, Lily sees the space-filling shadow (at about the time the Ramsays land at the Lighthouse), the visual effect is complete: " 'He must have reached it,' said Lily Briscoe aloud, feeling suddenly completely tired out. For the Lighthouse had become almost invisible, had melted away into a blue haze, and the effort of looking at it and the effort of thinking of him landing there, which both seemed to be one and the same effort, had stretched her body and mind to the ut-most" (318–19). The coalescence of visual and personal inquiry is accomplished; the fulfillment of her personal feelings—in particular, her repressed feeling for Ramsay—is achieved at the moment of vision: "Whatever she had wanted to give him, when he left her that morning, she had given him at last" (319).

Recognition of a dramatic moment like the climactic arrival depends not on direct observation but on reaching a kind of imaginative activity which blends thinking and seeing: ". . . the effort of looking at it and the effort of thinking of him landing there . . . seemed to be one and the same effort." The painter's vision is completed when it functions both optically and imaginatively, when it records both what is seen and what cannot be seen—and yet what does happen (the landing). This activity brings both certainty in thought and completion in form: " 'He has landed,' she said aloud. 'It is finished.' " (319). Lily turns again to the canvas to record this achievement, which must be both the visual (but unseen) landing and the formal unification of the work. She is no longer interested in solving the formal problem with the hedge or trees: "There it was—her picture. Yes, with all its greens and blues, its lines running up and across, its attempt at something" (319–20). The completion must come when the distant perspective is joined to the near, when the seen is united with the unseen, when the domestic subject in the garden is linked to the maritime subject of the journey. There is only one thing missing from the painting, and Lily adds it with a single stroke, "a line there, in the centre" (320). It is, can only be, the Lighthouse itself, which not only visually fills the space but connects one part of the painting to the other, the garden with the bay, the house with the Lighthouse, and completes the subject of the painting: the voyage to the Lighthouse. The journey to reach this vision, as realized in the painting itself, might well be titled, "To the Lighthouse."

□

Given the model of the painting, *To the Lighthouse* assumes a structure similar to that found in the fictional scene itself: ". . . the empty drawing-room steps, the frill of the chair inside, the puppy tumbling on the terrace, the whole wave and whisper of the garden became like curves and arabesques flourishing round a centre of complete emptiness" (275). Woolf was aware of this vacancy,[22] and in a letter to Roger Fry she acknowledges the structure and its unifying symbol, as enacted in the finale: "I meant *nothing* by *The Lighthouse*. One has to have a central line down the middle of the book to hold the design together."[23]

[22]The existential burden of this confrontation with nothingness has been considered in Lucio P. Ruotolo, *Six Existential Heroes: The Politics of Faith* (Cambridge, Mass., 1973), pp. 1 f., 13 f.—the latter passage with reference to *Mrs. Dalloway*. Although I believe these implications are latent in Woolf's texts, I have refrained from drawing them out, in the conviction that Woolf's own language makes a more satisfying expression of them than any theoretical reformulation.

[23]Quoted in Quentin Bell, *Virginia Woolf: A Biography* (London, 1972), ii, 129, 27 May 1927.

orlando: a biography

"The world

created by that

vision"

Virginia Woolf's career presents an almost unbroken sequence of biographical writing—a natural vocation for the daughter of England's leading practitioner, the first editor of the *Dictionary of National Biography*. Most of her literary essays take a biographical tack, although her approach is often at an angle to the standard estimate of her subjects. In her fiction proper she twice wrote works which trace the career of a single character among his contemporaries—in both cases placing the individual's name in the title—*Jacob's Room* and *Mrs. Dalloway*. She next turned to a new conception of the scope of a human life, expanding biography in *Orlando* (1928) to trace the process of personal formation through the course of a family's history.[1] While constantly experimenting with various modes in her fiction, she continued to turn biography on its head by writing the biography of Elizabeth Barrett Browning from the rather special perspective of a dog, Flush. And her last completed book was a full-scale biography of her friend, Roger Fry, begun shortly after his death.

There is also a more direct link between Woolf's biographical preoccupations and the model for *Orlando*: Vita Sackville-West's husband was a leading biographer and a reflective thinker on the subject.

[1] I have discussed the genetic and historical underpinnings in *The English Historical Novel* (Baltimore, 1971), pp. 233–45. For this reason, the present chapter is less detailed than the others.

In the same year that saw the appearance of *Orlando*, Harold Nicolson published *The Development of English Biography*, a brief outline of the field attempting to place his own predilections within the tradition. His concluding remarks on biography in the present and future are particularly relevant:

> The literary element will, of course, persist, but it will be driven into other directions. We may have some good satirical biographies, we may even have invective: I can well envisage the biography of hate. We shall have many sentimental biographies, a few idylls, a pastoral or an ecologue now and then. . . . in general, literary biography will, I suppose wander off into the imaginative, leaving the strident streets of science for the open fields of fiction. The biographical form will be given to fiction, the fictional form will be given biography. When this happens, "pure" biography, as a branch of literature, will have ceased to exist.[2]

From Nicolson's tone we can sense that he greeted this change with a mixture of regret, curiosity, and equanimity appropriate to the liberal-conservative diplomat he was. Rather than conclude that his prediction prompted Woolf to be first in the field, we may assume that they influenced each other; Woolf responded to Nicolson's anticipation of the mixture of styles and even genres in biography while he foretold the end of a clear demarcation between fiction and biography partially on the basis of his knowledge of Woolf's methods. *Orlando* may be called the first of the works in which "the fictional form will be given biography," just as her previous works had given biographical form to fiction.

Woolf's own views on biography were equally well formulated and open to the future. While working on her *Roger Fry*, she wrote an essay, "The Art of Biography," which sets out apparently long-standing convictions:

> By telling us the true facts, by sifting the little from the big, and shaping the whole so that we perceive the outline, the biographer does more to stimulate the imagination than any poet or novelist save the very greatest. For few poets and novelists are capable of that high degree of tension which gives us reality. But almost any biographer, if he respects facts, can give us much more than another fact to add to our collection. He can give us the creative fact; the fertile fact; the fact that suggests and engenders. Of this, too, there is certain proof. For how often, when a biography is read and tossed aside, some scene remains bright, some figure lives on in the depths of the mind, and causes us, when we read a poem or a novel, to feel a start of recognition, as if we remembered something that we had known before.[3]

[2]I quote the New York edition (1928), pp. 155–56.
[3]*Collected Essays*, IV, 227–28. Woolf also reviewed Nicolson's *Some People* (1927), finding his detachment and irony typical of "the new biography": *Collected Essays,*

The implied preference here is not only for the actual above the invented—a taste that goes back to Carlylian biography—but also for the self-revealing character, or what one might call the luminosity, of certain biographical facts. The "big" fact, the perceived "outline," the "creative" and "fertile" fact is seen as true intuition—or as Woolf has it, as generating "that high degree of tension which gives us reality." In response to such facts the mind is stimulated as only the greatest poets and novelists stimulate it; indeed, the esthetic enlargement of fact into fiction may be retrospectively seen as the objective equivalent ("scene" or "figure") of the biographical intuition.

Orlando is not merely an infusion of "the literary element" into the biographical form but a genuine fusion of fiction and biography, with all the attendant contradictions that a mixture of history and art entails. One of the ways in which literature and biography are mixed here is in the incorporation of literary texts, from passing allusions to lengthy quotations, into the fabric of the work. A number of scholars have shown that some of the verses which Orlando composes are based on the writings of the Sackville family, from the Renaissance Thomas Sackville's Induction to *The Mirror for Magistrates* (quoted in the manuscript but replaced by intentionally trivial lines in the published text) to passages from Vita Sackville-West's set of georgics, *The Land*, which is the original of Orlando's poem, "The Oak Tree."[4] The inclusion of portions of the biographical subject's writings is by no means unusual in the genre, but is here raised to a principle: ". . . biographers and critics might save themselves all their labours if readers would only take this advice. For when we read: [five lines of *The Rape of the Lock* quoted]—we know as if we heard him how Mr. Pope's tongue flickered like a lizard's, how his eyes flashed, how his hand trembled, how he loved, how he lied, how he suffered. In short, every secret of a writer's soul, every experience of his life, every quality of his mind is written large in his works . . ." (189–90). We have here an extension of the style-is-the-man dictum to biography,

iv, 229–35. At one point, Woolf engages the issues relevant to *Orlando*: ". . . he has devised a method of writing about people and about himself as though they were at once real and imaginary. . . . *Some People* is not fiction because it has the substance, the reality of truth. It is not biography because it has the freedom, the artistry of fiction" (232).

[4]For the unpublished quote, see Charles G. Hoffman, "Fact and Fantasy in *Orlando:* Virginia Woolf's Manuscript Revisions," *Texas Studies in Literature and Language*, x (1968), 442; for the published quotations and other relationships, see Frank Baldanza, "*Orlando* and the Sackvilles," *PMLA*, lxx (1955), 274–79. Other family poems that Woolf thought of quoting are the lyrics of the Restoration poet, Charles Sackville, Earl of Dorset; the manuscript contains stanzas from his "Song" ("May knaves and fools grow rich and great . . .") and "On the Countess of Dorchester" ("Tell me, Dorinda, why so gay . . .").

for if style fully revealed a man's traits and even inner experience it would be enough to incorporate samples of his work to evoke his authentic nature.

Woolf does not, of course, believe that any such simple equivalence of effect is likely, and the above quotation goes on to acknowledge, perhaps facetiously, the continued need for critics and biographers who will relate the text to the writer: ". . . yet we require critics to explain the one and biographers to expound the other. That time hangs heavy on people's hands is the only explanation of the monstrous growth" (190). Despite her limited expectations of successfully evoking the presence of the man by citing his work, Woolf does go on to quote entire paragraphs of Addison and of Swift, in each case claiming to "hold that gentleman, cocked hat and all, in the hollow of our hands" (190-91). Elsewhere, *Orlando* attempts to revivify the life and times of its biographical subject by directly or indirectly quoting his contemporaries. Not only is Shakespeare observed in the act of composition (22-23), but Orlando is described as seeing a street performance of *Othello*, which brings three lines of the post-murder speech into the fabric of the text (54) (from act 5, scene 2, 11. 99-101). Sir Thomas Browne's prose is not directly quoted but its effects are richly described: "Like an incantation rising from all parts of the room, from the night wind and the moonlight, rolled the divine melody of those words which, lest they should outstare this page, we will leave where they lie entombed, not dead, embalmed rather, so fresh is their colour, so sound their breathing . . ." (76).

In addition to these quotations and descriptions there are numerous references to the major figures of English literature. Through the perennial poetaster, Nick Greene, Orlando learns the gossip about the Renaissance poets (82-85); she becomes a patroness of Pope and his circle and sees the shadows of Johnson and Boswell (201); she marries a man who has Shelley's entire works by heart (235) and writes a mawkish kind of Romantic verse herself (but an inkpot blots it out) (215); her imagination is stocked with scenes from Victorian classics, like the passing of Arthur from Tennyson's *Idylls of the King* (223) and the climactic duel in Thackeray's *Henry Esmond* (256). (This last scene may, however, be derived from direct experience in the eighteenth century, given Orlando's longevity.) The narrative voice, as well, adds touches of literary history to fill in the medium of literature in which the heroine partly has her being: ". . . let other pens treat of sex and sexuality; we quit such odious subjects as soon as we can"— so ends the account of Orlando's sex change (128) (in a parody of the first sentence of the last chapter of *Mansfield Park*). The Victorians are knowingly described by a narrator who can generalize about the period as a whole: "For, of course, to the Victorians themselves Victorian literature meant not merely four great names separate and distinct but four great names sunk and embedded in a mass of Alexander Smiths, Dixons, Blacks, Milmans, Buckles, Taines, Paynes, Tuppers, Jamesons—all vocal, clamorous, prominent, and requiring as much attention as anybody else" (261). And the narrator is able to bring her literary constitution of her subject up to the phenomena of the moment, as she does in tilting at the recently published (and suppressed) *Lady Chatterley's Lover*: "Surely, since she is a woman, and a beautiful woman, and a woman in the prime of life, she will soon give over this pretence of writing and thinking and begin at least to think of a gamekeeper. . . . all of which is, of course, the very stuff of life and the only possible subject for fiction" (242).

These remarks and others like them are important less for their content than for their establishment of an esthetic mode: they help to build up a literary atmosphere, a world of words, in which the subject of this biography moves. *Orlando* is a literary biography not merely in recounting the life and times of a writer but in transforming that account into literature itself—making her biography a literary object which is her adequate symbol. *Orlando* is made of literature in somewhat the way Vita Sackville-West's sensibility as a writer was made of her own and her ancestors' literary experiences. Thus the work becomes as creatively historical—in the encyclopedic mode— as *The Cantos*, the "Oxen of the Sun" section of *Ulysses*, or (as we shall see) *Between the Acts*.

Orlando divides its subject's historical career into six untitled chapters, each of which bears the literary marks of the period it describes. Efforts to specify their precise dates by reference to the Sackvilles' history run into considerable complications in the seventeenth century,[5] and although the broad divisions between Elizabethan and Restoration earls are clear, many of the significant family developments are imaginatively recast. The relations of two nineteenth-century Sackvilles with a Spanish dancer and her daughter (*Pepita*—so Vita Sackville-West's book on her "gipsy" grandmother and mother is titled) are placed back in time and associated with Orlando's sex change: ". . . a woman, much muffled, but apparently of the peasant class, was drawn up by means of a rope . . . they embraced passionately 'like lovers,' and went into the room together. . . . Next morning, the Duke, as we must now call him, was found by his secretaries sunk in profound slumber. . . . But at length they came upon. . . . a deed of marriage, drawn up, signed, and witnessed between his Lordship,

[5]See Hoffman, "Fact and Fantasy in *Orlando*," pp. 438–39.

Orlando, Knight of the Garter, etc., etc., etc., and Rosina Pepita, a dancer, father unknown, but reputed a gipsy . . ." (121-22). The exotic marriage leads to the sex change in sleep—a comic climax marking the dilution of the family's aristocratic purity by alien but enlivening genetic strains. The transformation comes at the middle of chapter III, near the midpoint of the text, during the second of Orlando's three love affairs—chapter I being largely occupied with his courtship of the Russian ambassador's daughter, Sasha, and chapter v with her marriage to Marmaduke Bonthrop Shelmerdine, Esq. Between these mock-romantic passages the development of a writer is pursued; in chapter II Orlando reads and mixes with the Renaissance poets, in chapter IV with the Augustans, and in chapter VI with the Victorians and moderns—in each age developing her own talent by working at her manuscript of "The Oak Tree." To summarize this alternating rhythm of romantic and esthetic education:

Chapter	Page	Period	Historical references	Chief figure
I	15	Elizabethan-Jacobean	Elizabeth (21); James I (31)	Sasha
II	62	Seventeenth-century	Charles II (109: at close of chapter)	Nick Greene
III	110	Restoration	(Continued from chapter II)	Rosina Pepita
IV	140	Eighteenth-century	Anne (176)	Pope *et al.*
V	205	Nineteenth-century	"the Nineteenth century had begun" (204)	Shelmerdine
VI	237	Victorian and modern	Palmerston (241); to October 11, 1928 (295)	None ("The Oak Tree")

□

In a letter to Vita Sackville-West during the composition of *Orlando*, Virginia Woolf asks the subject of her imaginative biography to sit for her, like a painter's model, in a certain state of dress: "I want to see you in the lamplight, in your emeralds. Just to sit and look at you and get you to talk and then, rapidly and secretly, correct certain doubtful points."[6] The image of the subject set amid gems is the pre-

[6]Quoted in Aileen Pippett, *The Moth and the Star: A Biography of Virginia Woolf* (New York, 1957 [1953]), p. 256; date not given. Woolf associated the emerald with Edith Sitwell as well; *ibid.*, p. 184. The hint of a sexual vibration is confirmed in Vita's autobiographical memoir, published by her son, Nigel Nicolson, *Portrait of a Marriage: V. Sackville-West & Harold Nicolson* (New York, 1973).

dominant one in this work; it not only becomes the mark of Orlando's individuality—a gemlike flame enduring amid the phantasmagoria of change throughout history—but also evokes the very atmosphere in which he moves. The world of *Orlando* is as strange a place as it seems because it exists in a medium different from the flesh and blood, or even the paper, of history; its substance is stone, glittering and many faceted, opaque and burnished by time. In the initial scene the hero is shown illuminated by the light of the Sackville coat of arms:

Orlando stood now in the midst of the yellow body of an heraldic leopard. When he put his hand on the window-sill to push the window open, it was instantly coloured red, blue and yellow like a butterfly's wing. Thus, those who like symbols, and have a turn for the deciphering of them, might observe that though the shapely legs, the handsome body, and the well-set shoulders were all of them decorated with various tints of heraldic light, Orlando's face, as he threw the window open, was lit solely by the sun itself. (16)

Here the hero takes on the coloration of his aristocratic race and its visible symbol, the coat of arms; he becomes a jeweled centerpiece in the stained-glass windows of his ancestral home; and he acquires the symbolic attributes of the leopard and butterfly. Finally, the account is closed with a Latinate pun—"lit solely by the sun itself"—whose wry turn consigns the whole description to the realm of literary invention, while claiming enough credence to mark the hero as a semidivine being, like the sun itself. The style of *Orlando* is typified by this opening account, and wherever it operates to optimum effect, the jewel image will be found close at hand.[7]

Jewels have their place at the key moments in Orlando's career. When the sixteen-year-old boy does his service to Queen Elizabeth during the latter's visit to Knole, ". . . she read him like a page. Instantly she plucked a ring from her finger (the joint was swollen rather) and as she fitted it to his, named him her Treasurer and Steward; next hung about him chains of office; and bidding him bend his knee, tied round it at the slenderest part the jewelled order of the Garter" (25–26). When the Restoration earl is made a duke, the celebration is studded with the appropriate trappings: "gold plate . . . candelabras . . . pyramids of ice . . . fountains of negus . . . jellies made to represent His Majesty's ships . . . birds in golden cages . . ." (118). Orlando becomes identified as "the English Lord 'who dropped his emeralds in the well,' . . . who once, it seems, tore his jewels from him

[7]For other effects of the work's prose, see J. W. Graham, "The 'Caricature Value' of Parody and Fantasy in *Orlando*," *University of Toronto Quarterly*, xxx (1960–61), 345–66.

in a moment of rage or intoxication and flung them in a fountain . . ."
(115). But following Orlando's sex change, as she prepares to leave
society temporarily in favor of the gypsy life, she winds "about her
person several strings of emeralds and pearls of the finest orient which
had formed part of her Ambassadorial wardrobe" (128), and these
links with her past bring her through the succeeding adventures.

When Orlando reappears in society her position is made possible by
her jewels: ". . . with some of the guineas left from the sale of the
tenth pearl of her string, Orlando had bought herself a complete outfit
of such clothes as women then wore" (140). Under the onslaught of
the Archduke Harry's attentions, she adorns herself and escapes:
". . . she slipped her feet into pointed slippers, and drew an emerald
ring upon her finger. 'Now,' she said when all was ready and lit the
silver sconces on either side of the mirror . . . . she was like a fire, a
burning bush, and the candle flames about her head were silver
leaves; or again, the glass was green water, and she a mermaid, slung
with pearls, a siren in a cave . . ." (168-69). When she achieves Victorian respectability by marriage, following the keynote of the age,
her precious stones give way to the aegis of a golden ring: ". . . now
there was a clap of thunder, so that no one heard the word Obey
spoken or saw, except as a golden flash, the ring pass from hand to
hand" (236). Although she bears a child and fulfills herself as a poet
she does not recapture the singular intensity of a jewel until the
closing pages, when her bejeweled state serves as a beacon for her
adventurous husband's return: " 'Here! Shel, here!' she cried,
baring her breast to the moon (which now showed bright) so that her
pearls glowed like the eggs of some vast moon-spider. The aeroplane
rushed out of the clouds and stood over her head. It hovered above
her. Her pearls burnt like a phosphorescent flare in the darkness"
(295).

Jewels serve not only to decorate Orlando and to trigger her behavior at critical moments in her career but to form her image of herself. She recalls her initial vision of the family coat of arms near the
middle and end of the work, establishing a continuity of personality
through memory. The eighteenth-century Orlando, roaming through
Knole, "bathed her hand, as she had loved to do as a child, in the
yellow pool of light which the moonlight made falling through the
heraldic Leopard in the window" (156); and the modern Orlando similarly connects herself with her ancestral past: "Though she could
hardly fancy it, the body of the heraldic leopard would be making
yellow pools on the floor the day they lowered her to lie among her
ancestors" (285). In the same way, memories of her jewels enrich the
protagonist's self-image. As an Elizabethan adolescent, Orlando's

sexuality awakes while examining the family treasure: "Such indeed was the adventure that befel Orlando, Sukey, and the Earl of Cumberland. The day was hot; their loves had been active; they had fallen asleep among the rubies" (30); near the end of the work, she recalls her youth in the same scene: "How well she remembered the feel of rough rubies running through her fingers when she dabbled them in a treasure sack!" (270).

Orlando sees not only herself but others in the image of precious stones. Her vision of an Elizabethan poet—apparently Shakespeare—at work is set in such terms: "His eyes, globed and clouded like some green stone of curious texture, were fixed" (22). The queen herself is similarly described: "Such was [Orlando's] shyness that he saw no more of her than her ringed hand in water; but it was enough" (23). His first love, the Russian Sasha, bears this aspect, among others: "She was like a fox, or an olive tree; like the waves of the sea when you look down upon them from a height; like an emerald . . ." (45). And the irrepressible Archduke Harry presents himself in a mélange of gems and animality: "Not only had this magnanimous nobleman forgiven her, but in order to show that he took her levity with the toad [which she had dropped down his shirt] in good part, he had procured a jewel made in the shape of that reptile which he pressed upon her with a repetition of his suit . . ." (174).

These emblematic gems do not function merely as objective correlatives of the characters; they are part of what one might call the implicit metaphysic of the work. As a biography of individual existence through four centuries, *Orlando* must assume a movement of time different from that of ordinary human life. The biological clock of the Sackvilles runs slower than other mortals', endowed as the family is with powers of transpersonal persistence and slow growth.[8] We gradually derive a sense that things change for this race at about the tempo that they do for precious stones, which constantly change their lights or facets but remain essentially intact. One would be more inclined to describe the action of *Orlando* as the polishing of a precious object than as the growth of a living being.

As this is the mode in which the central figure is conceived, the world in which he/she moves should be seen in an appropriate light. This, it seems to me, is an explanation for the many scenes in the work that seem congealed or embalmed: static and apparently dead but

---

[8]Cf. Jean Guiguet, *Virginia Woolf and Her Works*, trans. Jean Stewart (London, 1965 [1962]), p. 341, on the static quality of Woolf's world. This is connected, in his view, to a phenomenological reduction of objects to their pure status in consciousness (p. 287).

luminous with a peculiar life. The most famous of these scenes is the widely praised account of the Great Frost:

The fields were full of shepherds, ploughmen, teams of horses, and little bird-scaring boys all struck stark in the act of the moment, one with his hand to his nose, another with the bottle to his lips, a third with a stone raised to throw at the raven who sat, as if stuffed, upon the hedge within a yard of him. The severity of the frost was so extraordinary that a kind of petrifaction sometimes ensued; and it was commonly supposed that the great increase of rocks in some parts of Derbyshire was due to no eruption, for there was none, but to the solidification of unfortunate wayfarers who had been turned literally to stone where they stood. (33–34)

This comic transformation touches the cultural style as well as the physical bodies of the men of the past; the delightful scenes of court revels at Greenwich during the Frost are couched in terms of bedizened ostentation, fitting the Renaissance taste. But a darker aspect of this lapidary style emerges with the remarkable underwater view of the frozen Thames:

So clear indeed was it that there could be seen, congealed at a depth of several feet, here a porpoise, there a flounder. Shoals of eels lay motionless in a trance, but whether their state was one of death or merely of suspended animation which the warmth would revive puzzled the philosophers. . . . The old bumboat woman, who was carrying her fruit to market on the Surrey side, sat there in her plaids and farthingales with her lap full of apples, for all the world as if she were about to serve a customer, though a certain blueness about the lips hinted the truth. (35–36). [The scene is recalled on pages 151 and 274.]

Such images of a state between life and death, partaking of both, serve to crystallize the dominant view of human time in *Orlando*—gelid and turgid, not merely static but dormant, yet hinting possibilities of millennial growth.

Other scenes sum up an entire age in a state of "suspended animation," sometimes with a hint of esthetic objectification—the view of Elizabethan London is an example: "As the sun sank, all the domes, spires, turrets, and pinnacles of London rose in inky blackness against the furious red sunset clouds. . . . there like a grove of trees stripped of all leaves save a knob at the end were the heads on the pikes at Temple Bar. Now the Abbey windows were lit up and burnt like a heavenly, many-coloured shield (in Orlando's fancy); now all the west seemed a golden window with troops of angels (in Orlando's fancy again) passing up and down the heavenly stairs perpetually" (50–51).

There is a similar evocation of the Victorian age, raised to sculpturesque permanence by a carefully placed heavenly light:

One afternoon in the early part of the century she was driving through
St. James's Park in her old panelled coach when one of those sunbeams,
which occasionally, though not often, managed to come to earth, struggled
through, marbling the clouds with strange prismatic colours as it passed. . . .
what was her surprise when, as it struck the earth, the sunbeam seemed to
call forth, or to light up, a pyramid, hecatomb, or trophy (for it had something
of a banquet-table air)—a conglomeration at any rate of the most heterogeneous
and ill-assorted objects, piled higgledy-piggledy in a vast mound where the
statue of Queen Victoria now stands! (209)

This late-baroque cartouche of prosaic objects is not only an amusing
satire of the Victorian spirit but one in a series of esthetic constructions which make up the vision of reality achieved in the book.

Given these views of reality as embalmed and yet scintillant, the
author—or her persona, the mock biographer—speculates on the temporal implications of the work:

Of the two forces which alternately, and what is more confusing still,
at the same moment, dominate our unfortunate numbskulls—brevity and
diuturnity—Orlando was sometimes under the influence of the elephant-
footed deity, then of the gnat-winged fly. Life seemed to him of prodigious
length. Yet even so, it went like a flash. . . . What made the process still
longer was that it was profusely illustrated, not only with pictures, as that of
old Queen Elizabeth, laid on her tapestry couch in rose-coloured brocade with
an ivory snuff-box in her hand and a gold-hilted sword by her side, but with
scents—she was strongly perfumed—and with sounds. . . . (92–93)

Not only are memories of the past both durably pictorial and
evanescently olfactory, but man himself is metaphorically conceived
as made up of both stonelike and immaterial substances: "Nature,
who has played so many queer tricks upon us, making us so unequally
of clay and diamonds, of rainbow and granite . . ." (73). This composite of antithetical substances not only characterizes the nature of
man and the movement of time in *Orlando* but extends to the dialec-
tics of sexuality.

□

So much has been written on Woolf's conception of the "androgynous mind" that there would seem little more to be said.[9] Yet most
such discussions become absorbed in timely considerations of
women's relations to men and thus inevitably, and probably rightly,
conclude by placing Woolf among the mothers of the women's libera-

[9]The fullest account is in Herbert Marder, *Feminism and Art: A Study of Virginia
Woolf* (Chicago and London, 1968). Still arresting is one of the earliest treatments
of Woolfian androgyny; Maud Bodkin, *Archetypal Patterns in Poetry: Psychological
Studies of Imagination* (London, 1963 [1934]), pp. 302–4, 307.

tion movement (like other mothers, open to abuse on certain counts). The sources of her commanding metaphor have been pushed back no farther than Coleridge's remark that great minds are androgynous, but reference to Coleridge only opens the field to further investigation. In our time, the psychological interdependence of male and female elements within each sex has been pursued most vigorously by Jung and his school, and their research into the history of the *anima* and related archetypes has yielded a rich fund of antecedents in literature and mythology. It is, fortunately, unnecessary to adopt the Jungian interpretation of this material to discover its relevance to Woolf's portrayal of an androgynous mind in the figure of Orlando.

A convenient summary of research on the subject is to be found in Mircea Eliade's essay, "Mephistopheles and the Androgyne, or the Mystery of the Whole," which synthesizes the work of historical and field anthropologists as well as that of the Jungians.[10] Eliade sums up the notions of bisexual cosmogony, divine androgyny, and ritual hermaphroditism as follows: "One finds such ideas, symbols and rites not only in the Mediterranean world of the ancient Near East but in a number of other exotic and archaic cultures. Such diffusion can only be explained by the fact that the myths offered a satisfactory picture of divinity, in other words of the ultimate reality, as an indivisible totality, and at the same time invited man to approach this plenitude by means of rites or mystical techniques of reintegration." Eliade's description of transvestite rituals as part of the process of initiation is a way of understanding the course of personality development in *Orlando*:

If we remember that transvestism was very widespread at Carnival, the spring festivity in Europe, and also in certan agricultural ceremonies in India, Persia and other Asiatic countries, we realize the principal function of this rite: it is, to be brief, a coming out of one's self, a transcending of one's own historically controlled situation, and a recovering of an original situation, no longer human or historical since it precedes the foundation of human society; a paradoxical situation impossible to maintain in profane time, in a historical epoch, but which it is important to reconstitute periodically in order to restore, if only for a brief moment, the initital completeness, the intact source of holiness and power.

[10]In *The Two and the One*, trans. J. M. Cohen (New York and Evanston, 1969 [1962]); quotations below are from pp. 108 and 113. Also see A. J. L. Busst, "The Image of the Androgyne in the Nineteenth Century," in Ian Fletcher, ed., *Romantic Mythologies* (New York, 1967), pp. 1-95; this record of literary treatments of the theme goes beyond the period indicated in the title. The most recent and sweeping survey is Carolyn G. Heilbrun, *Toward a Recognition of Androgyny* (New York, 1973).

As for the literary manifestation of similar impulses, Eliade sketches a sequence of works in which androgyny is conceived either as an ideal source or as an ultimate goal—a tradition that comes down from the *Symposium* through Neoplatonism, gnosticism, and hermeticism to medieval philosophers like Scotus Erigena, on to seventeenth-century theosophism, and through Boehme to German romanticism—ending with the statement that Balzac's "*Seraphita* is the last great work of European literature that has the myth of the androgyne as its central theme." We may excuse so learned a work for ignoring Woolf and place *Orlando* in this position.

One might remain content to consign such considerations to a vague background for *Orlando* were it not for the presence at the center of the text of a scene which has been aptly characterized as a "masque."[11] A close tracing of the scene in which the protagonist undergoes his famous sex-change suggests that Woolf dramatized the subject of her theories in precisely the forms employed in *rîtes de passage* the world over. The initiate goes into a seven-day "trance" (122), and a procession of maternal figures enters his chamber:

First, comes our Lady of Purity; whose brows are bound with fillets of the whitest lamb's wool; whose hair is an avalanche of the driven snow; and in whose hand reposes the white quill of a virgin goose. Following her, but with a statelier step, comes our Lady of Chastity; on whose brow is set like a turret of burning but unwasting fire a diadem of icicles; her eyes are pure stars, and her fingers, if they touch you, freeze you to the bone. Close behind her, sheltering indeed in the shadow of her more stately sisters, comes our Lady of Modesty, frailest and fairest of the three; whose face is only shown as the young moon shows when it is thin and sickle shaped and half hidden among clouds. (123-24)

The three figures proceed to speak of their powers: Purity as dropping a "veil," Chastity as killing by her glance, and Modesty as avoiding all fruition. Each is answered and annulled by the trumpets' call of "Truth, Candour, and Honesty, the austere Gods who keep watch and ward by the inkpot of the biographer . . ." (123). This force becomes personified as the antagonist of the triad of female deities; they chant "Truth come not out from your horrid den," and the trumpets respond "The Truth and nothing but the Truth" (125). The trio acknowledge defeat, declare their preference for a residence among the bourgeoisie, and name their endowments to it as "Wealth, Prosperity, Comfort, Ease" (126). In reply, "The trumpeters . . . blow one terrific blast:—

[11]Marder, *Feminism and Art*, p. 112. The quotation below is from p. 114.

'THE TRUTH!' at which Orlando woke. . . . he was a woman" (126). As Marder sums up the scene, "This whole sequence—the pompous ceremony [at the Embassy in Turkey] . . . the riot which disturbs it, the furtive love-affair [with Rosina Pepita], the seven-day sleep, and the final exorcism—illustrates a movement from repression to freedom." We might add that the revelation of the hero/heroine's true sexuality is a triumph not merely over the idols of the tribe—the conventions of sexual repression and bourgeois respectability, which Marder emphasizes—but also over the universal impulses represented by the archetypal sisters. The natural tendency to remain intact, purely potential, even infantile, is vanquished by the inevitable movement toward self-realization, maturity, and personal fulfillment. That this conflict should be dramatized as a theomachy between the triple goddess and the masculine "austere Gods" of truth suggests that we have here not merely a shift of sexual proclivities but a fusion in one person of the deepest propensities in human nature: on the one hand, the eternal feminine, the impulse toward security and permanence; on the other, the masculine dynamism of change and the intellectual faculties which drive toward truth.

The ritual that marks the emergence of the protagonist's dual sexuality is only the beginning of its adult career. It must be courted as a woman, love a man, and bear a child before it is mature enough to discover its artistic vocation. *Orlando* is a parodic *Künstlerroman*, among other models, and the return of the heroine to her adolescent poem, "The Oak Tree," marks the discovery of a vocation in the best romantic tradition. This fulfillment in art and life is symbolized by a curious and almost pathetic image: the wild goose, object of the well-known chase. It will be noted that the goose is associated initially with our Lady of Purity, who appears bearing "the white quill of a virgin goose" (123). Later, during Orlando's walk by the Serpentine, the image combines associations of the beloved—a Shelleyan figure, whose model is himself associated with the sea—and of sailing ships with their white wings (both Bonthrop's ship and the toy boat). Orlando immediately names this vision of adventure and creativity an "ectasy!" (258, 259). After she has completed her poem, the heroine identifies the image with her quest for an artistic ideal: "the goose flies too fast. . . . always I fling after it words like nets (here she flung her hand out) which shrivel . . . ; and sometimes there's an inch of silver—six words—in the bottom of the net" (282). Even when the poem wins a prize and she achieves "fame," confirming her status as an artist, Orlando is not satisfied that she has netted the goose. Instead, it elusively reappears at the close of the work, when her husband returns flamboyantly from his voyage: "And as Shelmerdine, now grown a fine sea captain, hale, fresh-coloured, and alert, leapt to the ground, there sprang up over his head a single wild bird" (295). On this image of esthetic irresolution—the heroine's artistic quest unsatisfied but her romantic life fulfilled in marriage—this biographical experiment ends.

□

After the death of her friend—and briefly, fiancé—Lytton Strachey, Woolf mused on his "failure" to mix "fact and fiction," to create "a book that was not only a biography but also a work of art":

It seems, then, that when the biographer complained that he was tied by friends, letters, and documents he was laying his finger upon a necessary limitation. For the invented character lives in a free world where the facts are verified by one person only—the artist himself. Their authenticity lies in the truth of his own vision. The world created by that vision is rarer, intenser, and more wholly of a piece than the world that is largely made of authentic information supplied by other people. And because of this difference the two kinds of fact will not mix; if they touch they destroy each other. No one, the conclusion seems to be, can make the best of both worlds; you must choose, and you must abide by your choice.[12]

[12]"The Art of Biography," *Collected Essays*, IV, 225–26; first published in 1939, well after the mixed forms of *Orlando* and *Flush*, while Woolf was writing the straightforward *Roger Fry: A Biography*.

the waves

"And penetrate
the buffeting waves
of the wind"

Jean Guiguet has demonstrated the relationship of *The Waves* to
Woolf's memories of her brother Thoby and by extension to the
theme of the dead youth in *Jacob's Room*.[1] Beyond this relation of
the two works, the donnée of following six characters through life,
tracing the phases of the archetypal man in childhood, maturity, and
decline, may be considered an almost geometric elaboration of the
individual's maturation and death. The books are further related in
their images of human beings as moths; the butterfly scenes of the
first are carried over in the later working title of *The Waves*, "The
Moths," and are retained in numerous instances of moth imagery (6,
8, 9, 38, 100 [where the metaphor for man is specific], 165, 190,

[1] *Virginia Woolf and Her Works*, trans. Jean Stewart (London, 1965 [1962]), pp. 91-93.
Guiget quotes diary passages in which Woolf thought of dedicating it to his memory.
This is also her closest approximation of a *roman à clef*, since not only the dead
Percival but Neville, Louis, and Bernard bear strong resemblance to members of the
Woolf circle, specifically to Lytton Strachey, Leonard Woolf, and the author herself.
Leonard Woolf makes the point about Neville and Percival, but goes no further, in
Sowing: An Autobiography of the Years 1880 to 1904 (London, 1960), p. 136. The
grounds for the first resemblance are apparent in sexual, literary, and other matters;
the grounds for the second are more tenuous but lie in the combination of a businessman's mentality with that of an intellectual (the bank-clerk, T. S. Eliot, has also
been suggested); the third resemblance has been generally observed, though it is
complicated by Woolf's connection with the neurosis and suicide of another character,
Rhoda.

208). The effect of these emotional and imaginative resources on
The Waves (1931) is to inspire a sense of determinism; the implicit
view of man as a moth is expressed in a form which traces human
lives through their inevitable genetic stages. The work sees human
life somewhat as Neville does, as a progressive narrowing of freedom:
". . . we could have been anything. We have chosen now, or sometimes it seems the choice was made for us—a pair of tongs pinched
us between the shoulders" (151).

In a work that thoroughly transmutes personal feeling into symbolic universality, temporal and local concreteness inevitably suffers
some diminution. The only historical indication given in *The Waves* is
the presence of Queen Alexandra's picture on the girls' schoolroom
wall (16, 23-24); this fixes the childhood scenes in the first decade
of this century (assuming, of course, that such pictures were changed
according to the reign). There are frequent indications of months and
seasons (part of the commanding cyclical metaphor to be discussed
below), like Susan's tearing sheets off the calendar in anticipation
of school holidays (29, 38), and references to October days at the
university (61). Temporal relations between events are occasionally
specified; e.g., Bernard's engagement precedes the first dinner by a
day (102), and his soliloquy in Rome follows his decision to go there
by five days (131). Geographical placement is lightly sketched in:
the girls' school is on the east coast (16) (but even here a doubt in-
trudes; it may be the south coast [175]), their finishing school is in
Switzerland (71), the boys' university is identified as Cambridge by
Byron's tree (60), Susan's home is in Lincolnshire (190), the first
dinner is held at a restaurant near Bond Street (101) and the second
at Hampton Court, and Bernard's summary soliloquy is delivered
near Shaftesbury Avenue (172). It is, however, possible to localize
the soliloquists more specifically by their areas of activity: Bernard
in the legal and journalistic quarter of Fleet Street (198), Louis in
the City, probably in a shipping firm (67), Jinny in West End society,
Neville and Rhoda (although more generally) as Londoners, as we follow them on walks through the city (113-17, 139-40).

The prose of *The Waves* has been described as "stream-of-consciousness" writing, as "impressionist" (but also as "expressionist"),
and inevitably as Woolf's "record [of] the atoms as they fall upon
the mind"; but the only detailed study of the text's language indicates how traditional are the means by which such effects are suggested: verbal repetition, grammatical parallelism, and a host of
other conventional tropes prominently appear in the writing.[2] It has

[2]Irma Rantavaara, *Virginia Woolf's The Waves* (Port Washington, N.Y. and London,
1969 [1960]), pp. 50 ff. This self-described "philological" analysis yields more

also been perceived that this is the most finished, the most formal of Woolf's experimental efforts, not only in the control of its several styles, but in the coherent elaboration of its governing metaphors: the rise and fall of a wave and the passage of the sun as the course of an individual life. So thorough is the transmutation of the entire span of a life into the patterns of art that the work can afford to be explicit about its modes and materials. This, more than any other of Woolf's books, is an *ars poetica* for fiction—although the question whether it is a prose poem or a narrative remains open.

The most striking stylistic innovation of *The Waves* is its alternation of passages of italicized prose with sections of the main text in roman type. Great care must be taken in describing these italicized passages, for to assume that they are prologues, prose poems, or any other conventional form is to prejudice our judgment of the work's unique achievement. The main text is divided into nine sections, entirely without chapter heading or number. These convey not a narrative but a series of soliloquies, each within quotation marks. The speakers of these soliloquies are not the same as conventional dramatic characters; Woolf was quite explicit on the point: "Odd that they (*The Times*) should praise my characters when I meant to have none" (*Diary*, p. 175, 5 Oct. 1931). The body of the work is, then, a series of statements by certain soliloquists, never directly described as acting (although they may allude to their own actions). These verbal events are reported by some mechanism that can record inner experience, since most of the soliloquies are silent and undramatic—that is, they occur in the presence of others without inspiring direct responses. This recording mechanism is not a conventional omniscient narrator who gives us both inner and outer events; there are no external events here, only silent speeches. The recorder interrupts the soliloquists only to say "he said" and "she said," but even this locution is equivocal since the speeches are thought, not spoken. (There are, however, two instances of direct address by Rhoda and Louis which we are justified in calling dramatic action. These occur on pages 100-101 and 160-61 and are indicated by parentheses around the dialogue.) The world posited by the soliloquies is not, then, the world of things and acts; it has been reduced

---

insight into Woolf's procedures—and often into the meaning of the work—than the more *au courant* exercises in stylistics that have begun to crop up. Another monograph on this novel is: Magdalene Brandt, *Realismus und Realität im modernen Roman: Methodologische Untersuchungen zu Virginia Woolfs The Waves* (Berlin and Zurich, 1968).

to consciousness-of-the-world and then translated into symbolic terms like those ordinarily used in speech—but which are not spoken. There is a double distancing—or in phenomenological terms, "bracketing"—at work: the world is given only as lived by minds, and their expression of experience is composed as an ideal summary, not an active communication to other men.[3]

The ten italicized passages are, on the contrary, rendered in a voice resembling that of a conventional omniscient narrator, except that it is blankly objective in its treatment of natural phenomena. (This voice does, to be sure, bear marks of a subjective consciousness in the form of frequent metaphors, similes, and "as if" constructions.) Woolf acknowledged the problematic aspects of her arrangement: "Who thinks it? And am I outside the thinker? One wants some device which is not a trick" (*Diary*, page 146, 25 Sept. 1929). She thought of calling these passages "Choruses" or "Interludes" but rejected both terms, presumably because of their conventional associations.[4] Instead of likening these unusual texts to traditional prose forms, we may find it more useful to see how they operate in their own right in the rhythm of the fiction.

The subject matter of the two prose series is juxtaposed, so that the passage from dawn to dusk is paralleled by the passage from youth to age; it may even be possible to specify such parallel moments as sunrise and birth, sunset and death. If we put these two series on the same plane, the narrator of the italicized passages becomes another soliloquist; the experience represented is not that of any person but that of the entire earth.[5] The hypostatized figure that stands behind these passages is neither Virginia Woolf, nor one or all of the "characters," nor an omniscient narrator (for it knows little of human life), but an impersonal consciousness, reporting the eternal rhythms of the earth: sun and sea, days and seasons, birth and death.

For convenience in reading the work and in following the present discussion a purely heuristic table of contents may prove useful:

---

[3]It is noteworthy that another novel work, similarly composed of ideal equivalents of the fictional characters' speech—comparable to the invented speeches that historical figures "would have" spoken, which historians from Thucydides down have created—was almost exactly contemporaneous with *The Waves*: Faulkner's *As I Lay Dying* (1930). The two have been compared in Robert Humphrey, *Stream of Consciousness in the Modern Novel* (Berkeley and Los Angeles, 1962 [1954]), pp. 104–5.

[4]Ms. in the Berg Collection of the New York Public Library.

[5]There is a good description of the "natural time" of the italicized passages, and its effects on objects, in Michael Payne, "The Eclipse of Order: The Ironic Structure of *The Waves*," *Modern Fiction Studies*, xv (1969), 210 f.

virginia woolf

The major parallel movements, the passage of a day and the course of a life, are complemented by others, the most prominent of which is the changing of the seasons from spring to winter: *"As the light increased a bud here and there split asunder and shook out flowers"* (21); *"the birds sang in the hot sunshine"* (78); *"The afternoon sun . . . reddened the corn"* (130); *"a scattering of leaves fell to the ground"* (167). A similar movement is the gathering and dissolution of a wave (although with waves breaking throughout, this is largely a matter of emphasis): *". . . The grey cloth became barred with thick strokes, one after another, beneath the surface, following each other, pursuing each other, perpetually"* (5); the sun *"now bared her brows and with wide-opened eyes drove a straight pathway over the waves"* (53); *". . . the waves, as they neared the shore, were robbed of light, and fell in one long concussion, like a wall falling"* (147); *"The waves broke on the shore"* (211). Accompanying this account of the waves is a series of allusions to the creation and annihilation of the earth, from the opening allusions to Genesis (*"The sea was indistinguishable from the sky . . ."* [5]) to the penultimate account of apocalypse:

As if there were waves of darkness in the air, darkness moved on, covering houses, hills, trees, as waves of water wash round the sides of some sunken ship. Darkness washed down streets, eddying round single figures, engulfing them; blotting out couples clasped under the showery darkness of elm trees in full summer foliage. Darkness rolled its waves. . . . (168)

Most of the italicized passages have a common structure: a first paragraph on the sea's appearance and the waves' motion, a second on the effects of light in a garden and the response of birds to it, and a third on the passage of light through a house and over household objects. This pattern holds exactly, however, only for the first two occasions before it is varied by the elaboration of special phenomena, e.g., the birds tapping on snail shells and ravening a worm in III, the midday sun's power in V, or the coming of darkness in IX. (The variations in paragraphing in VII, VIII, and IX do not break the thematic sequence.)

Although these structures indicate a fairly uniform system of recording natural processes, they do not necessarily imply a cyclical theory of human life or history, as some readers have assumed. The thrust of all sequences in this work is linear, tracing a sequence of changes through one cycle—whatever may come afterward. There is no suggestion that these lives are to be followed by others in a humdrum round, nor is there an effort to draw the moral that there is nothing new under the sun. The waves moving toward the land and dissolution, the seasons and sun moving through their appointed rounds, and individuals forming their identities in the order of life's stages are all treated as the only instances in question. It is as if they occur once and for all time, quintessentially and not repetitively. Woolf successfully resisted the tendency of Pound, Yeats, and others of the period toward cyclical notions of self and history—despite hints of determinism here, as in *Orlando* and *Between the Acts*.

When we come to the main body of the text, the existence of Rantavaara's and others' studies make it unnecessary to follow the careers of the soliloquists in detail. I shall concentrate on an aspect of their lives that has been relatively neglected: their imaginative development. Each soliloquist has a dominant image (or scene) from his first speech onward. For Louis it is an extraordinarily clear survival of an archetype, related to him as the underside of his worldly identity: "Up here my eyes are green leaves, unseeing. I am a boy in grey flannels. . . . Down there my eyes are the lidless eyes of a stone figure in a desert by the Nile. I see women passing with red pitchers to the river . . ." (8) (cf. 48, 69, 91, 119, 143-44, 160, 201). The imagination of the apparently professional writer in the group is curiously limited: Neville's fantasy extends to crime—the vision of a murdered or hung man which he calls "death among the apple trees" (17) (cf. 89, 108, 171)—and to sex, in a homosexual fantasy of naked cabin boys disporting themselves (128, 140). The girls' minds are also fairly limited: Susan's imagination moves amid beech trees (9, 10, 96, 122), and to the twisted handkerchief she holds in anguish at the primal kiss (9, 10, 11, 102, 170, 176)—although she later develops a sense of herself as a "field bearing crops" (94) and as a container or cocoon enclosing her young (122). Jinny's mind focuses on her own bodily movements (30): e.g., she imagines her body being carried in the flood of traffic at Piccadilly (125, 137-39).[6] Rhoda initially sees herself as the observer of ships or flowers in a bowl (13, 76, 159, 170), but this image gives way to her vision of a column set on a mountain or in a desert near a fountain, by which she lives as a nymph (99, 179, 183, 195, 199, 205). The scene is enriched by her ascent of a Spanish mountain (145-47) and provides the imaginative setting for her apparently executed suicide leap (205).

Bernard's imaginary landscape is the most elaborate; he imagines a dream world he calls Elvedon: "There is the white house lying among the trees. It lies down there ever so far beneath us. . . . The waves close over us, the beech trees meet above our heads. . . . The lady sits between the two long windows, writing. . . . gardeners sweep the lawn with giant brooms. . . . We must escape to the beech wood. . . . That is only the murmur of the waves in the air. That is a wood-pigeon breaking cover in the tops of the beech trees" (11-13) (cf. 16, 19, 89, 137, 152, 170-71, 176, 190-91, 202). A number of peculiarities of Bernard's imagination may be noted here: it is narrative (he makes up a story as he sets the scene—in the places represented by ellipses above); it is social, being addressed to Susan and inviting her to participate in his fantasy (indeed, it is unclear whether she borrows the beech trees from his mind or vice versa); it is close in tone to the prose of the italicized passages, perhaps because his novelistic point of view is akin to the recorder of those passages); and it is esthetic, ending in the making of poems (Bernard eventually writes a poem about the wood pigeon [171]).

The particular interest of these imaginative clusters or self-images is that they are all connected with the dominant symbol of the work, the waves. Descending into Elvedon, Bernard finds that "the waves close over us" (11); on reascending he hears "the murmur of the waves in the air" (12). Rhoda rocks the water in the basin "so that my ships may ride the waves" (13); ascending the Spanish hill, she sees "innumerable waves spread beneath us. . . . We may sink and settle on the waves. . . . Rolling me over the waves will shoulder me under" (147). Susan's memory of her pastoral home includes the notion that "the waves are a mile long. On winter nights we hear

[6]She also thinks of herself as a nightingale singing "jug, jug, jug" (126)—in a close approximation of the nightingale in *The Waste Land*. This and other references to Eliot are cited in Allen McLaurin, *Virginia Woolf: The Echoes Enslaved* (Cambridge, 1973), pp. 134-35.

them booming" (32). Jinny's sense of movement is that of being adrift on the tide: ". . . the brisk waves that slap my ribs rock more gently, and my heart rides at anchor, like a sailing-ship whose sails slide slowly down on to the white deck" (33). Louis's repeated image of a "great beast" (6-7, 42, 49, 91) is associated with, or is itself, the sound of the waves: ". . . I always hear the sullen thud of the waves; and the chained beast stamps on the beach" (42). Neville's lack of a strong imagination yields him a weaker sense of the waves; but on re-calling a Cambridge punting scene, which remains with him and with Bernard through life (59, 176-79, 201, 202), he develops the waves' rhythm: "Now begins to rise in me the familiar rhythm; words that have lain dormant now lift, now toss their crests, and fall and rise, and fall and rise again" (59).

The implication of these imaginative activities in *The Waves* is that the soliloquists are themselves waves, not in the putative sense of a simile—men's lives pass and expire like waves on the shore—but in a deeper symbolic relation. The soliloquists imagine themselves as waves, think in wavelike rhythms, and model the scenarios for their lives on the sound or structure of the waves. The waves are not merely the ambience in which they move but become the texture of their being. In this way, the title of the work comes to refer at once to its dominant metaphor, its structural ordering, its "characters" or soliloquists, and its vision of the rhythmic nature of life. Rarely in the history of fiction have form and content—indeed, all the diverse elements of a fictional work—been so closely bound together to form one substance.

□

A great deal of ground on the narrative mode has been covered in a searching article by J. W. Graham, "Point of View in *The Waves*: Some Services of the Style."[7] The main points of his study may be summarized as follows: the soliloquists' prose is not stream-of-consciousness writing, for the styles of the speakers are not suffi-ciently differentiated to allow subjective expression; moreover, "the rhythm, sentence structure, and vocabulary of any one speaker do not change noticeably between childhood and middle age" (page 194); the soliloquies are largely in the "pure present" tense, which empha-sizes states of feeling and only momentary external action—"The cumulative effect of this is to bestow on *all* the activities narrated in *The Waves*, whether internal or external, the aura of a meditating mind" (page 196). And as a final point, the soliloquies are conveyed

[7]*University of Toronto Quarterly*, xxxix (1969-70), 193-211; further citations will be made parenthetically. This is one in a series of articles on Woolf that Graham has published over the years, which deserves collection in book form.

by a narrative device which merely resembles the traditional omniscient narrator—but which Graham prefers to call a "translator": ". . . they have their characteristic images and expressions, which the translator faithfully mirrors; but the words we actually *hear* are his, and are strongly coloured by the nuances and rhythms of his own vocabulary and voice. In the published text of *The Waves*, the translator appears explicitly only in the use of the word 'said' [as in "he said," "she said"], which implies that someone is reporting the speeches, and in the interludes . . ." (page 196).

In the manuscript of the work, from which Graham quotes key passages showing the author's narrative stances, we see such expressions as "the mind was certain of this" (quoted on page 198) and "the lonely mind" (quoted on page 201); this and other evidence points to Woolf's pursuit of a narrative mode that would render things differently from the subjective points of view in her earlier fiction. In Woolf's diary—and within *The Waves*, in Bernard's meditation at Rome, which uses the same imagery as that of the diary—Graham finds a "surrender to what is contemplated—a submission that was uncritical, responsive, passive; in a very real sense an impersonal recognition of something moving 'far out' " (page 203).[8] This encounter with reality is the ultimate goal of Woolf's long-drawn-out effort to discover a new style for *The Waves*: "In contrast to . . . authorial omniscience, the narrative continuum that Virginia Woolf sought to establish might be termed omnipercipience: *a perception* (not an understanding) of the characters' inner experience fused with a *perception* (not an understanding) of what they do not perceive—the background of time and the sea against which they are set" (page 204).

Further, Graham quotes the manuscript as follows: "I am telling myself the story of the world from the beginning. I am not concerned with the single life, but with lives together. I am trying to find, in the folds of the past, such fragments as time, having broken the perfect vessel, still keeps safe" (page 205). Without dilating on the myth of lost childhood or ideal past implied here, or on the archetypal significance of a "story of the world from the beginning," Graham takes these sentences to typify the "bardic voice" which marks the work's style, featuring hypnotic rhythms and incantatory repetitions; abrupt transitions in time, place, character, and event; "a heavy use of appositions (one might almost call them kennings); and at all times, the tireless driving voice . . ." (page 206). Because

[8]A more modish description ("A vision of absolute phenomenality") is given in Frank D. McConnell, " 'Death Among the Apple Trees': *The Waves* and the World of Things," *Bucknell Review*, xvi (1968), 23–39.

of this omnipercipient narrator, the reader's relation to the soliloquists is not immediate but proximate: "It *seems* that he is present in the consciousness of each character at the moment when the psychic action occurs; but he is actually stationed close to—not *in*—an omniscient consciousness which recounts to itself, without comment, the consciousness of six speakers . . ." (page 206). Some of Graham's remarks on this consciousness sound mystical, e.g., "When the containing consciousness in which *The Waves* takes place examines the inner life of the six speakers, it is examining itself: they are not meant to be 'human beings' but figures who act out the dilemma of consciousness for its own enlightenment" (page 206). But there may be some basis for this claim in Woolf's tendency toward fusion of consciousness in a state I have elsewhere described as "indirect perception," a McTaggartian union of love.[9]

Woolf takes another approach to such fusion in Bernard's closing soliloquy, which Graham finds distinguished from the other soliloquies by its incorporation of both narrative in the past tense and explanatory commentary in the present tense and by its direction to a silent listener to whom Bernard overtly speaks. The fusion occurs in the medium of language, not merely because the other soliloquists exist only in Woolf's language, not merely because Bernard's summary is the conscious design of a speaker (himself a novelist), but because Bernard here finds "higher ground than any he has found." Combining past and present, dramatic speech and meditation, this soliloquy can bring together two other impulses which are essential to Woolf's vision of life: "the fundamental dramatic opposition between 'life itself' and the course taken by its creature, which 'intersects,' cuts across and counter to, the impersonal rhythm of time" (page 210). Presumably, Graham is addressing himself to the final heroism of Bernard's exclamation of individuality in the face of death—although here as elsewhere further exemplification from the text would have been in order.

Despite the penetration and wide significance of Graham's analysis, some of its observations are open to challenge. Far from exhibiting a uniform and static style, as Graham implies, the move-

---

[9]Another viewpoint on the uniformity of the speakers' styles, their ability to influence (and even to "create") each other, and the possibilities of their fusion or "cosmic communication" is presented in Susan Gorsky, " 'The Central Shadow': Characterization in *The Waves*," *Modern Fiction Studies*, xviii (1972), 449–66. Also see James Naremore, *The World without a Self: Virginia Woolf and the Novel* (New Haven and London, 1973), whose general view of Woolf's narrative stance I have discussed in my Foreword. I must here acknowledge that Naremore's (and Alice Kelley's) discovery of the ultimate assimilation by Bernard of the point-of-view of the italicized passages antedates my own in publication.

ment of the work through its formal program is accompanied by perceptible development in the styles in which that program is carried out. The main change in the soliloquies' prose is from the simplicity of the opening passages—the "I see a ring . . . I hear a sound" of childhood (6)—to a richness resembling that of the italicized passages, even to the point of assimilating the latter's metaphors and rhythms, as in Bernard's final soliloquy. Along the way, the soliloquists take up the themes of sun and wave, birds and garden, and even some of the more idiosyncratic references, e.g., to natives with assegais (100) (the italicized metaphor is on page 54). Jinny remarks on the light on the windows (7), Louis on the garden sounds at dawn (48), Susan on the "bird chorus" (70), Rhoda on the foam racing over the beach (even using it as a metaphor of herself [93]), and Neville on the depths of the sea (152). But it is Bernard who most thoroughly responds to the natural phenomena that occupy the italicized passages:

In the beginning, there was the nursery, with windows opening on to a garden, and beyond that the sea. [169] . . . a bird sings close to the window. I heard those songs. I followed those phantoms. . . . And from among them rise one or two distinct figures, birds who sang with the rapt egotism of youth by the window; broke their snails on stones, dipped their beaks in sticky, viscous matter; hard, avid, remorseless; Jinny, Susan, Rhoda. [175] . . . I saw the first morning [Percival] would never see—the sparrows were like toys dangled from a string by a child. To see things without attachment, from the outside, and to realise their beauty in itself—how strange! [187] . . . it seems we are spent; our waters can only just surround feebly that spike of sea-holly; we cannot reach that further pebble so as to wet it. It is over, we are ended. But wait—I sat all night waiting—an impulse again runs through us; we rise, we toss back a mane of white spray; we pound on the shore; we are not to be confined. [189-90] . . . our life adjusts itself to the majestic march of day across the sky. [193] . . . The moment was all; the moment was enough. And then Neville, Jinny, Susan and I, as a wave breaks, burst asunder, surrendered. . . . [197] . . . I could not recover myself from that endless throwing away, dissipation, flooding forth without our willing it and rushing soundlessly away out there under the arches of the bridge, round some clump of trees or an island, out where seabirds sit on stakes, over the roughened water to become waves in the sea—I could not recover myself from that dissipation. So we parted. [198] . . . How then does light return to the world after the eclipse of the sun? Miraculously. Fraily. In thin stripes. . . . So the landscape returned to me; so I saw fields rolling in waves of colour beneath me, but now with this difference; I saw but was not seen. [203] . . . Day rises; the girl lifts the watery fire-hearted jewels to her brow; the sun levels his beams straight at the sleeping house; the waves deepen their bars; they fling themselves on shore; back blows the spray; sweeping their waters they surround the boat and the sea-holly. The birds sing in

160

chorus; deep tunnels run between the stalks of flowers; the house is whitened; the sleeper stretches; gradually all is astir. Light floods the room and drives shadow beyond shadow to where they hang in folds inscrutable. What does the central shadow hold? Something? Nothing? I do not know. [207] . . . The stars draw back and are extinguished. The bars deepen themselves between the waves. The film of mist thickens on the fields. A redness gathers on the roses, even on the pale rose that hangs by the bedroom window. A bird chirps. Cottagers light their early candles. Yes, this is the eternal renewal, the incessant rise and fall and fall and rise again. And in me too the wave rises. It swells; it arches its back. . . . Against you I will fling myself, unvanquished and unyielding, O Death! (210–11)

It should be clear from this abundant quotation that the identification of Bernard as a wave in the closing lines of the work is not a mere figure of speech or momentary effect but the close of a long development of consciousness and expression in the main soliloquy.

Shall we conclude from this development that the author has manipulated her effects in order to shift from a contrast of styles to a harmony? Graham seems to make the closing tendency toward unity of perspective into a merely formal resolution which Woolf adopts on esthetic grounds, but his own analysis points to a deeper impulse in the work: i.e., that *The Waves* manifests the process by which we discover an omnipercipient view of human life. Just as the author found herself engaged in such a quest, so the soliloquists go through life in search of meaning and form; but only Bernard discovers the images and rhythms which animate the larger vision of the italicized passages.

Another question partially begged by Graham is that of the relation that may be said to obtain between the "omnipercipience" of the italicized passages and the "translator" of the soliloquies. If we assume that the former is a receptive openness to external being, how does this influence the impersonal point of view required to report the subjectivities of the soliloquies? As we have seen, the soliloquists enter into the images and rhythms of the italicized prose; they approximate—and Bernard (if I am right) acquires—the point of view from which those passages are written. That point of view is defined by Bernard in the question, "But how describe the world seen without a self?" (204); his immediate response is, "There are no words." But he then goes on to find them; i.e., there is only a momentary despair of his or the artist's ability to render such a point of view in language. It is powerfully evocative and yet restrained language that makes possible the formation of an ordered view of life in the italicized passages; without the recurrent rhythms of that controlled prose, there would be only a set of impressionistic prose-poems (as, indeed, these passages have erroneously been taken to be). The omnipercipient view that establishes the rhythmic parallels between external nature and man's career is thereby enabled to act as the "translator" who can express the quintessence of the soliloquists' states of mind. The soliloquists can express only their own subjective perceptions, but these acquire both generality and concreteness because they are reported by a translator who gives form to their subjectivity. I would go further than Graham and claim that there would be no translation of subjectivity into the objectivity of the soliloquies were it not for the similar translation of the bare stuff of nature into the crystalline structures of the italicized passages.

In this double translation, Woolf has abstracted herself from the work in a more radical way than any of her predecessors in the tradition of the dramatic novel. The author expresses nothing; the italicized passages convey no attitudes, only a formal set of descriptions of successive stages of certain phenomena together with a set of metaphors which suggest the connection of those phenomena with the stages of human life. As the chief soliloquist, Bernard, takes on the language of the voice of the italicized passages, he also acquires its impersonality and loses much of the charming boyishness by which he had earlier been marked. At the same time, Bernard's growth of consciousness leads not to an obliteration of personality in a Spinozistic vision of the universe *sub specie aeternitatis* but to a sharper definition of his identity than he had previously been able to achieve. And, paradoxically, his gain in self-definition provides an opportunity for the recorder of the soliloquies and the voice of the italicized passages to acquire identity in their own right. In sum, as Bernard achieves the cosmic viewpoint of these narrators—and thereby qualifies as a genuine artist—the artist who has suppressed herself and taken on the chaste and perhaps stilted tone of the italicized passages comes into being as a heroic figure in her own work. In this final soliloquy it is Virginia Woolf herself who finds—or rather creates—a medium in which to embody herself, for Bernard's repeated call to arms in resistance to death, "Fight! Fight!" (160, 191), is made in Woolf's own words (*Diary*, page 148, 11 Oct. 1929), just as his metaphor of the artist's vision, the "fin in the waste of water" (134, 174, 194, 201), is Woolf's image of her own quest (*Diary*, page 101, 30 Sept. 1926, also page 169, 7 Feb. 1931).

□

This major movement of the prose toward the author's self-constitution is accompanied by minor movements of self-creation within

162

the soliloquies. These proceed from community to individuality, from an initial homogeneity to increasing differentiation, and we may deduce from this that life is conceived here as a process of individuation. The process is dialectical: the self is made out of experience, and experience includes others, so that the loss of the initial unreflective unity is compensated by the return of the differentiated others in an internalized form, a process by which they constitute the created self. This dialectic is the plan on which the work proceeds, and it is articulated by the chief soliloquist, Bernard, in the course of his extensive speculations on identity.

The initial prose style of the soliloquists is homogeneous: they utter similar sentence structures recording similar sense perceptions (6–8) in a series of short soliloquies which we may call a medley. (Medleys occur also on pages 104–5 and 159–65, but they are considerably more complex interplays.) Differentiation begins in self-perception, when sensations are first received with a shock of recognition and lead to consciousness of one's own body: "Bright arrows of sensation shoot on either side. I am covered with warm flesh" (19) (Bernard remembers being bathed on pages 83, 89, 112, 170, 205, and Jinny refers to her body in the same terms on page 126). These sensations occur in a sequence that suggests, through use of the metaphor of flowing water, the well-known stream of consciousness. But, significantly for the movement toward individuation, this term has a different meaning for each soliloquist. For Louis it connotes disruption: "The streamers of my consciousness waver out and are perpetually torn and distressed by their disorder" (67); for Bernard it means relaxation into the "general life" (Arnold's phrase): "I will let myself be carried on by the general impulse. The surface of my mind slips along like a pale-grey stream reflecting what passes" (81). Later, Bernard employs it to describe the unconscious: "There is always deep below . . . a rushing stream of broken dreams, nursery rhymes, street cries, half-finished sentences and sights—elm trees, willow trees, gardeners sweeping, women writing—that rise and sink even as we hand a lady down to dinner" (181) (he uses the metaphor again on page 183); and finally, it becomes for him the rhythm of life murmured by the mind: ". . . murmuring Pillicock sat on Pillicock's hill, or Hark, hark, the dogs do bark, or The World's great age begins anew, or Come away, come away, death—mingling nonsense and poetry, floating in the stream" (200).

The emergence of self-consciousness in bright arrows of sensation is further articulated by the forces of sex and guilt. The primal fall for four of the six soliloquists is Jinny's kissing Louis behind a hedge

(9), which so upsets Susan that Bernard must comfort her by creating the imaginary world of Elvedon (12-13).[10] The incident, trivial and amusing in itself, assumes archetypal import in the soliloquists' prose. It is remembered by Louis as the occasion of his awakening and as a disaster: "I woke in a garden, with a blow on the nape of my neck, a hot kiss, Jinny's; remembering all this as one remembers confused cries and toppling pillars and shafts of red and black in some nocturnal conflagration" (69); and later it becomes connected with his failure at social integration: "Jinny broke the thread when she kissed me in the garden years ago" (155). For Susan, the scene becomes negatively associated with Jinny's sophisticated sexuality: "They dance in London. Jinny kissed Louis" (72); but she also recognizes that she can assimilate it into her pastoral domesticity: "The violent passions of childhood, my tears in the garden when Jinny kissed Louis, . . . are rewarded by security, possession, familiarity" (135). For Jinny, it remains a height of passion, both of love and of hate: "It is love, . . . it is hate, such as Susan feels for me because I kissed Louis once in the garden. . . . But our hatred is almost indistinguishable from our love" (98). And for Bernard, it is one of the experiences of others he uses to make his identity: "Here on the nape of my neck is the kiss Jinny gave Louis. My eyes fill with Susan's tears" (205).

Having sifted the elements of a human life—sensation, the subconscious, self-consciousness, sex, guilt, among others—the chief soliloquist undertakes a sustained inquiry into the nature of selfhood. It is Bernard's achievement to gain in theoretical clarity while realizing himself in practice: just as his life is a steady growth in imaginative and expressive power, so his sense of self develops through a number of alternative theories to a final statement (which we can identify with the author's own). This parallel process is one of the finest achievements of *The Waves'* design and affords a summa of Woolf's views of the individual's relations to death, art, and the universe.[11]

Bernard begins his questioning at college: "What am I? I ask. This? No, I am that" (54). This may be called his first theory: the notion that the self is not everything but is something, though indefinable

[10]One of the few efforts to assess this and other iterative images in *The Waves* is found in Ralph Freedman, *The Lyrical Novel: Studies in Herman Hesse, Andre Gide and Virginia Woolf* (Princeton, 1966 [1963]), pp. 252 n. But Freedman's analysis leaves important questions open by reducing the italicized passages to "prose-poems," in line with the thesis announced by his title.

[11]Another instance of Woolf's propensity for multiple analysis of the aspects of the self is found in the essay "Evening over Sussex: Reflections in a Motor-car," *Collected Essays*, II, 290-92.

because merely an abstract negativity—this, because not that. Almost immediately Bernard makes an attempt to fill this negativity by describing his own procedures in living: ". . . I have to effect different transitions; have to cover the entrances and exits of several different men who alternately act their parts as Bernard" (55). This is the now popular theory of role-playing, conveyed in theatrical metaphors, but it will be seen that it is only a provisional theory for Bernard and is not that of the author, although it comes up as a possibility again in *Between the Acts*. It may be observed in passing that two of the roles Bernard takes on are the sexual poles, made much of by Woolf's recent critics: " '. . . joined to the sensibility of a woman' (I am here quoting my own biographer), 'Bernard possessed the logical sobriety of a man' " (55).[12]

Almost immediately, he produces a third theory in contradiction to the preceding one: "But *you* understand, *you*, my self, who always comes at a call (that would be a harrowing experience to call and for no one to come . . .), you understand that I am only superficially represented by what I was saying to-night" (55); and later, "What I was to myself was different; was none of these" (184). This irreducible self-consciousness—Woolf calls it the "Captain self" in *Orlando*—is one's intimate companion and apparently authentic guarantor, but like the negative self it lacks substance: it is there, but what is it? "When I say to myself, 'Bernard,' who comes? . . . A man of no particular age or calling. Myself, merely." (58). At this stage in his career Bernard is not prepared to define this central self, and his self-images are limited to a succession of roles: "Once you were Tolstoi's young man; now you are Byron's young man; perhaps you will be Meredith's young man . . ." (63) (this is from Neville's description but the terms are first used by Bernard and are repeated on pages 57, 60, 64, 182, 193).[13]

Besides these personae from literature, there are a number of persons with whom Bernard has social relationships, and in response to them he constructs another theory: "The truth is that I need the stimulus of other people. . . . which of these people am I?" (58). In this initial version of the theory he appears to take on these other people as roles in order to stimulate his storytelling imagination;

[12]The invention of a biographer gives Bernard the opportunity to repeat the satire of conventional biography found in *Orlando*: " 'The birth of children made it highly desirable that he should augment his income.' That is the biographic style, and it does to tack together torn bits of stuff . . ." (184).

[13]Louis is also addicted to this mode of self-imaging—"I was an Arab prince . . . I was a great poet in the time of Elizabeth. I was a Duke at the court of Louis the Fourteenth" (91)—and he adopts this style in life by inhabiting the Surrey estate of a businessman and the garret of a bohemian poet.

but he uses the word "integrate" in a way that implies more than mere role-playing: "The real novelist . . . would not integrate, as I do" (58). He goes on to suggest a variety of generative relationships with others: "Let me then create you. (You have done as much for me.)" (61); "I only come into existence when the plumber, or the horse-dealer, or whoever it may be, says something which sets me alight. . . . Thus my character is in part made of the stimulus which other people provide . . ." (95); "To be myself (I note) I need the illumination of other people's eyes, and therefore cannot be entirely sure what is my self" (83); "I am not one person; I am many people; I do not altogether know who I am . . ." (196).

This dependence on others for one's identity is more threatening to Bernard than the other modes of being. He even experiences an intensified form of this social self, a fusion of the individual's movements with those of the group, entering into the rhythm of the community's habitual movements: "This is my calling. This is my world. All is decided and ready; the servants, standing here, and again here, take my name, my fresh, my unknown name, and toss it before me. I enter" (73); "Having dropped off satisfied like a child from the breast, I am at liberty now to sink down, deep, into what passes, this omnipresent, general life" (81).[14] But this assimilation of the self in its social roles is disturbed by the fact of death: "This then is the world that Percival sees no longer. Let me look. The butcher delivers meat next door; two old men stumble along the pavement; sparrows alight. The machine then works; I note the rhythm, the throb, but as a thing in which I have no part, since he sees it no longer" (109). A compromise is reached, whereby the self is alternately in and out of the common life: "One cannot live outside the machine for more perhaps than half an hour. Bodies, I note, already begin to look ordinary; but what is behind them differs—the perspective" (110). Other men make up a system of which he is part, but since they are subjective in their own ways, they always see their own roles differently and therefore are never merely a passive medium in which Bernard can merge.

This sense of being both inside and outside society marks the origin of his theory of opposites, which resembles Yeats's in some respects: "Now through my own infirmity I recover what [Percival] was to me: my opposite" (111). For Bernard this antiself is the man of action, the perfectly unself-conscious man, and Percival is posited in this

[14]A similar account of the identity formed amid the "general life" is given in Woolf's own voice in "Street Haunting: A London Adventure," *Collected Essays*, IV, 155-66, especially pp. 161 and 164. The entire piece, written while *The Waves* was in progress, would bear detailed comparison with the latter's themes.

role. (Bernard also evokes, in Yeatsian language, the figure of Rhoda as his opposite [199], but she is closer to being himself than he thinks.) One's opposite is even more strongly felt as the presence, distinct from oneself, of one's own body: ". . . it is only my body—this elderly man here whom you call Bernard—that is fixed irrevocably— so I desire to believe" (153). This view reaches a climax (in an image later to be developed in a poem by Delmore Schwartz): "There is the old brute, too, the savage, the hairy man who dabbles his fingers in ropes of entrails; and gobbles and belches; whose speech is gut- teral, visceral—well, he is here. He squats in me" (205).[15]

Bernard's closing soliloquy not unexpectedly serves as a summary of his theories of self, but it also moves beyond them to a new theory, one in accord with the step he is taking in the very enact- ment of the soliloquy. He begins with the primary distinction of self from not-self: " 'Hullo,' one says, 'there's Jinny. That's Neville. . . . Therefore . . . I am myself, not Neville,' a wonderful discovery" (170). He entertains other notions of personality and development along the way, including the empiricist *tabula rasa* ("the virginal wax that coats the spine melted in different patches for each of us . . ." [171]) and the social theory of personality that tends to deny individuality ("We exist not only separately but in undifferentiated blobs of mat- ter. With one scoop a whole brakeful of boys is swept up and goes cricketing, footballing" [174]). He then runs through the next stages of thought and experience in his career, restating the role theory when describing his youth: "I changed and changed; was Hamlet, was Shelley, was the hero, whose name I now forget, of a novel by Dostoevsky; was for a whole term, incredibly, Napoleon; but was Byron chiefly" (177). But he quickly renounces role-playing in favor of a central self: "I rose and walked away—I,I,I; not Byron, Shelley, Dostoevsky, but I, Bernard. I even repeated my own name once or twice" (180). This effort of will immediately relapses into an identifi- cation with others: "How impossible to order them [friends, faces] rightly; to detach one separately, or to give the effect of the whole— again like music. What a symphony with its concord and its discord, and its tunes on top and its complicated bass beneath, then grew up! Each played his own tune. . . . With Neville, 'Let's discuss Hamlet.' With Louis, science, With Jinny, love" (182). This symphonic union

---

[15]People like Jinny are capable of expressing imagination in body, which Yeats held up as an ideal in images of the dancer and in his theory of the primary self. The view is explicit here: ". . . we who live in the body see with the body's imagination" (125). This mode of being is distinguished from that of Susan, who lives simply according to the body's natural rhythms but who says: ". . . sometimes I am sick of natural happi- ness. . . . I am sick of the body . . ." (136).

of others' tunes is extended into an identification with the larger community of historical tradition: ". . . the whole of life, its masters, its adventurers, then appeared in long ranks of magnificent human beings behind me; and I was the inheritor; I, the continuer; I, the person miraculously appointed to carry it on" (180).

As Bernard recalls marriage, Percival's death, and his own career, almost the same sequence of ideas is passed through again: the self as role-player—"Better burn one's life out like Louis, desiring perfection; or like Rhoda leave us, flying past us to the desert; or choose one out of millions and one only like Neville; better be like Susan and love and hate the heat of the sun or the frost-bitten grass; or be like Jinny, honest, an animal" (189); the central self—"What I was to myself was different; was none of these. I am inclined to pin myself down most firmly there before the loaf at breakfast with my wife" (184); the social self—". . . it is not one life that I look back upon; I am not one person; I am many people; I do not altogether know who I am—Jinny, Susan, Neville, Rhoda, or Louis; or how to distinguish my life from theirs" (196) (but there also comes the thought, "Was this, then, this streaming away mixed with Susan, Jinny, Neville, Rhoda, Louis, a sort of death?" [198]); the communal self—"We are become part of that unfeeling universe that sleeps when we are at our quickest and burns red when we lie asleep" (199); the anti-self—"While [the barber] brushed the fluff from my coat I took pains to assure myself of his identity, and then, swinging my stick, I went into the Strand, and evoked to serve as opposite to myself the figure of Rhoda . . ." (199).

Bernard's final theory is a step beyond the others but includes something of them all—that is to say, it is logically dialectical, as well as being dialectically related to his life-experience. It begins with a negation of both life and theory: "I said life had been imperfect, an unfinished phrase. It had been impossible for me . . . to keep coherency. . . . I addressed myself as one would speak to a companion with whom one is voyaging to the North Pole" (201) (this *Doppelgänger* is perhaps derived from the reference in section 5 of *The Waste Land* to the "third who walks always beside you," although Eliot derived him from Shackleton's South Pole expedition). This companion is the undiscovered self for whom Bernard has all along been searching: "I spoke to that self who had been with me in many tremendous adventures; the faithful man who sits over the fire when everybody has gone to bed, stirring the cinders with a poker; the man who has been so mysteriously and with sudden accretions of being built up, in a beech wood [a repeated association with Susan, Elvedon, and the primal kiss], sitting by a willow tree on a bank [this is Byron's tree at Cambridge, connected with Neville, poetry, and maturation], leaning over a parapet at Hampton Court [at the reunion dinner]; the man who has collected himself in moments of emergency and banged his spoon on the table, saying, 'I will not consent' " (201) (the spoon-banging is anticipated on page 160). In this seventh theory the self is formed not—as previous theories would have it—by simply tacking on aspects of others but by joining in developmental experiences and sharing an imaginative formation with others. It has been "built up" in an esthetic process which brings something to life that is greater than the sum of existing attributes— by "accretions of being" a new man is created.

Yet this created self, too, is marked by lack of personality, so that it is felt as an absence, a negation: "This self now as I leant over the gate looking down over fields rolling in waves of colour beneath me made no answer. He threw up no opposition. He attempted no phrase. His fist did not form. I waited. I listened. Nothing came, nothing. I cried then with a sudden conviction of complete desertion, Now there is nothing. No fin breaks the waste of this immeasurable sea" (201). It is at this point, when Bernard takes up Woolf's own image of her quest for reality, that the language of the italicized passages fully takes over Bernard's prose: having emptied himself of the personality of this or that self, having created a self which is entirely open to the world, he takes on the point of view of the artist, of the cosmic spectator, and of Woolf herself. He is "a man without a self" (202) and so can "describe the world seen without a self" (204); he "saw but was not seen . . . walked alone in a new world, never trodden" (203), as did, in the beginning, newly created man.

Bernard however, suffers feelings of doubt and alienation: "There are no words" to describe the world seen without a self (204); "All this little affair of 'being' is over" (204); "I begin to doubt . . . the reality of here and now" (204); "Am I all of them? Am I one and distinct? I do not know" (205); "There is the old brute, too, the savage, the hairy man" (205). But despite his waverings, he experiences a transformation that resembles traditional heroic exaltation:

But no more. Now to-night, my body rises tier upon tier like some cool temple whose floor is strewn with carpets and murmurs rise and the altars stand smoking; but up above, here in my serene head, come only fine gusts of melody, waves of incense, while the lost dove wails. . . . When I look down from this transcendency, how beautiful are even the crumbled relics of bread! [Bernard had made bread pellets into people for his early stories (pages 18, 50); no other reference to the doctrine of transubstantiation is required.]

Immeasurably receptive, holding everything, trembling with fullness, yet clear, contained—so my being seems, now that desire urges it no more out and away; now that curiosity no longer dyes it a thousand colours. It lies deep, tideless, immune, now that he is dead, the man I called "Bernard". . . . (206)

In this state of transcendency Bernard acquires the sublimity of Lear reunited with Cordelia in prison (act 5, scene 3, lines 16-17): "So now, taking upon me the mystery of things, I could go like a spy without leaving this place . . ." (207). Where he goes, *what he sees, is the opening* of *The Waves* itself: "Day rises; the girl lifts the watery fire-hearted jewels to her brow; the sun levels his beams straight at the sleeping house; the waves deepen their bars . . ." (207). We reach here the fusion of style and expansion of vision toward which the entire work has tended: the consciousness of one favored character has been developed so as to approximate a universal perspective.

Yet problems remain, both for the creator of the scene and for the self in the world: "What does the central shadow [in the house of the italicized passages] hold? Something? Nothing? I do not know" (207); "I catch your eye. I, who had been thinking myself so vast, a temple, a church, a whole universe, unconfined and capable of being everywhere on the verge of things and here too, am now nothing but what you see . . ." (207).[16] The silent listener's Sartrian stare returns Bernard to himself, but now in the form of the two symbols of human life which have predominated throughout: "Once more, I . . . find that the wave has tumbled me over, head over heels, scattering my possessions, leaving me to collect, to assemble, to heap together, summon my forces, rise and confront the enemy" (208); ". . . this shadow which has sat by me for an hour or two, this mask from which peep two eyes, has power . . . to send me dashing like a moth from candle to candle" (208). Solitary, watching the earth's and the sun's changes, sitting with "bare things" (210), he again confronts the dawn, the deepening bars between the waves, the "eternal renewal" (211). He is united with the rhythm of the waves yet opposed to one of its necessary moments, the fall into death; he identifies with the universal course of life and yet remains an individual, now made heroic by his assertion of human values in the face of the order of things:

And in me too the wave rises. It swells; it arches its back. I am aware once more of a new desire, something rising beneath me like the proud horse whose rider first spurs and then pulls him back. What enemy do we now perceive advancing against us, you whom I ride now, as we stand pawing this

---

[16]This tendency to expand to include everything is present in Bernard's desire "to allow our lives to spread out and out beyond all bristling of roofs and chimneys to the flawless verge" (186), but despite his expansion toward being an infinite container, he is drawn back to identity and life, as Rhoda, with similar tendencies, is not.

stretch of pavement? It is death. Death is the enemy. It is death against whom I ride with my spear couched and my hair flying back like a young man's, like Percival's, when he galloped in India. I strike spurs into my horse. Against you I will fling myself, unvanquished and unyielding, O Death! (211)

The imagery of chivalry rampant here is not fully accounted for by associating it with the chivalric Percival or by identifying Bernard with Percival as rider, hero, enemy of death. For the soliloquist addresses the horse directly—"you whom I ride now"—as one with human rather than equine understanding. The image carries associations of Plato's *Phaedrus* (which the hero reads in *Jacob's Room*), where it is a symbol of the soul; it also suggests Pegasus, on which poets have traditionally made their leap at immortality. What is most remarkable in the context of this work is the fusion of the horse and rider with the commanding symbol of the waves: the wave "arches its back" like a horse, the rider's hair flies back like a wave's crest, and the pair fling themselves against death like the waves breaking on the shore. Thus, the waves' destructive dissolution is transmuted into an image of the human soul riding heroically into life and death. The desire, pride, and unyielding affirmation of the soliloquy's prose is balanced by the flat finality of the closing italicized passage: *"The waves broke on the shore."*

□

In an essay or sketch written apparently at about the time of *The Waves*,[17] Woolf follows a consideration of the qualities of the "moment" with this remarkable paragraph:

Then comes the terror, the exultation; the power to rush out unnoticed, alone; to be consumed; to be swept away to become a rider on the random wind; the tossing wind; the trampling and neighing wind; the horse with the blown-back mane; the tumbling the foraging; he who gallops for ever, nowhither travelling, indifferent; to be part of the eyeless dark, to be rippling and streaming, to feel the glory run molten up the spine, down the limbs, making the eyes glow, burning, bright, and penetrate the buffeting waves of the wind.

---

[17]For the basis of this conjecture, see Guiguet, *Woolf and Her Works*, p. 289 n. Guiguet also points out other relationships between the shorter and the longer work. The quotation that follows is from *Collected Essays*, II, 296.

the years

"And I saw again

the current which took . . .

the dead leaves"

A suspicion lingers about this fiction. Appearing in the decade spanned by *The Waves* and *Between the Acts*, it seems less an avant-garde experiment than a reversion to traditional realism. The knowledge that its composition cost Woolf enormous pain and interminable rewriting only tends to confirm the impression that *The Years* (1937) is not an authentic product of the Woolfian imagination. And its extraordinary success with the public appears to place it in a class with Conrad's *Chance* and other novels whose superior but less accessible predecessors passed in relative obscurity while they reached the bestseller lists on the strength of more superficial appeal. There is no avoiding the fact that this is a family-chronicle novel of the type that became popular in the wake of *The Forsyte Saga*—or the fact that it is longer than any other Woolf work except *Night and Day*—with an amplitude that encourages the reader to become intimate with its characters in a way ruled out by the tight economy and unsettling inventiveness of her preceding fictions. Yet, with sustained attention, *The Years*, composed with many of the same techniques, will be found to express its meaning in much the same terms as the greater members of the canon.

Although conceived on the scale of a historical novel presenting the social fortunes of an English upper-middle-class family from 1880 to the "present day,"[1] *The Years* is also modeled on the autobiographical novel, for its broad social canvas carries many touches of Woolf's attitude toward her own class, family, and personal relationships. The most obvious case of portraiture from life is the Pargiters' family friend, Nicholas Pomjalovsky; with his eastern European manner and his vision of a "New World" of human brotherhood, he bears many of the traits of that sage of St. John's Wood, S. S. Koteliansky (although the homosexuality that prevents Pomjalovsky from marrying Sara Pargiter bears some resemblance to Lytton Strachey's relations with Virginia Stephen).[2] The Kensington setting, the extended family structure, the Oxbridge connections (although the placing of Edward Pargiter at Oxford seems a deliberate effort to vary the scene from the habitual Cambridge), and especially the tendency of this respectable clan to lose caste by virtue of its feminist, pacifist, and other bohemian tendencies all mark this fiction as being of a piece with the Stephen family's experience. In portraying a variety of bluestocking reformers— from the beautiful-souled Eleanor to the slightly demented Sara, from the aggressive Parnellite Delia to the disillusioned "new woman," Peggy—Woolf can present a gallery of possibilities which her own feminist sentiments had led her to contemplate and occasionally to encounter. On another tack, the tendency of the Pargiter males to become officious and stuffy—the bourgeois Morris successful in the law, the retired colonial Martin comfortably keeping a mistress, the donnish Edward with "the look of an insect whose body has been eaten out, leaving only the wings, the shell" (437)—is an expression of the antipathy toward traditional, masculine-oriented institutions, which Woolf was simultaneously indulging in the writing of *Three Guineas*.

Woolf was unusually explicit with herself about the mixture of genres which she was undertaking: ". . . I have entirely remodelled my 'Essay.' It's to be an Essay-Novel, called *The Pargiters*—and it's to take in everything, sex, education, life etc.: and come, with the most powerful and agile leaps, like a chamois, across precipices from 1880 to here and now."[3] The outlines of the plan remain in the finished

---

[1]The dating of the final section, entitled "Present Day," can be made more precise by using the age of one of the characters: Peggy Pargiter is sixteen or seventeen in 1911 (220) and is said to be thirty-seven or thirty-eight at the time of the concluding family party (425); i.e., the "present day" is 1931–33.

[2]On Koteliansky, see Leonard Woolf, *Beginning Again: An Autobiography of the Years 1911–1918* (London, 1963), pp. 248–53. See also *The Quest for Rananim: D. H. Lawrence's Letters to S. S. Koteliansky, 1914–1930*, ed. G. J. Zytaruk (Montreal, 1970).

[3]*Diary*, p. 189, 2 Nov. 1932; the last three words of this sentence served later as a working title. The quotation below is from *Diary*, p. 221, 7 Aug. 1934.

work, but additional genres were employed for special effects: "I want a chorus, a general statement, a song for four voices. . . . I am now almost within sight of the end, racing along: becoming more and more dramatic. And how to make the transition from the colloquial to the lyrical, from the particular to the general?" The effects of these generic features—in addition to the infusions of short story and other forms—will be discussed in their place, but the manifestation of such versatility should dispel the impression that *The Years* is not an experimental fiction. The experiment's success remains to be estimated.

□

In keeping with a historical perspective that mixes the universal and the concrete, the narrative point of view in *The Years* takes on the quality of both the "bardic voice" of *The Waves* and the topical allusiveness of *Orlando*. The paragraphs of general description which appear at the opening of each section of *The Years* vary in tone from the "cosmic consciousness" found in Woolf's visions of the universe—e.g., "Time Passes" in *To the Lighthouse*—to the brisk worldliness in the account of Clarissa Dalloway's walk. The first of these introductory paragraphs catches more of the former note:

It was an uncertain spring. The weather, perpetually changing, sent clouds of blue and of purple flying over the land. In the country farmers, looking at the fields, were apprehensive; in London umbrellas were opened and then shut by people looking up at the sky. . . . The stream of landaus, victorias and hansom cabs was incessant; for the season was beginning. In the quieter streets musicians doled out their frail and for the most part melancholy pipe of sound, which was echoed, or parodied, here in the trees of Hyde Park, here in St. James's by the twitter of sparrows and the sudden outbursts of the amorous but intermittent thrush. (1)

The elements of the scene—changing seasons, age-old street musicians, chattering and dimly communicative birds—are gathered up from Woolf's earlier fictions and will be developed to create a sense of the recurrent rhythms of human life.

Other opening paragraphs serve the function of setting the historical situation, and even the descriptions of the weather are made to suggest the passage of time and the onset of a new year or age. This habitually temporal placement of the characters generates a wide view of them, the perspective moving freely from one to the other as if to indicate their coexistence in a larger scheme of things, in spite of their separation by location and activities. Such a "panning" from character to character opens the "1891" section (94-95), where we move with the autumn wind sweeping over England from Kitty Lasswade in the North, to Milly Pargiter in Devonshire, to Edward at Oxford, and to Morris at the law courts in London. Frequently, the opening sets up a subtle historical atmosphere: the account of "1910," for example, opens with a London "waiting for something to happen; for a curtain to rise" (172). At times, too, the initial paragraph is used in a more conventional way, merely serving to introduce a scene by giving something of its social and temporal background, as in the first paragraphs of the "1907" section, which introduce a party at the Digby Pargiters's as part of the London social scene (138-40). Toward the end of the work the introductory texts become more concise (being reduced to brief paragraphs from "1913" onward) and evocative of hope and mystery, up to "Present Day": "It was a summer evening; the sun was setting; the sky was blue still, but tinged with gold, as if a thin veil of gauze hung over it, and here and there in the gold-blue amplitude an island of cloud lay suspended" (329).

The introduction of the decades, characters, and scenes of *The Years* is not, however, the only function of these passages. The persistence in them of geographical, meteorological, and social phenomena which are traced from season to season and from year to year generates a rhythm of its own, and this rhythm—conveying both transience and stability, change and durability—becomes one of the central themes of the fiction. The rhythm of human existence is made up of repetitions of all sorts: the movement of air, clouds, and birds across the skies at various times and seasons; the course of cabs, lights, and other hints of human journeys across London from West End to East End and back (1, 138-39, 172); and most important of all, the passage of each year (2, 96, 172).

The persistence of these terms in the introductory passages is part of a pervasive rhythm in the body of the work in which sounds, words, and situations are repeated in order to convey an impression of the continuity of the present and the past (with or without conscious memory). The most clearly recognized of these recurrences is the carefully-staged appearance of a man escorting a woman home— apparently more than fifty years after he calls on her in a cab on the Pargiters' street (18, 469) (also recalled on page 361). We remind ourselves that the street is not the same, that the latter-day young man cannot be the same young man, and that the two events have been artfully placed to frame the action near the beginning and end; but the impression of an enduring rhythm of courtship and marital fulfillment is conveyed. In much the same way, sounds—like the pigeons' "take two coos, Taffy" (79, 80, 123, 190, 202, 467), the parental "grubby little ruffian" (11, 135), the hammerings of a young carpenter and of the Wagnerian Siegfried (70, 197, 204)—progressively create in the reader the sense of an audible music of humanity, of continuity and harmony in human life.[4]

In support of this music and its expressive meaning are the myriad happenstances of family life that recur in collective or individual memory. An instance of collective remembering is the sharing of memories by cousins—Maggie recalling elements of the Abel Pargiter menage, in which her cousin Rose grew up, like the house on Abercorn Terrace, the maid Crosby, and the necklace her uncle had given her, and Rose remembering objects in Maggie's house like the old Italian mirror (177-79). The reader's response to these reversions to scenes and objects which have previously appeared in the fiction may be similar to Rose's feeling of mingled reality and unreality: "They talked as if they were speaking of people who were real, but not real in the way in which she felt herself to be real. It puzzled her; it made her feel that she was two different people at the same time; that she was living at two different times at the same moment" (180).

The rhythmic reappearance that assumes most general significance in *The Years* is that of the street singer; indeed, its evocative power in this fiction is almost as great as the effect of the better-known apparition in *Mrs. Dalloway*. The music is heard as early as the eighth page of the text: "The elderly street singer, who had been swaying along the kerb, with a fisherman's cap stuck jauntily on the back of his head, lustily chanting 'Count your blessings, Count your blessings——' turned up his coat collar and took refuge [from the rain] under the portico of a public house where he finished his injunction: 'Count your blessings. Every One.' Then the sun shone again; and dried the pavement" (8). This omen of good fortune—the return of the sunshine—is not in itself a guarantee of what is to come, but the lusty chanting provides an appeal to a folk wisdom in its insistence on the blessings to be counted amid the chances of life and death. In the same vein, another street figure appears in the middle of the book, not singing, but rhythmically offering flowers for sale:

In the alley that led into the old square off Holborn an elderly man, battered and red-nosed, as if he had weathered out many years at street corners, was selling violets. . . .

"Nice vilets, fresh vilets," he repeated automatically as the people passed. Most of them went by without looking. But he went on repeating his formula automatically. "Nice vilets, fresh vilets," as if he scarcely expected any one

[4]This phenomenon is carefully developed in Allen McLaurin, *Virginia Woolf: The Echoes Enslaved* (Cambridge, 1973), pp. 162-63. See also Alice van Buren Kelley, *The Novels of Virginia Woolf: Fact and Vision* (Chicago and London, 1973), pp. 206 ff., for analysis of the musical refrains and other repetitive patterns.

to buy. Then two ladies came; and he held out his violets, and he said once more "Nice vilets, fresh vilets." (187)

He repeats his formula "automatically," but the twice-used word does not convey the horror of automatism found in Eliot or Bergson; rather it is a comfortable, self-sustaining ritual, indifferent to loss and gain, and with an age-old dignity. The gradually emerging fact that the ladies are Rose and Sara Pargiter and the flower seller's subsequent intuition of Sara's oddness (for it is she who picks up a bunch of violets, though Rose pays for them) are less important in this scene than the persistence of the street sounds, like a natural music. Here as elsewhere the fiction's title acquires layers of depth as it is placed in relation to the recurrent processes of human living: ". . . he had weathered out many years at street-corners, was selling violets. . . ."

The appearance of another flower seller, this time a woman, produces a different impression: "They passed the woman selling violets. She wore a hat over her face. [Martin] dropped a sixpence in her tray to make amends to the waiter [whom he had refused to tip]. He shook his head. No violets, he meant; and indeed they were faded. But he caught sight of her face. She had no nose; her face was seamed with white patches; there were red rims for nostrils. She had no nose—she had pulled her hat down to hide that fact" (253). The dramatic shock of this experience is less significant than the fact that the shock remains in Martin's imagination: "An old straw hat with a purple ribbon round it, he thought opening his paper. The sight persisted" (254). The image persists in our minds, too, and becomes part of the larger image of street folk which the text generates; here the horror of poverty and the decadence that is part of the rhythm of nature find their appropriate places in the fictional world.

The final version of this figure appears in Eleanor's enigmatic encounter on a bus: "The omnibus moved on. She found herself staring at an old man in the corner who was eating something out of a paper bag. He looked up and caught her staring at him. 'Like to see what I've got for supper, lady?' he said, cocking one eyebrow over his rheumy, twinkling old eyes. And he held out for her inspection a hunk of bread on which was laid a slice of cold meat or sausage" (324). The most peculiar point about this passage is its position in the text: it comes at the end of a section, set off by white space—precisely at the close of an account of the war years, which is dated "1917." Evoking, as he does, some of the ambiguous responses generated by the noseless flower seller, this old man brings to further distinctness the image of the poor that has all along been forming in this record of middle-class life. The archetypal rhythms of street singers and violet sellers become less important than their furtiveness and degradation, which the man in the bus vigorously casts off by his gesture. Gradually, without sentimentality, another of the earth's continuities emerges from these repeated images: a conviction akin to that of the biblical phrase, "the poor you always have with you." It is not an expression of political resignation but a perception that this, too, is a part of the years' rhythmic round.

□

Although these and other repetitions of word, image, and incident establish a rhythm that *The Years* proposes as its model of human life, there are other impulses at work which in turn generate their own structural forms. The dated sections of the text—eleven in all, although the penultimate one, "1918," is only a short transitional passage marking the end of World War I—are each composed with an eye to the integrity of the unit. Instead of an unfolding, continuous narrative, *The Years* is a series of vignettes, catching up a number of characters at varied moments in their lives. Each of these sections might be taken as a short story, not, of course, of the Poe or even Chekhov type, but of the kind that had been established as the norm of the English short story by Joyce and Mansfield in the period of Woolf's own finest stories. The hallmark of this fictional mode is a progression—often through desultory mental channels or apparently insignificant incidents—to a moment of insight or intense awareness on the part of the protagonist: a revelation that has been given the name "epiphany." An appreciation of the wide range of short-story techniques in the sections of *The Years* would gain much from an analysis of Woolf's career as a writer of brief fictions, but such an analysis remains to be done in detail. Here we can only consider the scenes in which a character reaches a point of generalization or broad questioning about his own or mankind's life—occasions which can fruitfully be described as epiphanies.[5]

With one exception, the sections of *The Years* are constructed with an epiphany as an end-in-view, although some have more than one such moment. The stimulus for widened awareness of or intense concern for meaning in life is most often a visit by one character to another or to a series of people and places. It will be found that, just as each section leads up to an epiphany, each starts with (or is largely occupied with) a visit. The accompanying table summarizing these may prove useful.

[5]Woolf's epiphanies are set within the larger scope of this generic development in Morris Beja, *Epiphany in the Modern Novel: Revelation as Art* (Seattle, 1971).

Page	Date	Visit	Epiphany
1	1880	Abel to Mira; Kitty to the Robsons	Delia, Rose, and Eleanor (questionings); Kitty is ambivalent about becoming a don's wife
94	1891	Eleanor to Mrs. Potter; Abel to Eugénie and Digby	Eleanor asks: "Why do we do it?"
138	1907	Maggie to Sara's room	Both ask: ". . . what's 'I'?"
157	1908	Martin to Eleanor and Rose	They recall childhood relationships
172	1910	Rose to Maggie and Sara; Kitty to Eleanor's meeting	They recall childhood relationships; Kitty reaffirms her way of life
206	1911	Eleanor to Morris and Celia	Eleanor sees the irrevocability of the past, etc.
230	1913	Crosby to Martin	Martin sees the lie of master-servant relations
241	1914	Martin and Sara to Maggie in the park; Kitty to her country home	Martin imagines a world without "I"; Kitty reawakens to country life
301	1917	Eleanor to Maggie and Renny	Eleanor is first skeptical, then hopeful, about the future
325	1918	[Crosby hears of Armistice]	
329	Present day	North to Eleanor and Sara	North recognizes mystery of Sara
		Peggy to Eleanor	Peggy recognizes mystery of Eleanor
		Maggie and Renny to Sara	Maggie senses the coherence in things
		Eleanor to Delia's party	Eleanor gains a series of insights
		Peggy to Delia's party	Peggy sees civilization as "heart of darkness"
		North to Delia's party	North sees people as bubbles in the stream of life

The opening section, "1880," is the second longest in the work and is almost as varied as the closing section, "Present Day." Most of the characters are introduced as Woolf develops the milieu of Abel Pargiter's family on the day of his wife's death; later scenes add the family's Oxford extension, including Edward and his possible fiancée, Kitty Malone. The first scene, in which Abel visits his mistress, Mira, leads to no epiphany, but the following scenes, in which the children react to their mother's impending death, are among the most explicitly revelatory in the work. First, Delia visits the sickroom, and while musing resentfully on her mother's refusal to die, she dreams of addressing a public meeting under the tutelage of Parnell (22–23). Her mother wakes and asks, "'Where am I?' . . . For a moment Delia was bewildered too. Where was she?" The ambiguity of the pronoun suggests that Delia is bewildered not only about her mother's condition of death or life but also about the status of her own dreams—is she still addressing the meeting or merely attending her mother in death? The revelation is incomplete; no sure conclusions are to be drawn from this event alone; but Delia's subsequent career as a lifelong Parnellite and her marriage to an Irish republican takes something from this heightened moment.

Delia's experience is followed by the most flamboyantly dramatic event in the book: Rose's encounters with an exhibitionist while running an errand. On the way, she imagines herself in the role of her legendary ancestor, "Pargiter of Pargiter's Horse . . . riding to the rescue" (27), and when the man approaches her she makes him part of her fantasy: "'The enemy!' Rose cried to herself. 'The enemy! Bang!' she cried, pulling the trigger of her pistol and looking him full in the face as she passed him. It was a horrid face: white, peeled, pock-marked; he leered at her" (28). As in Delia's case, this scene provides no easy explanation of Rose's subsequent career as a suffragette and spinster, but the experience is clearly formative in some way. Its power is heightened by the repetition of the exhibitionist's approach on Rose's homeward journey (29) and, worst of all, by her inability to express her feelings to others; her attempt to tell Eleanor is difficult enough and is rendered vain by an interruption: "'I saw . . .' Rose began. She made a great effort to tell her the truth; to tell her about the man at the pillar-box. 'I saw . . .' she repeated. But here the door opened and Nurse came in" (43).[6]

The experience is bottled up inside Rose and remains with her—and with the reader—in some form of conscious or unconscious memory (the two are never strictly distinguished in Woolf's psychology). Sometimes surpassing the limits of psychology, moreover, memories of events in Woolf's works have the capacity to enter the minds of persons other than those who first experienced them. In the present case, Rose's "I saw" and Delia's "Where am I?" both became part of their sister Eleanor's thinking: "'I saw . . .' What had she seen? Something

[6]The incident and possibly the anguish are from life: see Quentin Bell, *Virginia Woolf: A Biography* (London, 1972), I, 35.

horrible, something hidden. But what? . . . A blankness came over her. Where am I? she asked herself, staring at a heavy frame. What is that? She seemed to be alone in the midst of nothingness; yet must descend, must carry her burden . . ." (44). And Eleanor's lifelong role as the bearer of others' burdens—both as champion of good causes and as moral center of her family—is here crystallized.

The other moment of awareness in the "1880" section occurs in the Oxford scenes; it shapes Kitty's decision not to marry Edward and settle into the life of a don's wife, like her mother's. First Edward and his friends are introduced (one of them, Hugh Gibbs, will subsequently marry Milly Pargiter). Then the Malones' characteristic home life is established—and broadly satirized—in their entertainment of a visiting American professor and his wife. The key scene is that in which Kitty visits the home of a friend, Nelly Robson, and meets her oddly matched father and mother and her rough-hewn but attractive brother. Kitty's response is complex:

"Not a patch on her," [Mr. Robson] repeated, pinching Nell on the shoulder. As she stood there with her father's hand on her shoulder under the portrait of her grandmother, a sudden rush of self-pity came over Kitty. If she had been the daughter of people like the Robsons, she thought; if she had lived in the north—but it was clear they wanted her to go. . . . She looked at him standing there with his heavy watch-chain, like a schoolboy's. You are the nicest man I have ever met, she thought, holding out her hand. (77)

The complexity of Kitty's response is spelled out in a number of ways: her pleasure in this particular don's family life is not enough to dispel her resistance to a ménage of her own (66), and she eventually decides against marrying a scholar, choosing to become Lady Lasswade instead; she maintains her attraction to earthy manners by making her home in northern England a place of withdrawal from the rigors of London society; she retains her sense of the male force of Jo Robson and connects his hammering of hencoops with the hammering of the heroic Siegfried in an opera performance at Covent Garden (197, 199); and in "Present Day" she hears with unstated emotions that Nelly Robson has died: " 'Died, did she—died—' said Lady Lasswade. She paused for a moment" (457). Although the consciousness of liking the Robsons is only a transitory feeling, it works its way into Kitty's life in devious ways, becoming what might be called a proleptic epiphany, significant not immediately but potentially.

The second section of *The Years*, while considerably shorter than the opening, also has a multiple focus: Eleanor's visit to a poor old woman in the course of her social work, and Abel's visit to his brother and sister-in-law. The "1891" section seems to be loosely structured, but its meaning emerges subtly in its parts. The two events, which are neatly divided by the announcement of the death of Parnell, have little in common. The point of Eleanor's encounter with the whining Mrs. Potter is to bring into question the *raison d'être* of her philanthropy: "Why do we do it? she asked herself as Mrs. Potter went on talking. Why do we force her to live? she asked, looking at the medicine on the table. She could stand it no longer. She withdrew her hand" (105–6). Eleanor is of course only temporarily checked in her lifelong effort to relieve human suffering, but she gains in attractiveness and authenticity by showing herself capable of questioning her own idealism.

After reading Martin's letter about his adventures in India and watching Morris perform at the law courts, Eleanor hears the news of Parnell and thinks of her sister's devotion: "Delia had cared. Delia had cared passionately. What was it she used to say—flinging out of the house, leaving them all for the Cause, for this man? Justice, Liberty? [These words appear in Delia's childhood daydream of addressing a meeting (22–23).] She must go to her. This would be the end of all her dreams" (121). Eleanor emerges as a kind of super-philanthropist, a friend to the friends of mankind, without losing any of her self-awareness or even her touch of irony.

The concluding episode of this section is almost too fragile for description, but it manages to bring forward an object that will acquire evocative power in later sections. Abel visits his more successful brother's house, responds to his sister-in-law's warm reception, and soon recognizes that it is time to leave, since Digby and his wife are going out to dinner. The displacement of the elderly man whose wife has died and whose children have grown up is rendered scenically by framing him in a mirror: "They had been to Italy, he remembered. A looking-glass stood on the table. It was probably one of the things she had picked up there: the sort of thing that people did pick up in Italy; an old glass, covered with spots. He straightened his tie in front of it" (125–26). This mirror adds its silvery and mottled aura to the scene as Eugénie sees herself in it while describing her daughter's birthday games (129). Its aura remains hovering over the house as Maggie and Sara watch their parents' garden party in "1907" ("'Did anybody give you a piece of glass,' [Sara] said, 'saying to you, Miss Pargiter . . . my broken heart?'" [148]); and it is taken up again in "1910" when Rose visits her recently impoverished cousins in their slum flat after their parents' death: "'And that glass——' said Rose, looking at the old Italian glass blurred with spots that hung between the windows, 'wasn't that there too?'" (177–78). The closing scene of the "1891" section does not, then, reach a climax of illumination, but it sets in motion an element of imaginative continuity that eventually embraces characters emotionally unconnected with Abel Pargiter.

Another effect of the continued presence of the old Italian mirror in succeeding sections is to help in establishing what might be called a color range or tonality. The next section, "1907," is a scene of muted reverie, in which the children of Digby Pargiter, Maggie and Sara, look down at their parents' guests in the garden and muse on love and life. No visit occurs—unless one sister's joining the other in her room is to be called a visit—and the epiphany that crowns the encounter is a moment of questioning rather than of revelation. Yet there is a sense of heightened consciousness throughout, and this impression is allied to the mirrorlike silvery sheen that covers the scene: "It was midsummer; and the nights were hot. The moon, falling on water, made it white, inscrutable, whether deep or shallow. But where the moonlight fell on solid objects it gave them a burnish and a silver plating, so that even the leaves in country roads seemed varnished. . . . All the windows were open. Music sounded. From behind crimson curtains, rendered semi-transparent and sometimes blowing wide came the sound of the eternal waltz . . ." (138). This atmosphere is sustained by partial repetitions of phrase and image in the following pages, in the course of which the vague romantic mood is articulated in metaphysical terms.

The first widening of reference occurs with the introduction of a human subject—Sara, alone. She picks up a "faded brown book" (perhaps a Schopenhauer) from her bed and comments on it: "'And he says,' she murmured, 'the world is nothing but . . .' She paused. What did he say? Nothing but thought, was it? . . . she would let herself *be* thought. It was easier to act things than to think them. Legs, body, hands, the whole of her must be laid out passively to take part in this universal process of thinking which the man said was the world living" (142). The connection between this metaphysical rumination and the opening imagery is elaborated as Sara goes on thinking of her body and imagining herself a tree; but unlike the opening view of moonlit trees and semitransparent curtains, her self-image is a tree with leaves lit by the sun. This impressionistic reverie is broken, however, by a sharp swing to cold reality; Sara opens her eyes and looks at the garden, no longer seeing it as a luminous vision, no longer seeing herself as a radiant and growing thing. Instead, she sees the tree in the garden as a stark fact: "She opened her eyes in order to verify the sun on the leaves and saw the actual tree standing out there in the garden. Far from being dappled with sunlight, it had no leaves at all. She felt for a moment as if she had been contradicted. For the tree was black, dead black" (142). Sara's character, in which illusion and reality both appear but do not quite mesh—what is called her "queerness"—may well be crystallized in these formative scenes, although their philosophic resonance remains obscure.

The next stage of imaginative expansion occurs with the entry of Maggie, coming to Sara's room to share impressions of the party. Sara asks her the question, quoted above, about being given a "piece of glass," and the sisters stand illuminated by the moon in a scene conveying the poignancy of adolescent romance and unfulfilled desire: "'It's the moon,' [Maggie] said. It was the moon that was making the leaves white. They both looked at the moon, which shone like a silver coin, perfectly polished, very sharp and hard" (149). Sara reverts to her metaphysical book and its doctrine that "the world is nothing but thought," and Maggie turns the idea to the self:

She had been thinking something of the kind when the cab crossed the Serpentine; when her mother interrupted her. She had been thinking, Am I that, or am I this? Are we one, or are we separate—something of the kind. . . .

"Would there be trees if we didn't see them?" said Maggie.

"What's 'I'? . . . 'I' . . ." She stopped. She did not know what she meant. She was talking nonsense.

"Yes," said Sara. "What's 'I'?" She held her sister tight by the skirt, whether she wanted to prevent her from going, or whether she wanted to argue the question.

"What's 'I'?" she repeated. (150)

At this point their mother enters and the sisters turn to her for some imaginative release; they ask her to tell them more about a youthful romance that she seems to have had, but the story—and the section—peters out inconclusively. The action is undramatic, the images remain merely impressions, the questionings suggest no clue of an answer; yet this remains one of the most beautiful chapters in all Woolf's writings, bearing comparison with Mansfield's "Prelude" at the peak of the epiphanic style.

□

The section which follows, "1908," is relatively brief, turning largely on the changed state of affairs that follows the death of Digby and Eugénie the preceding year. The occasion is again a visit, as Martin, home from India, calls on his sister Eleanor at the house on Abercorn Terrace—where she and their father still live—and their sister Rose joins them in the course of the visit. The reunion encourages a number of reflections on the family past—"What awful lives children live" (171) (and Rose, who was unable to tell about the exhibitionist, adds, "And they can't tell anybody"). The effect of the reunion is also to renew certain childhood habits, e.g., Eleanor's fraying a wick to make the flame burn brighter and Martin's irritated denial that it does any good (162-63); Eleanor's reflection that Rose was made in the image of their heroic ancestor, "Pargiter of Pargiter's Horse" (169); and Martin's familiar phrase for his sister's moods, "Eleanor's broody" (169). There is also a summing up of the fortunes of the Digby Pargiter family: the finality of Eleanor's view that "it was better to die, like Eugénie and Digby, in the prime of life with all one's faculties about one" (165) is contested by Martin's reminder of the uncompleted story of Eugénie's youthful love affair from the previous section—"Wasn't there some story . . . about a letter?" (165)—with its hint of something unfulfilled and unspoken in her life and death. Despite this grouping of characters and review of past experience, the "1908" section remains transitional and achieves no heightened moment of illumination.

In keeping with Woolf's dictum that "human nature changed" in or around 1910, the next section is a crowded and vigorous one. From the opening sentences on, there is a feeling of summation and new beginnings: "In the country it was an ordinary day enough; one of the long reel of days that turned as the years passed from green to orange; from grass to harvest. . . . In London, however, the stricture and pressure of the season were already felt, especially in the West End, where flags flew; canes tapped; dresses flowed . . ." (172). This moderate-sized section covers four distinct visits or movements, and it is further enriched by the fact that two of these scenes are public activities which give a wider social dimension to the characters' actions. First Rose visits Maggie and Sara in their shabby south-bank flat; then Rose and Sara go off to a women's rights meeting at which Eleanor is a leader; next Kitty appears at the meeting, mainly to see Eleanor but also to sample and reject the rhetoric; Kitty moves on to her evening at the opera and memories of heroic hammering; finally, as a reprise, Sara returns home and reviews the day's events with Maggie. With such a crowded schedule there is little time for lingering meditation, and the epiphanic moments are confined to brief flashes of recognition of the tendency of one's tastes or the drift of one's life. Nothing is revealed here, but there is a sense of expectancy at the closing cry, "The King's dead!" (205). The buildup of impressions does not cohere in a single attitude, but Sara has a fit of depression which sums up one view of the entire section: "In time to come . . . people, looking into this room—this cave, this little antre, scooped out of mud and dung, will hold their fingers to their noses . . . and say 'Pah! They stink!' " (203).

The year "1911" is another of the few remaining to the memory before the full onset of an iron time in the first of the world wars. After conveying the incidental information (206) that Maggie has married, the section concerns itself exclusively with Eleanor's visit to her brother's family in Dorsetshire. Although Morris, his wife Celia, their children Peggy and North, Celia's mother, Mrs. Chinnery, and another houseguest—an old family friend, Sir William Whatney—are present, the point of view is almost exclusively Eleanor's. Much of the narrative is taken up with her reactions to the domestic English scene before her, drawing on her reflections on a recent trip abroad. She also muses on her passage into middle age and seems vaguely regretful that she will not marry a man like Whatney, who had once praised her eyes and never will again. Above all, she resents being typed in her new role: "But now I'm labelled, she thought—an old maid who washes and watches birds. That's what they think I am. But I'm not—I'm not in the least like that, she said" (218).

After dinner and its desultory talk of the past and current doings of family and friends, Eleanor retires to her bedroom and experiences an epiphanic meditation. The scene is set in terms appropriate to an ecstasy of the imagination: "The candle burnt its little pear-shaped flame on the table by her side" (226); ". . . three moths . . . made a little tapping noise as they dashed round and round from corner to corner" (227); ". . . the liquid call of an owl going from tree to tree looping them with silver" (228) (the owl has been anticipated on pages 217-18). At this point she picks up one of the bedside books her hostess has prepared for her, a translation of Dante:

She read a few lines, here and there. But her Italian was rusty; the meaning escaped her. There was a meaning however; a hook seemed to scratch the surface of her mind.

> chè per quanti si dice più li nostro
> tanto possiede più di ben ciascuno.

What did that mean? She read the English translation.

> For by so many more there are who say 'ours'
> So much the more of good doth each possess.

Brushed lightly by her mind that was watching the moths on the ceiling, and listening to the call of the owl as it looped from tree to tree with its liquid cry, the words did not give out their full meaning, but seemed to hold something furled up in the hard shell of the archaic Italian. (228)

Eleanor fails to absorb the doctrine of medieval organicism which these lines render in quintessential form: that the individual is fulfilled and ennobled only insofar as he participates in a community transcending the individual—in this case, the community of souls making their way up the penitential mountain toward the "good" in which they find their personal pilgrimages fulfilled. This summary statement by Vergil to Dante in "Purgatorio" (canto 15) acts as a rhetorical and dramatic peak in *The Divine Comedy*; its resounding affirmation creates a similar crescendo at this, the central, point of *The Years*.[7]

Eleanor does not respond directly to the doctrine, but its gravity affects her attitude toward her impending old age and the passage of time. Passing beyond the man she might have married, she finds herself still open to the future: "Sir William was getting into bed next door, his life was over; hers was beginning" (229). And despite her expression of weariness at life's endless round, Eleanor accepts change, including her own passage from youth to age, with curiosity and expectancy: "Things can't go on for ever, she thought. Things pass, things change, she thought, looking up at the ceiling. And where are we going? Where? Where? . . . ." (229). Although the Dantean faith is incompletely registered in Eleanor's consciousness, its ideal vision of a heavenly community reinforces her own secular hopes.

The section that follows is the one most closely patterned on the model of a Joycean short story. From the opening lines, "1913" reveals its probable inspiration by "The Dead": "It was January. Snow was falling; snow had fallen all day. The sky spread like a grey goose's wing from which feathers were falling all over England" (230). This ubiquitous snow, knitting together not only the visual scene but the fateful community of mankind, becomes a consistent motif in the section. Eleanor sells the house in Abercorn Terrace under its aegis: "The light was unbecoming to them [her and the house agent], yet the snow—she saw it through the window at the end of the passage—was beautiful, falling" (230-31). The old family retainer, Crosby, passes under it to her retirement at Richmond: "Snow was falling as the cab trotted along the streets" (233). She visits her former master, Martin, and leaves under the same sign: "She stood for a moment, like a frightened little animal, peering round her before she ventured to brave the dangers of the street. At last, off she trotted. [Martin] saw the snow falling on her black bonnet as she disappeared. He turned away" (240). The snow becomes a carrier of the common fate as surely under these circumstances as it does for the lovers and loveless of the *Dubliners* tale.

The snow serves to focus a more salient epiphany in the "1913" section. As Martin muses on Crosby, his family, and his class after her departure, he summarizes a judgment of the Pargiters and their age that has been gathering in the course of the fiction:

---

[7]Woolf was reading the "Purgatorio" while writing *The Years*: ". . . I cannot make the transition from *Pargiters* to Dante without some bridge": *Diary*, p. 242, 27 March 1935.

It was a lie. . . . One always lies to servants, he thought, looking out of the window. The mean outlines of the Ebury Street houses showed through the falling sleet. Everybody lies, he thought. His father had lied—after his death they had found letters from a woman called Mira tied up in his table-drawer. . . . Why had his father lied? What was the harm in keeping a mistress? And he had lied himself; about the room off the Fulham Road where he and Dodge and Erridge used to smoke cheap cigars and tell smutty stories. It was an abominable system, he thought; family life; Abercorn Terrace. No wonder the house would not let. It had one bathroom, and a basement; and there all those different people had lived, boxed up together, telling lies. (239)

This is from Martin's point of view, to be sure, and Martin is fated to remain a bachelor, keeping a mistress and a kind of shabby dignity along with his ironic detachment. But his summary view of family life expresses a dominant attitude in this least sentimental of family novels.

Martin's skepticism also helps to propel the fiction toward its next stage, as he reads and interprets the newspaper: "The war in the Balkans was over; but there was more trouble brewing—that he was sure" (237). The next section, "1914" shows the last of the prewar world in a pastoral state of retirement and relaxation—if only in Kensington Gardens and a country house in the north of England. It is set in the spring of that year, before the guns of August and the end of the family's highly compromised innocence. It is one of the more complex and lengthy segments of the text, and while it is focused on two characters it involves many more. It may be considered a last long look at a departing age.

The first part of "1914" centers on Martin as he makes his way through London alone, stopping for a look in at St. Paul's, where he meets Sara and invites her to lunch at a City chophouse; it continues as he joins her in meeting her sister Maggie, sunning her baby in the park. Moments of self-awareness come fairly regularly, as Martin regrets his lost vocation of architect while under the impress of Wren's achievement; recognizes his own snobbishness under the influence of Sara's puckish irony (and on his own, after a run-in with a cheating waiter, for he regrets leaving no tip); and finally comes to his moment of self-definition and self-effacement in the park: "What would the world be, he said to himself . . .—without 'I' in it? . . . A primal innocence seemed to brood over the scene. The birds made a fitful sweet chirping in the branches. . . . The sun dappling the leaves gave everything a curious look of insubstantiality as if it were broken into separate points of light. He too, himself, seemed dispersed" (261). The imagination of a world seen without a self, which had become a graphic possibility in *To the Lighthouse* and *The Waves*, here amounts to no more than an illusion. But this unsettling doubt about the normal order of life allows Martin a temporary intimacy with Maggie as they sit together. He is thus able to tell her of his difficulties with his mistress, to comment on his father's peccadillos, and to reach an intuition that his father loved Maggie's mother: "Are we brother and sister?" she asks (266)—casting another light on Eugénie's phantom lover.

In spite of Martin's now wider vision of himself in relation to his family, the city, and the universe, he slips back into the social role of a man-about-town, even though he has always held the role in contempt. He attends Kitty's party that evening and is swallowed up in the desultory and shallow talk around him. His dissolution in the social atmosphere allows the scene to be shifted to Kitty, and she dominates the remainder of the section. So thoroughly is this transition effected, through gossip about adults and reports of Kitty's children's doings, that by the time we see Martin again he is rendered from Kitty's point of view: " 'A very brilliant party, Lady Lasswade,' he said with his usual tiresome irony" (282). The climax of this long and meandering section comes as Kitty dashes to catch a train, falls asleep with difficulty in a Pullman, and awakes to embrace the countryside where she has her true life. Although Kitty enters the section as an apparent afterthought, she comes to dominate the fiction at this point and becomes the chorus for one of its central themes—the passage of the years.

The sense of passing time in this section is built up with Proustian regularity by a succession of soundings of that resonant word: " 'It's time,' said Maggie. . . . 'Time is it?' she sighed" (266); " 'I'm just on time,' [Martin] thought" (268); "Time was passing; if they stayed much longer she [Kitty] would miss her train" (284); "Just in time, she said to herself. . . . 'Only just in time,' " the railway guard says (290); " 'Just in time,' Kitty said to herself . . ." (291); "They'll learn in time," her chauffeur says as he narrowly misses running down a dog (294). Accompanying this widespread awareness of time is a display of consistent attention to the clocks of London, beginning with the opening paragraph: "And from all the spires of all the London churches . . . the hour was proclaimed. . . . But the clocks were irregular, as if the saints themselves were divided. There were pauses, silences. . . . Then the clocks struck again" (241). Thereafter, Martin marks the time on "all the clocks of the city" (244), especially at Charing Cross Station (254); he hears the clocks around the park striking three (255), four (262), and five (266); just to be sure, he checks his watch again on his way to the party (267). Kitty, for her part, hears the clock chiming "a succession of petulant little strokes" on her rush to the station (285); sees the station clock giving her five minutes to spare (290); and makes her train in a temporary triumph over time.

Unlike Martin, who is dominated by the clock, Kitty longs for an escape from time. As she tries to sleep, the sense of life's transiency and vapid repetition seizes her, echoing the titular theme: "The years changed things; destroyed things; heaped things up—worries and bothers; here they were again" (292). But in the retirement of her country house she can enjoy not only solitude but freedom from time: "What did it matter what [Martin] said, what they said, what anybody said, since she had a whole day to herself?—since she was alone?" (298). And in the setting of the undulating and seemingly unpopulated North Country, with at least temporary freedom and an image of the earth's permanence, she arrives at her final epiphany:

All passes, all changes, she thought, as she climbed up the little path between the trees. Nothing of this belonged to her; her son would inherit; his wife would walk here after her. . . . She threw herself on the ground, and looked over the billowing land that went rising and falling, away and away, until somewhere far off it reached the sea. Uncultivated, uninhabited, existing by itself, for itself, without towns or houses it looked from this height. . . . A deep murmur sang in her ears—the land itself, singing to itself, a chorus, alone. She lay there listening. She was happy, completely. Time had ceased. (299-300)

The vision is like those hill-top views of Orlando which take in all England; it is the elevated perspective appearing periodically in Woolf's writings that removes man momentarily from the evanescence of personal existence and allows him to envision an enduring social, historic, or in this instance, geocosmic order.[8]

After the increasing universality of the characters' vision in the pre-war sections, the atmosphere of "1917" is fully particularized: it is life lived under the pressures of war. The occasion is another of the visits of cousin to cousin—this time it is Eleanor having dinner with Maggie and her husband, Renny (René), Maggie's sister, Sara, and their friend Nicholas Pomjalovsky. At dinner the talk is of war and attitudes toward war: Sara reports that their nephew North has visited her on his way to the front, and there is bitter repartee on the pacifist position. The dinner is interrupted by an air raid, the company adjourns to the cellar, and Eleanor returns home amid searchlights and a partial blackout. A larger illumination comes from Eleanor's anticipations of the postwar world; in the course of articulating a vision of the future,

[8]For a study of these passages and their implications for Woolf's narrative art, see the unpublished dissertation by Penelope Cordish, "The View from on High: A Study of a Metaphor of Perception in Virginia Woolf," The Johns Hopkins University 1973.

she expresses to the company the timid hopefulness which marks her throughout and which is one of the fiction's leading motifs.

Much of Eleanor's thinking is governed by her responses to Nicholas's idealistic goal of human reformation: "We cannot make laws and religions that fit because we do not know ourselves" (304). After the talk, the raid, and the reemergence from the cellar, "a feeling of great calm possessed her. It was as if another space of time had been issued to her, but, robbed by the presence of death of something personal, she felt—she hesitated for a word; 'immune?' Was that what she meant?" (317). The feeling is vague, the response inarticulate, but Eleanor tries to define it by examining Nicholas's idealism: "About the new world . . . D'you think we're going to improve? . . . But how . . . how can we improve ourselves . . . live more . . . live more naturally . . . better . . . How can we?" (319). He dilates vaguely upon the soul's desire to expand, but she responds with skepticism mixed with exaltation: "When, she wanted to ask him, when will this new world come? When shall we be free? When shall we live adventurously, wholly, not like cripples in a cave? He seemed to have released something in her; she felt not only a new space of time, but new powers, something unknown within her" (320). Thus, the utopian claims are found valid not as prediction but as inspiration: despite Eleanor's persistently skeptical estimate of human nature, she is inspired by something of Nicholas's idealism: "We shall be free, we shall be free, Eleanor thought" (320).

Even more striking than this sudden bout of visionary emotion is Eleanor's intensity of feeling for Nicholas, unexpected in one who loves so widely: "That is the man, she said to herself, with a sudden rush of conviction, as she came out into the frosty air, that I should like to have married. . . . For a moment she resented the passage of time and the accidents of life which had swept her away—from all that, she said to herself" (323). But Eleanor is jolted back to reality as the old man in the bus displays his meager sandwich and returns her to her sense of vocation.

After the transitional "1918," in which a minor character, the old servant Crosby, hears of the armistice with hardly a break in the rhythm of dailiness—"The war was over—so somebody told her as she took her place in the queue at the grocer's shop" (328)—the narrative takes a long leap ahead and we are cast into "Present Day."

□

This, the longest and—in its mingling of perspectives—the most complex section of *The Years*, is also one of the most tightly patterned and distinctive in its revelatory utterances. With dancelike formality, the postwar Pargiters—first North, then Peggy—visit members of the

191

elder generation and gain fresh insights from the contact. Then all gather at a grand reunion of family and friends and severally achieve larger perspectives on themselves and their social roles. At the party, "Present Day" reverts to the dual focus of earlier sections, as Peggy and North generalize their comments on individuals to sweeping views of the state of civilization and the course of human life. There is a gradual build-up toward a moment of total revelation, and when this moment comes it upsets our expectation in a brilliant comic display. For all its narrative turnings and mixture of modes, "Present Day" stands with the "Wandering Rocks" section of *Ulysses* as a grand attempt to synthesize a vision of life from the varied perspectives of a modern multitude.

The beginnings of the family reunion are unpromising. North, just returned from a colonial position in Africa, visits Eleanor, just back from a tour of India, and all she can find to talk about—while among her other guests—is the installation of a shower bath: "Eleanor is just the same, he thought: more erratic perhaps" (331). Similarly, on his visit to Sara he feels the distance caused by his revulsion at her slum flat and miserable dinner; moreover, communicating with the elusive Sara is difficult: "She broke off; for now a trombone player had struck up in the street below, and as the voice of the woman practising her scales continued, they sounded like two people trying to express completely different views of the world in general at one and the same time" (340). But the expectations of an insight for North appear early: "She left the room without looking in the glass. From which we deduce the fact, he said to himself, as if he were writing a novel, that Miss Sara Pargiter has never attracted the love of men. Or had she? He did not know. These little snapshot pictures of people left much to be desired . . ." (341). He is on his way to more sensitive observation still, as she tells him laughingly of her life's humiliations: "'How much of that was true?' he asked her. But she had lapsed into silence. The actual words he supposed—the actual words floated together and formed a sentence in his mind—meant that she was poor; that she must earn her living, but the excitement with which she had spoken, due to wine perhaps, had created yet another person; another semblance, which one must solidify into one whole" (368).

Meanwhile, in a series of intercalated passages recounting Peggy's simultaneous visit to Eleanor, North's sister is reaching much the same complication of feeling toward another older woman of the prewar generation. For Peggy, the age gap is more difficult to bridge, partly because she has had scientific training, which has encouraged a degree of detachment, even coldness, and partly because of her bitterness at the loss of her brother Charles in the war. She encourages

Eleanor to talk of the past, but she sees it as a world remote from reality, a fairy tale realm of childhood: ". . . they had been talking about Eleanor's childhood—how things had changed; one thing seemed good to one generation, another to another. She liked getting Eleanor to talk about her past; it seemed to her so peaceful and so safe" (350-51). While Eleanor recalls the conversation with Nicholas on the utopian new world (354-55 [also referred to on pages 332, 337, 339, 374, and 417]), Peggy reflects on a picture of her grandmother (352). (This is presumably the portrait that appeared previously on pages 160 and 162, to which Martin had responded in the detached way Peggy now does.) But it is the present that focuses their attitudes, when they react differently to the rise of Fascism, represented by a picture of Mussolini. "What a queer set they are," Peggy thinks, after Eleanor tears the newspaper photo in her anger; and she reflects further: "It was as if she still believed with passion—she, old Eleanor— in the things that man had destroyed. A wonderful generation, she thought, as they drove off. Believers . . ." (357). But this observation of their differences does not disturb Peggy in her calculated sum- marizing of Eleanor's generation: "It's the sense of the family, she added, glancing at Eleanor as if to collect another little fact about her to add to her portrait of a Victorian spinster" (359).

Peggy's skepticism prompts her to give up the problem of human personality as too difficult for detached investigation: "I'm no use at describing people, she said to her friend at the Hospital. They're too difficult . . . Where does [Eleanor] begin, and where do I end? she thought. . . . On they drove. They were two living people, driving across London; two sparks of life enclosed in two separate bodies. . . . But what is this moment; and what are we? The puzzle was too diffi- cult for her to solve it" (360). But Peggy's admission of defeat is a step in the same direction her brother North is taking. At the party, sur- veying other members of the family, her curiosity triumphs over her skepticism, and she continues asking the important questions about people, even though she cannot answer them: "I'm good, she thought, at fact-collecting. But what makes up a person—, (she hollowed her hand), the circumference,—no I'm not good at that. . . . Why did Delia marry Patrick? she wondered. How do they manage it—love, child- birth? . . . But none of the lines on his face was sharp enough, she thought, to explain how they came together and had three children" (380-81).

While the members of the younger generation pursue the mystery of personality and the difficult business of living among other people, some of the older family members are making their own estimations of life, their own lives, and each other. Maggie has the most ethereal of these epiphanies as she leaves Sara's apartment to go to the party: "She switched off the light. The room now was almost dark, save for a watery pattern fluctuating on the ceiling. In this phantom evanescent light only the outlines showed; ghostly apples, ghostly bananas, and the spectre of a chair. Colour was slowly returning, as her eyes grew used to the darkness, and substance . . ." (377). Maggie enjoys a temporary abstraction from reality, seeing things without color and substance, but she is also able to return to the present and her habitual attempts at "collecting, gathering, summing up into one whole" (376).

As the party develops, Eleanor's sense of life expands into a comprehensive skepticism that questions all but the present moment and the concrete particular: "My life, she said to herself. That was odd, it was the second time that evening that somebody had talked about her life. And I haven't got one, she thought. Oughtn't a life to be something you could handle and produce?—a life of seventy odd years. But I've only the present moment, she thought. . . . She clenched her hands and felt the hard little coins she was holding. Perhaps there's 'I' at the middle of it, she thought; a knot; a centre . . ." (395).[9] But as with her previous heightened vision under the influence of Dante, Eleanor's imagination can take her only so far: ". . . is there a pattern; a theme, recurring, like music; half remembered, half foreseen? . . . a gigantic pattern, momentarily perceptible? The thought gave her extreme pleasure: that there was a pattern. But who makes it? Who thinks it? Her mind slipped. She could not finish her thought" (398).

Nevertheless, Eleanor puts her notion of a pattern of experience together with her previous intimation of the Dantean vision of a community of souls and reaches a formulation of the ruling power in family life that has never before been so explicit in *The Years*:

This is their love-making, Eleanor thought, half listening to their laughter, to their bickering. Another inch of the pattern, she thought, still using her half-formulated idea to stamp the immediate scene. And if this love-making differs from the old, still it has its charm; it was "love," different from the old love, perhaps, but worse, was it? Anyhow, she thought, they are aware of each other; they live in each other; what else is love, she asked, listening to their laughter. (399)

Given this striking identification of family life with organicist doctrines of community—and even a McTaggart-like definition of "love"—Eleanor ends her vision on a peak of elation, affirming life and opening herself again to the future: "It seemed to her that they were all

---

[9] A rare critical perception of significant details like these coins is found in Herbert Marder, "Beyond the Lighthouse: *The Years*," *Bucknell Review*, xv (1967), 61-70.

young, with the future before them. Nothing was fixed; nothing was known; life was open and free before them. 'Isn't that odd?' she exclaimed. 'Isn't that queer? Isn't that why life's a perpetual—what shall I call it?—miracle? . . . it's been a perpetual discovery, my life. A miracle' " (412-13).

The perspective at this point shifts abruptly to Peggy, reading randomly in a French book and coming upon this Baudelairian sentiment: *"La médiocrité de l'univers m'étonne et me révolte . . . la petitesse de toutes choses m'emplit de dégoût . . . la pauvreté des êtres humains m'anéantit"* (413). Partaking somewhat of this attitude, her response to the family and to the larger world about them will be opposite to Eleanor's:

Far way she heard the sounds of the London night; a horn hooted; a siren wailed on the river. The far-way sounds, the suggestion they brought in of other worlds, indifferent to this world, of people toiling, grinding, in the heart of darkness, in the depths of night, made her say over Eleanor's words, Happy in this world, happy with living people. But how can one be "happy"? she asked herself, in a world bursting with misery. On every placard at every street corner was Death; or worse—tyranny; brutality; torture; the fall of civilisation; the end of freedom. . . . Thinking was torment; why not give up thinking, and drift and dream? But the misery of the world, she thought, forces me to think. Or was that a pose? Was she not seeing herself in the becoming attitude of one who points to his bleeding heart? to whom the miseries of the world are misery, when in fact, she thought, I do not love my kind. (418-19)

It is the literary allusions that do most to carry this remarkable sequence of thought forward. Peggy begins with a Conradian vision of the social world, using terms strikingly like those used in "Heart of Darkness" to describe a pervasive moral condition. Woolf's expansion of that title takes almost the same form as her later use of the phrase at the conclusion of *Between the Acts*: ". . . in the heart of darkness, in the fields of night" (*Between the Acts*, page 256). Peggy then reacts in horror to the political dangers of the moment in a way she had previously scorned in Eleanor as outmoded Victorian idealism. The threat to freedom and the profusion of suffering become nearly as vivid to her as the loss of her brother in the most recent outbreak of genocide. But her ironic stance extends to herself at this stage, and she suspects herself of self-indulgence in her dark thoughts —applying to herself the stock phrase "bleeding heart."

Peggy goes on to muse on a well-known passage from Keats's "The Fall of Hyperion." In making the distinction between the dreamer and the ideal poet—

"The poet and the dreamer are distinct,
Diverse, sheer opposite, antipodes.
The one pours out a balm upon the World,
The other vexes it."

(Canto 1, 11.199-202)

—the prophetess Moneta speaks of "those to whom the miseries of the world/Are misery, and will not let them rest," and Keats identifies the latter with his description of the serious and constructive poet. But Peggy associates the lines with the sentimentalist "dreamer," with whom she sees herself ranked in her new-found concern for human misery. She turns away from this self-image to another, which Woolf had used earlier for the protagonist of a short story, "The Man Who Loved His Kind."[10] In that story, Woolf describes a humanitarian member of the Dalloway set with some of the scorn that Peggy employs for Eleanor and other "bleeding hearts." But as Peggy continues, sympathy with rather than detachment from the human community becomes her hallmark.

Peggy's heightened involvement with humanity and her potential idealism are shown developing only in relation to individuals, not on a public scale. Joking with her brother, North, she experiences a moment of sudden exhilaration: "She felt, or rather she saw, not a place, but a state of being, in which there was real laughter, real happiness, and this fractured world was whole; whole, and free. But how could she say it?" (420). The best she can do with her utopian vision is to speak with Tolstoyan fervor to North: " 'You'll write one little book, and then another little book,' she said viciously, 'instead of living . . . living differently, differently.' She stopped. There was the vision still, but she had not grasped it. She had broken off only a little fragment of what she meant to say, and she had made her brother angry. Yet there it hung before her, the thing she had seen, the thing she had not said" (421). The future is not grasped; the utterance is incomplete; yet Peggy can say, with Lily Briscoe, "I have had my vision."

North, for his part, pursues his observations of the family members and muses on the new thrust of Peggy's idealism until, randomly opening a book in Delia's library, he receives a vision of his own:

He opened the little book. Latin, was it? He broke off a sentence and let it swim in his mind. There the words lay, beautiful, yet meaningless, yet composed in a pattern—*nox est perpetua una dormienda*. He remembered his master saying, Mark the long word at the end of the sentence. There the

[10]*A Haunted House and Other Short Stories*, pp. 109-15.

words floated; but just as they were about to give out their meaning, there was a movement at the door. . . . The younger generation following in the wake of the old, North said to himself as he put the book back on the shelf and followed. Only, he observed, they were not so very young; Peggy—there were white hairs on Peggy's head—she must be thirty-seven, thirty-eight? (424-25)

The quotation is from Catullus's fifth poem and reads, in context:

> Soles occidere et redire possunt,
> Nobis cum semel occidit brevis lux,
> Nox est perpetua una dormienda.

It may be translated: "Suns may rise and set; we, when our short day has closed, must sleep on in one perpetual night." With this meaning on the verge of consciousness, North's succeeding awareness of the passage of the generations—and of his own place in the train of the younger generation—comes as a fulfillment of the grave truth of the Latin text.

North's meditation turns next from death to life; as he drinks a glass of champagne, images of fecundity and renewal come to mind:

For them it's all right, he thought; they've had their day: but not for him, nor for his generation. For him a life modelled on the jet (he was watching the bubbles rise), on the spring, on the hard leaping fountain; another life; a different life. . . . To keep the emblems and tokens of North Pargiter—the man Maggie laughs at; the Frenchman holding his hat; but at the same time spread out, make a new ripple in human consciousness, be the bubble and the stream, the stream and the bubble—myself and the world together—he raised his glass. (442-43)

The reduction of such ancient symbols as the fountain of generation and the stream of life to the scale of a champagne glass adds a note of comic verve to the epiphany. North's growth of self-consciousness underscores his own vitality at the moment of accepting the mortality of the generations. The generations pass, but one may distinguish oneself among them; the stream flows, the bubbles are evanescent, but there is a source that renews—if not the "abounding jet" of Yeats's version of the topos.

This further stage of self-articulation does not lead North into full possession of his youthful power; instead, he reverts to images that had marked his sister's flounderings in skepticism: "He felt that he had been in the middle of a jungle; in the heart of darkness; cutting his way towards the light; but provided only with broken sentences, single words, with which to break through the briar-bush of human bodies, human wills and voices, that bent over him, binding him, blinding him . . ." (444). At this point occurs one of the most subtle of classical references in Woolf's oeuvre. The *Antigone*, which has been mentioned in the text in connection with Edward's rise to "the top of his tree" at Oxford (54, 144), is now quoted by him in the original to demonstrate the mellifluousness of the Greek:

> North looked up.
> "Translate it," he said.
> Edward shook his head. "It's the language," he said.
> Then he shut up. It's no go, North thought. He can't say what he wants to say; he's afraid. They're all afraid; afraid of being laughed at; afraid of giving themselves away. . . . That's what separates us; fear, he thought. (446–47)

The quoted words (line 523 of the *Antigone*) are the heroine's reply to Creon's statement of hostility ("A foe is never a friend—not even in death"): "'Tis not my nature to join in hating, but in loving" (in Sir Richard Jebb's translation).[11] This grand moment of self-definition stands in contrast to the timidity of Edward and others, whom North finds wanting in the qualities that distinguish the classical heroine. For Woolf, Antigone's choice of love over aggression is an affirmation of the power that could overcome alienation, which North sees as the ruling force in modern life. The limitations of the modern world are implied—and a way of transcendence pointed to—in the simple act of reciting a classical passage which, unknown to the speaker, holds the key to these revelations.

The focus of attention is now extended beyond North to the family as a whole. A number of reminiscences are woven together to establish the community of experience which is the medium of family life: among them are Rose's childhood identification with "Pargiter of Pargiter's Horse" (449, 453), Kitty's decision not to marry Edward (451), and her distaste for the suffragette movement (453). In this end-of-the-party mood of communion Kitty turns to Nicholas, urging him to propose a toast. With utmost gentility and charming idealism, he acknowledges the hosts, the company, and finally the human race, " 'which is now in its infancy, may it grow to maturity! Ladies and gentlemen!' he exclaimed, half rising and expanding his waistcoat, 'I drink to that!' He brought his glass down with a thump on the table. It broke" (460).

---

[11]The line is also quoted in the nearly contemporaneous *Three Guineas* (published 1938), p. 303, where it is praised as "worth all the sermons of all the archbishops" (148) in the course of comparing the classical heroine to modern suffragettes and anti-Fascist martyrs and while describing Sophocles as using "freely all the faculties that can be possessed by a writer" (302). For further discussion of Woolf on *Antigone*, see above, pp. 17–18.

The undercutting of this humanitarian gesture is not, however, allowed to dissipate the feeling of community and openness to the future that Eleanor has acquired; it leads her to a further stage of her speculations:

There must be another life, she thought, sinking back into her chair, exasperated. Not in dreams; but here and now, in this room, with living people. . . . This is too short, too broken. We know nothing, even about ourselves. We're only just beginning, she thought, to understand, here and there. . . . She held her hands hollowed; she felt that she wanted to enclose the present moment; to make it stay; to fill it fuller and fuller, with the past, the present and the future, until it shone, whole, bright, deep with understanding.
. . . It's useless, she thought, opening her hands. It must drop. It must fall. And then? she thought. For her too there would be the endless night; the endless dark. (461-62)

Here in simplest and most poignant form are stated the essential themes of Woolf's vision of life: the fragmentariness of human existence under the conditions of mortality, the ideal of a life in which the flight of time is filled with meaning and brought into formal order, and the impossibility of attaining that ideal—the necessity of sinking back into that fragmentariness. The theme is nothing new— the close of the passage recalls the line from Catullus cited earlier: *nox est perpetua una dormienda.* What is remarkable is Woolf's ability to state both the ideal *and* its impossibility with renewed commitment throughout her work.

Eleanor's meditation on life and death comes to an end with the renewal of ongoing life: though her mind envisions the "endless dark," her eyes become filled with the "growing light" of dawn. At this point one of the most bizarre episodes in all of Woolf's fiction occurs. A new element enters the Pargiters' party; the children of the caretaker, rising early, peep into Delia's flat to see the grownups at play. Responding to Nicholas's generalizations about the human race in its infancy, the company asks the children to speak or sing for them. The song they sing is of unsettling ethereality:

> Etho passo tanno hai,
> Fai donk to tu do,
> Mai to, kai to, lai to see
> Toh dom to tuh do—
> Fanno to par, etto to mar,
> Timin tudo, tido,
> Foll to gar in, mitno to par,
> Eido, teido, meido—
> Chree to gay ei,
> Geeray didax. . . . (463-64)

As may be imagined, the adults greet this communication with bewilderment—and appropriate comments on the inadequacies of current education. There is also a note of disturbance: "Nobody knew what to say. There was something horrible in the noise they made. It was so shrill, so discordant, and so meaningless" (464). It is left to two of the more sensitive characters to express some of the wonderment traditionally felt toward communications—sometimes made in angelic children's voices—from a realm outside the normal order of life:

> "But it was . . ." Eleanor began. She stopped. What was it? As they stood there they had looked so dignified; yet they had made this hideous noise. The contrast between their faces and their voices was astonishing; it was impossible to find one word for the whole. "Beautiful?" she said, with a note of interrogation, turning to Maggie.
> "Extraordinarily," said Maggie.
> But Eleanor was not sure that they were thinking of the same thing. (465)

Some day this extraordinary song may be discovered to be a transformation of a classic text, mingling as it does a number of Greek and Latin syllables and words. But it may be possible to tell what the song conveys even without understanding the words. Throughout her fiction, Woolf was intrigued by the sound of birds stridently expressing their vitality: from Septimus's hallucination of sparrows singing "freshly and piercingly in Greek words how there is no crime and . . . how there is no death" (*Mrs. Dalloway*, page 28), to the succession of birds in the italicized passages of *The Waves* who sing "stridently, with passion, with vehemence. . . . They sang as if the edge of being were sharpened and must cut . . ." (pages 78 et seq.). At times, Woolf gave words to the birds, always the same words: "What's life, we ask, leaning on the farmyard gate; Life, Life, Life! cries the bird, as if he had heard, and knew precisely . . ." (*Orlando*, page 243); "The tree became a rhapsody, a quivering cacophony, a whizz and vibrant rapture, branches, leaves, birds syllabling discordantly life, life, life, without measure . . ." (*Between the Acts*, page 245). There is no sure identity of the birds' song and the children's, which is obviously a more complex utterance, but they share the violence and even ugliness of a passionate urge to speak to the absolute fact that besides age, besides death, there is life.

After this manifestation and the failure to interpret it, life goes on. The sun rises, the party ends, and in words heard before, time is acknowledged: " 'It's time,' said Maggie, touching [Sara] on the shoulder. 'Time, is it?' she sighed" (466). Despite this renewed awareness of transiency, the party has had the cumulative effect of providing an image of permanence, not only for the reader but for the participants in the action. As the company disperses, Sara points up at the remaining guests framed in the window above: "The group in the window, the men in their black-and-white evening dress, the women in their crimsons, golds, and silvers, wore a statuesque air for a moment, as if they were carved in stone" (467). But it is only a momentary impression; ". . . they changed their attitudes; they began to talk." And with a renewal of the pigeons' chant, "take two coos," and the return by cab of the young couple across the street, life starts up again.

The sun had risen, and the sky above the houses wore an air of extraordinary beauty, simplicity and peace.

□

In the course of a series of lectures on feminism some time before *The Years*, Woolf had written:

Nothing came down the street; nobody passed. A single leaf detached itself from the plane tree at the end of the street, and in that pause and suspension fell. Somehow it was like a signal falling, a signal pointing to a force in things which one had overlooked. It seemed to point to a river, which flowed past, invisibly. . . . Now it was bringing from one side of the street to the other diagonally a girl in patent leather boots, and a young man in a maroon overcoat; it was also bringing a taxi–cab; and it brought all three together at a point directly beneath my window; where the taxi stopped; and the girl and the young man stopped; and they got into the taxi; and then the cab glided off as if it were swept on by the current elsewhere.

The sight was ordinary enough; what was strange was the rhythmical order with which my imagination had invested it; and the fact that the ordinary sight of two people getting into a cab had the power to communicate something of their own seeming satisfaction. The sight of two people coming down the street and meeting at the corner seems to ease the mind of some strain, I thought, watching the taxi turn and make off.

* * *

And I saw again the current which took . . . the dead leaves; and the taxi took the man and the woman, I thought, seeing them come together across the street, and the current swept them away, I thought, hearing far off the roar of London's traffic, into that tremendous stream.[12]

---

[12]*A Room of One's Own*, pp. 144-45, 157-58.

between the acts

"England was

earth merely, merely

the world"

Although *Between the Acts* (1941) may be considered as a late experimental development within the tradition of historical fiction[1], the work deserves to be discussed in broader terms as a synthesis of fiction and drama, of contemporary satire and literary parody, of psychological analysis and esthetic fantasy. Within the confines of a conventional modern tale—the marital tensions and sexual hankerings of Giles and Isa Oliver—a typical village fête is placed; the performance is not simply reported, but its text is inserted into the narrative so as to render the latter a mere frame to the pageant. The mixture is a rich—not to say, murky—one, and it will be useful to have something resembling a program to follow the sequence and order its elements. Such a program is mentioned and quoted in the text itself: the audience of the pageant—including the Olivers, their gentry set, and the author, Miss LaTrobe—"brooded over the blurred carbon sheet which had been issued for their information" (184) (also mentioned on page 106). This is a difficult document to interpret, both for the audience in the fiction and for the reader outside it, but it provides a structure for the text of the pageant, which is italicized, and thereby helps to order the roman text of the narrative proper.[2]

[1]See Fleishman, *The English Historical Novel* (Baltimore, 1971), pp. 245-55.
[2]An alternative structure is provided by counting only the sequence of fully dramatized scenes—Elizabethan, Restoration, Victorian—as high points in a depiction of English

The pageant begins with a Prologue (94–96), consisting of a child speaker representing young England (played by an otherwise undesignated Phyllis Jones) and a chorus of villagers chanting of the settlement of the land and the unvarying prehistoric round of life and death ("*Dug ourselves in to the hill top . . . Ground roots between stones . . . Ground corn . . . till we too . . . lay under g-r-o-u-n-d . . .*" [96]). The second number (97–99) takes the same form; an older girl (Hilda, the carpenter's daughter) represents an England grown medieval but still youthful, while a chorus, more articulate now, represents the common folk with a harvest charade and song ("*I kissed a girl and let her go, / Another did I tumble . . .*" [99]). After spanning vast ages in broadly allegorical fashion, with only a faint reference to literature, the pageant devotes four numbers to the Elizabethan-Jacobean period: a tableau of Elizabeth herself (played by Eliza Clark, the tobacco shop keeper [101–3]); an interlude resembling the interruption of a court jester or stage fool (impersonated without much difficulty by Albert, the village idiot [104–5]); a "scene from a play" of a naively stylized, post-Shakespearian sort (106–11) (the players include a Mrs. Otter [who later acts Lady Harraden] as an aged crone, one Sylvia Edwards as a disguised-and-revealed princess, and Mr. Albert Perry as her lost-and-found prince); and finally, "a mellay; a medley" danced to a folk tune ("A-maying, a-maying" [113]), followed by a procession of the actors from the stage.

At this point, the conventions of the charity-lawn-party demand an intermission for refreshment. (This interval is apparently marked number seven in the program.) The performance continues with another tableau, this time enthroning not England or its Queen but Reason (played by a Miss Mabel Hopkins [146]), who is somewhat incongruously paired with a chorus chanting the generalized rhythms of the farm laborer ("*Digging and delving, ploughing and sowing . . .*" [147–48]) (this chant is taken up again in the next number [164]). Then follows the longest and most brilliant of the parodies, a nearly full-fledged Restoration comedy, *Where there's a Will there's a Way* (in which Mrs. Otter is joined by the shop assistant Millie Loder in the role of Flavinda [159]). "The Victorian age," which follows, begins with "Number Ten. London street cries it was called. 'A Pot Pourri'" (184); it consists largely of recorded music of the recent past, pre-

history. But this arrangement is not to be taken as more than a set of clichés. Woolf's amusement at the inveterate problems of periodization and cultural homogeneity is displayed not only in her two "historical" fictions but in her biography of a dog: "The whole question of dogs' relation to the spirit of the age, whether it is possible to call one dog Elizabethan, another Augustan, another Victorian, together with the influence upon dogs of the poetry and philosophy of their masters, deserves a fuller discussion than can here be given it" (*Flush: A Biography*, p. 162).

sumably more readily available than music from the other ages. A transition between the Restoration and Victorian eras is provided by the standard chorus of common folk: "The Nineteenth Century . . . Look, there's the chorus, the villagers, coming on now, between the trees" (187). The prologue proper is spoken by a Victorian traffic policeman (played by Budge, the publican [188]) and a picnic skit includes a Mrs. Rogers and one Hammond (180), playing Mrs. Hardcastle and Sir John presumably, and Albert the idiot, representing the hindquarters of a donkey (199).

The methods used to bring the pageant into the modern age are appropriately unconventional and even expressionistic. The program indicates "Another interval. . . . And after that . . . Present time. Ourselves" (206), but the distinction between the two is blurred. "Nothing happened" (205) in either; in Miss La Trobe's script they are regarded as a single event: " 'After Vic.' she had written, 'try ten mins. of present time' " (209). She accomplishes another such incorporation of spectators into spectacle before the finale by having the actors turn a collection of mirrors toward the audience, which brings the modern age into the play and possibly reveals the men of the present to themselves (214-15). The next scene is another ensemble: this time each character, in costume, offers a reprise of "some phrase of fragment from their parts" (215-16). (The reprise is thickened—as will be discussed below—by the addition of a number of immortal lines and ragtag rhymes from the jumble of English civilization [216].) The final number is the author's direct address to her audience; although at the outset it seems mysterious and "Whose voice it was no one knew" (218), after a while it becomes unmistakably Miss La Trobe's voice: *"Do I escape my own reprobation, simulating indignation, in the bush, among the leaves?"* (219). The performance closes with the harmonies of music: "The tune began; the first note meant a second; the second a third. Then down beneath a force was born in opposition; then another. On different levels they diverged. On different levels ourselves went forward . . ." (220).

Three ritual actions follow the pageant: first, an attempt at interpretation by Reverend Streatfield (221-25); then, a collection, "for the illumination of our dear old church" (225) (which is interrupted by a flight of war planes overhead); and finally, the playing of "God Save the King" (227-28). Even here the line between art and life is blurred; as the actors mingle with the audience, "each still acted the unacted part conferred on them by their clothes" (228). The audience moves off to the tune of *"Armed against fate / The valiant Rhoderick . . . ,"* which has been sounded from the beginning onward (96, 114-15, 229-31); their chatting gropes for a simple formula for the mélange they have experienced and is accompanied by a grinding down of the tune to elementary positive and negative notes: *"Unity— Dispersity.* It gurgled *Un . . . dis . . .* And ceased" (235).

□

This outline of the program indicates that the content of the staged scenes alone gives a very incomplete impression of what transpires in the pages devoted to them. Since the scenes are presented as viewed and interpreted by the audience, and since the latter is not a monolithic entity but an assemblage of individuals interested in the play and interesting in themselves, the problem of interpreting the pageant is multiplied: the reader must deal not simply with the linear sequence of the scenes but with the depth of their fictional context.

Proceeding from the least to the most sophisticated responses, we may begin with Bond, the "cowman" (the ambiguity suggested by the epithet is probably deliberate). At the opening prologue, when a little girl forgets her lines, "Only Bond the cowman looked fluid and natural" (94); his attitude had been the same during the preparations: "He contemplated the young people hanging roses from one rafter to another. He thought very little of anybody, simples or gentry" (36). Almost as detached, but more inquisitive, is Cobbet of Cobb's Corner, "retired, it was understood, on a pension from a tea plantation. Not an asset" (91)—but one who is envied by his neighbors for his success at flower shows (231). His attitude toward the play derives from his attitude to mankind: ". . . he had known human nature in the East. It was the same in the West. Plants remained . . ." (131) (he is also shown "automatically" remembering to water his plants on page 118). At the opposite extreme of receptivity is Mrs. Manresa, the "wild child" of nature (97). She is well-versed in history (99) and thoroughly enjoys herself at the spectacle (103), but her response to it is essentially narcissistic, for she sees herself reflected in the action ("Somehow she was the Queen; and he (Giles) was the surly hero" [112])—just as she evades the revelation of the mirrors at the finale by using them to powder her nose (217).

Almost equally egoistic in their responses are Giles and Isa Oliver, the quarreling couple of the frame story, who react according to the moods occasioned by their mutual hostility and sexual adventurousness. Giles is sullen, partly because of the news of gathering war clouds, partly because of his wife's attention to their visitor, William Dodge, and perhaps because he also knows of her interest in their neighbor, Rupert Haines. He is capable of literary responses, remembering lines of poetry when they are alluded to in discussion (104); and he is among the few spectators to grasp one of the main points of the pageant, for when Mrs. Parker objects to the performance of the idiot by saying, "Surely, Mr. Oliver, we're more civilized?" he replies, *"We? . . . We?"* (132). Yet Giles's essentially kinetic rather than esthetic nature causes him to seize on the similarities between his own situation and what is enacted in the pageant and to act on this recognition, as when he muses on the elopement in the mock-Restoration play: "A moral. What? Giles supposed it was: Where there's a Will there's a Way. The words rose and pointed a finger of scorn at him. Off to Gretna Green with his girl; the deed done. Damn the consequences. 'Like to see the greenhouse?' he said abruptly, turning to Mrs. Manresa" (174-75). Isa's self-projection onto the action is less dramatic, more verbal. She enters into the rhythm of the verse and repeats snatches of it that nourish her abundant self-pity—"There is little blood in my arm" (109)—or invents poetic tags of her own, e.g., "On little donkey, patiently stumble" (183). Her poetic sensibility is sentimental rather than esthetic; she does not value the scenes except as an aid in fostering her image of herself as an alienated spirit, wandering "in some harvestless dim field where no evening lets fall her mantle; nor sun rises. All's equal there" (181).

Two members of the elder generation exhibit another pair of responses to the play. Giles's father, Bart Oliver, is the man of reason—when Reason speaks, he applauds mightily (146)—and he remains skeptical about the myths and pieties of English history (smirking at the absence of reason in the Restoration scene [157]). He correctly interprets the chuffing of the phonograph as "marking time" (100); he is stamped as learned by the collection in his "country gentleman's library" ("A great harvest the mind had reaped; but for all this, compared with his son, he did not care one damn" [138]); and he expresses suspicion of the performance, along with distaste for its subject: "What's the object . . . of this entertainment? . . . Nothing's done for nothing in England" (206-7). In contrast, his sister, Lucy Swithin, is all enthusiasm: "He would carry the torch of reason till it went out in the darkness of the cave. For herself, every morning, kneeling, she protected her vision" (240). This distinction refers not merely to Mrs. Swithin's Catholic faith, for which her brother gently chides her, but to their broader habits of mind: ". . . she belonged to the unifiers; he to the separatists" (140). For her, the pageant is a revelation of man's beauty ("I'd no notion we looked so nice" [100]); the appearance of swallows flying through the performance is to be welcomed as one of the constants of nature ("'They come every year'. . . . As they had come, she supposed, when the Barn was a swamp" [123]); theatrical art is capable of great symbolic power ("Actors show us too much. The Chinese, you know, put a dagger on the table and that's a battle" [167]); and Miss La Trobe's art is a revelation of the unfulfilled selves that everyone harbors within ("What a small part I've had to play! But you've made me feel I could have played . . . Cleopatra!" [179]). Some of Mrs. Swithin's other responses are more general and more questionable: "The Victorians. . . . I don't believe that there ever were such people. Only you and me and William dressed differently" (203) (Dodge rightly observes, "You don't believe in history"); she goes off on a "circular tour of the imagination—one-making" and comfortably concludes "that *all* is harmony, could we hear it. And we shall" (204); and her final inference from Miss La Trobe's concluding speech is that "we act different parts but are the same" (251).

Two other characters rise above a personal mode of response to an esthetic one. There is a considerable difference, however, between the creative spirit of Miss La Trobe as she interprets her own work and the passive enjoyment of the homosexual William Dodge, which remains hedonistic and superficial. For Dodge, the esthetic value of art is sufficient: "Beauty—isn't that enough?" (100); the mellay is a source of pure delight: "an entrancing spectacle . . . of dappled light and shade on half clothed, fantastically coloured, leaping, jerking, swinging legs and arms. He clapped till his palms stung" (112). He can respond to Isa's poetic mutterings by quoting speeches of the play (125), but there is no indication that he perceives anything beyond the camp elements of the performance. Miss La Trobe, on the contrary, seeks to instill a deeper response: "Hadn't she, for twenty-five minutes, made them see? A vision imparted was relief from agony . . ." (117) (although she acknowledges almost immediately that their seeing is inadequate, her vision a failure). Her means are the sensuous and rhythmic elements of her medium, but she recognizes her mistake in trying to appropriate the materials of nature whole, without modifying them by esthetic design: "She wanted to expose [the audience], as it were, to douche them, with present-time reality. But something was going wrong with the experiment. 'Reality too strong,' she muttered. 'Curse 'em!'" (209). Her address to the audience, nevertheless, sums up not only her impulse toward moral revelation but her ultimate distrust of esthetic media in favor of direct communication: ". . . *let's talk in words of one syllable, without larding, stuffing or cant. Let's break the rhythm and forget the rhyme. And calmly consider ourselves*" (218).

There are, besides the principals, the less vocal members of the audience, who may be taken in characteristic groupings. Those named include Mrs. Elmhurst (105, 149–50, 166, 175) and Mrs. Parker (122–23, 132, 226, 229, 235), who dislike Albert's appearance in the play;

Mrs. Herbert Winthrop (106-7) and Mrs. Lynn Jones (185-87, 191, 201-03, 229), who, along with Mrs. Elmhurst, contribute to the pageant by reading from the program to introduce the scenes; and Colonel and Mrs. Mayhew (184, 209, 217, 230) and Etty Springett (185, 192, 202, 226), who are the only ones to judge the play unfavorably. (The Colonel objects to the omission of the British Army and Miss Springett finds the Victorian scene "cheap and nasty.") There is also one speechless but distinguished spectator, Lady Haslip, of Haslip Manor (117): "The great lady in the bath chair . . . —so indigenous was she that even her body, crippled by arthritis, resembled an uncouth, nocturnal animal, now nearly extinct—clapped and laughed aloud—the sudden laughter of a startled jay" (112) (similar descriptions are given on pages 157 and 238).[3]

□

The most prominent participant is, however, neither a protagonist of the frame story nor one of the invited neighbors but an anonymous voice that emerges from the audience as a whole. This collective point of view is assigned a special way of being introduced and of speaking, so that it develops a personality of its own, a synthetic identity formed from the response of divergent perspectives to a common experience. In other Woolf fictions, a dinner party or the apparition of an old woman can fuse disparate characters into a unitary consciousness; here, an ongoing work of art performs that function. Despite its amateurishness and gimmickry, the pageant stimulates a new awareness in the men of contemporary England—not least because its materials are drawn from the collected experience of the nation's history. From the outset, the members of the audience take their places in relation to their forebears: ". . . had Figgis [the guidebook writer] been there in person and called a roll call, half the ladies and gentlemen present would have said: '*Adsum*; I'm here, in place of my grandfather or great-grandfather,' as the case might be" (92).

The medium which maintains this continuity is time, represented mechanically by the revolutions of the phonograph: "Then the play began. Was it, or was it not, the play? Chuff, chuff, chuff sounded from the bushes. . . . Some sat down hastily; others stopped talking guiltily. All looked at the bushes. For the stage was empty" (93). Introduced to the rhythm of the drama and its representation of the passage of history, the audience becomes esthetically and historically responsive at the same time. After some initial resistance ("They

[3]Jean O. Love, in *Worlds in Consciousness: Mythopoetic Thought in the Novels of Virginia Woolf* (Berkeley, Los Angeles and London, 1970), pp. 225-27, comments on the animal imagery accompanying the characters in this work.

glared as if they were exposed to a frost that nipped them and fixed them all at the same level" [94]), they gradually fall in with the music and spectacle: "Muscles loosened; ice cracked. The stout lady in the middle [Mrs. Manresa] began to beat time with her hand on her chair" (96). At this point, the audience begins to speak in its own voice, rendered by the narrative voice in *erlebte Rede*: "Everyone was clapping and laughing. From behind the bushes issued Queen Eliza-beth—Eliza Clark, licensed to sell tobacco. Could she be Mrs. Clark of the village shop?" (101). Assimilating the quoted dialogue of the in-dividual characters, this *erlebte Rede* becomes the dominant mode of discourse in which the middle portion of *Between the Acts* is com-posed:

Were they about to act a play in the presence of Queen Elizabeth? Was this, perhaps, the Globe theatre?
"What does the programme say?" Mrs. Herbert Winthrop asked, raising her lorgnettes.
She mumbled through the blurred carbon sheet. Yes; it was a scene from a play. (106)

Despite the unification effected by this mode of discourse, the audience relapses into discrete elements, separated from the rhythms of the play and of history. At the interval—to which Miss La Trobe had objected—the group fragments to the tune of the "armed against fate" song: "The music chanted: *Dispersed are we* . . . as they streamed, spotting the grass with colour, across the lawns, and down the paths: *Dispersed are we*" (114–15). Yet even here they are in the same *Stimmung*, as it were, for they respond uniformly to the rhythm and rhyme of the song, each mentally adapting it to his own concerns: "Freely, boldly, fearing no one, . . . I'm for tea" (Mrs. Manresa); "All is over. The wave has broken. . . . Now I follow . . . that old strum-pet . . . to have tea" (Isa); "Shall I . . . go or stay? . . . Or follow, follow, follow the dispersing company?" (Dodge); "What made her indue the antique with this glamour—this sham lure, and set 'em climbing, climbing, climbing up the monkey puzzle tree?" (Cobbet); "Bart, my dear, come with me. . . . D'you remember, when we were children, the play we acted in the nursery?" (Mrs. Swithin says this aloud); and even Miss La Trobe: "Hadn't she, for twenty-five minutes, made them see? A vision imparted was relief from agony . . ." (115–17).

The interlude of small talk and sexual pursuits in and about the Barn returns the members of the audience to their habitual ways of life, but they are still unconsciously under the common spell. After a nursery tune and a waltz are sounded (the latter being practiced in the house), the martial music that dispersed them brings them together again

(141). Now they achieve a new mode of speech, described as an "inner voice" that accompanies their spoken words: "Feet crunched the gravel. Voices chattered. The inner voice, the other voice was saying: How can we deny that this brave music, wafted from the bushes, is expressive of some inner harmony? 'When we wake' (some were thinking) 'the day breaks us with its hard mallet blows.' 'The office' (some were thinking) 'compels disparity . . .' " (142). In response to the music, these individual memories of separation are swallowed up in a general sense of unity: "For I hear music, they were saying. Music wakes us. Music makes us see the hidden, join the broken. . . . And the trees with their many-tongued much syllabling, their green and yellow leaves hustle us and shuffle us, and bid us, like the starlings, and the rooks, come together, crowd together, to chatter and make merry while the red cow moves forward and the black cow stands still" (143). The music and elements of nature—especially the cows and birds, which later perform crucial aleatory roles when assimilated by the pageant (165–66)—become part of the unity of consciousness which the audience is shown to be forming.

With this unification, the manner of presenting the audience's speech finds its definitive form: it is no longer the direct statement (sometimes unspoken) of its individual members, or the *erlebte Rede* which assimilates the several voices into the narrator's point of view, but the quoted speech of the ensemble: " 'Where did we leave off? D'you remember? The Elizabethans . . . Perhaps she'll reach the present, if she skips. . . . D'you think people change? Their clothes, of course . . . But I mean ourselves . . . Clearing out a cupboard, I found my father's old top hat . . . But ourselves—do we change?' " (144). Although some individual voices are still discernible, speaking in the first person singular and recounting personal experiences, there is in these speeches a new awareness of a shared involvement in the play and a growing identification with the historical community which lies behind it. This consciousness of connection with the men of the past and with the men of the present is signaled by the use of the term "ourselves." This clannish term is then widened to include more remote groups and gives signs of encompassing the entire race: " 'And what about the Jews? The refugees . . . the Jews . . . People like ourselves, beginning life again . . . But it's always been the same . . .' " (145).

Again the pageant's scenic action begins, and the individual spectators fall back into their private points of view and make their charactertistically insipid remarks. But as the pageant reaches the Victorian age, which many of them can remember, a new response occurs: "Yet somehow they felt—how could one put it—a little not quite here or there. As if the play had jerked the ball out of the cup; as if what I call myself was still floating unattached, and didn't settle. Not quite themselves, they felt" (175). They are both in and out of the play and in and out of history and thus feel not quite individual but not yet a community. When the transitional music returns, however, they are held together merely by the rhythm of the passage of time, without the content of theatrical or historical experience: "Chuff, chuff, chuff went the machine. Time was passing. How long would time hold them together?" (177). At this point, as men of the present, they discover resources of unity in their common fears of the future and shared memories of the past:

Over the tops of the bushes came stray voices, voices without bodies, symbolical voices they seemed to [Miss La Trobe], half hearing, seeing nothing, but still, over the bushes, feeling invisible threads connecting the bodiless voices.
"It all looks very black."
"No one wants it—save those damned Germans."
There was a pause. . . .
"They say there's been a garden here for five hundred years. . . ." (177)

Having arrived at the present and being thrust into immediate reality by Miss La Trobe's experiment with "ten mins. of present time," the audience dissipates not only its esthetic attention to the play but also its awareness of itself in history: "All their nerves were on edge. They sat exposed. The machine ticked. There was no music. . . . They were neither one thing nor the other; neither Victorians nor themselves. They were suspended, without being, in limbo. Tick, tick, tick went the machine" (207). Forced to face themselves outside the well-known patterns of history, the individual members of the audience gradually reassert their egoism and separateness: " 'Ourselves . . .' They returned to the programme. But what could she know about ourselves? The Elizabethans yes; the Victorians, perhaps; but ourselves; sitting here on a June day in 1939—it was ridiculous. 'Myself'—it was impossible. Other people, perhaps. . . . But she won't get me—no, not me" (208-9). This egoism leads Miss La Trobe to curse the audience and imagine an ideal play without them (210), but they soon regain their sense of a common destiny in a cathartic shower: "Down it poured like all the people in the world weeping. Tears, Tears. Tears. . . . they were all people's tears, weeping for all people. Hands were raised. Here and there a parasol opened. The rain was sudden and universal" (210).

After the shower, there occurs one of the more remarkable events in a constantly surprising work: the music that had come from the house at the end of the interval begins again, not merely playing but speaking—for it has already been described as a voice: "Another voice, a third voice, was saying something simple. And they [Isa and Dodge] sat on in the greenhouse, on the plank with the vine over them, listening to Miss La Trobe or whoever it was, practising her scales" (137). Now the piano returns, playing the same tune; it is again described as a voice, but of an even stranger sort: ". . . it was the other voice speaking, the voice that was no one's voice. And the voice that wept for human pain unending said:

> The King is in his counting house,
> Counting out his money,
> The Queen is in her parlour . . ." (211)

This "other voice" is the same as that "inner voice, the other voice" (142) of the audience which speaks below its audible remarks. If this is so, then the audience has become identified, in the course of its experience, with "the voice that wept for human pain unending"; this voice that is "no one's voice" is now everyone's voice.

Having achieved this degree of articulation and of universality, the audience relapses into its fragmentary state with the end of the pageant. When all the after-pieces are over, and while the recessional music provides them a rhythm of both unity and dispersal, these "scraps, orts and fragments" of a community express the sum of their responses:

"I do think," someone was saying, "Miss Whatshername should have come forward and not left it to the rector. . . . After all, she wrote it. . . . I thought it brilliantly clever. . . . O my dear, I thought it utter bosh. Did you understand the meaning? Well, [Reverend Streatfield] said she meant we all act all parts. . . . He said, too, if I caught his meaning, Nature takes part. . . . Then there was the idiot. . . . Also, why leave out the Army, as my husband was saying, if it's history? And if one spirit animates the whole, what about the aeroplanes? . . ." (230-31)

The several members of the audience thus assemble a response to the pageant that comes close to wisdom. For they are each partly right: the pageant is at once brilliant and utter bosh; it suggests that "we all act all parts" and that "Nature takes part," although it says neither of these exclusively. Only the sum of the audience reactions approximates the pageant's meaning; only the group consciousness formed in esthetic response to historical experience can approach the universal perspective at which the pageant—and *Between the Acts* itself—aims.

Yet there is no way of maintaining this communal wisdom in society at large. "What we need is a centre [as a spectator observes].

Something to bring us all together" (231)—but in our time a "centre" is likely to mean an activity hall rather than a cultural ideal. Moreover, the communal wisdom, which includes scraps and fragments of the leading ideas of modern culture (e.g., relativity and psychoanalysis [232-33]), can at best arrive at the proper questions, not the answers to them: "He said she meant we all act. Yes, but whose play? Ah, that's the question! And if we're left asking questions, isn't it a failure, as a play? . . . Or was that, perhaps, what she meant? . . . Ding dong. Ding . . . that if we don't jump to conclusions, if you think, and I think, perhaps one day, thinking differently, we shall think the same?" (233). Like the "ding dong" of the church bells, which "always stopped, leaving you to ask: Won't there be another note?" (242), the question is left in the air.

□

Despite its thirteen numbers and three after-pieces, its individual and collective observers and their intercalated responses, the pageant is nevertheless only the central section of *Between the Acts*. On either side lies the frame story of Giles and Isa Oliver, their family, friends, and house, Pointz Hall. From one standpoint, this story—of a rather callous stockbroker and his unfulfilled, poetic wife—is so conventional that it pales by comparison with the vivid and complex pageant; in this view, the realistic contemporary plot is mere stage play, and the real subject, the pageant, lies "between the acts" of its flummery. From another point of view, the pageant is a mere entr'acte between the realistically portrayed actions of the Olivers' falling-out and reconciliation. Both perspectives reduce the frame story and the pageant to a common plane of mimesis; they are equally real in affecting the historical imagination of their observers and equally fictional as symbolic equivalents of their respective historical ages. The effect is to make the entire span of history into a series of dramatic representations, all part of the vast cosmic drama which is human life. The Renaissance (ultimately Platonic) *topos* of the world as a stage lies in the background of the work throughout—though it emerges explicitly only in the most appropriate place, at the performance, in the pageant, of mock-Elizabethan play (106).

Though there is no way of deciding whether it is the frame story that lies among the acts of the larger pageant of history, or the pageant that lies between the acts of the frame, there is a thread common to both. At the center of the pageant is the Restoration play, and at the center of that play is a moment of stillness. It is the moment of the conventional lovers' embrace: " 'All that fuss about nothing!' a voice exclaimed. People laughed. The voice stopped. But the voice had seen; the voice had heard. For a moment Miss La Trobe

213

behind her tree glowed with glory" (163). This perception of an
emptiness at the center of the pageant—which itself lies between the
acts of ongoing life—suggests a state of negativity at the core of
human affairs. But the continued impulse to action, however
illusory—to make a "fuss about nothing"—brings renewed life to the
theatrical situation, just as it does to man's life in history; when
illusion fails, Miss La Trobe finds, "This is death" (165). What is
perhaps most remarkable in this dramatization of the analogy
between life illusion and theatrical illusion is the audience's perception of it, for the voice that perceives the underlying vacancy—a voice
that is said to hear and see (163)—can be none other than the collective mind that has been formed of the individual observers by the
action of the play.

What is the motive force that urges this pursuit of illusion, this
dramatic action with nothing at the center? Though marked by its
author's delicacy, *Between the Acts* answers firmly that this force
is sex—or, more broadly, natural desire. Virginia Woolf nowhere else
makes so much of the raw materials of which art and civilized life are
composed; nowhere is nature as roughly introduced into her work—
neither in *The Voyage Out*, where it breeds death, nor in *The Waves*,
where it provides an encompassing order. In *Between the Acts*, the
wayward mooing of cows is thrust into the highly patterned forms of
the pageant (159). Later, planned release from esthetic control by
the introducion of "ten mins. of present time" is saved from bathos
by an unexpected shower of rain. In both cases, the happy accident
does more than supersede esthetic order; just as the rain expresses
universal tears, so the cows speak of universal need: "From cow after
cow came the same yearning bellow. The whole world was filled with
dumb yearning. It was the primeval voice sounding loud in the ear of
the present moment. . . . as if Eros had planted his dart in their
flanks and goaded them to fury. The cows annihilated the gap;
bridged the distance; filled the emptiness and continued the emotion" (165-66). What the cows convey is the impulse that moves men
and beasts alike; responding to the erotic impulse, man fills the
nothingness that underlies his world, brings art and history into
being, gives form to what would otherwise be inchoate matter.

While the participation of cows and rain helps to universalize
human yearning—abundantly represented in the love scenes of the
pageant and the extramarital and marital urges of the frame story—
other elements of nature play a more passive, yet nonetheless
prominent, role in this vision of human life. Just as "Nature had
provided a site for a house" (15), so "the terrace, rising, made a
natural stage. The trees barred the stage like pillars" (93). These

trees are omnipresent in the scenes and behind them; the actors and author are usually "hidden behind the tree" (94), and the chorus is conceived by Miss La Trobe as "winding in and out between the trees" (71). Moreover, the trees are suggestive of human spaces and rhythms: they are "magnificently straight. They were not too regular; but regular enough to suggest columns in a church; in a church without a roof; in an open-air cathedral, a place where swallows darting seemed, by the regularity of the trees, to make a pattern, dancing, like the Russians, only not to music, but to the unheard rhythm of their own wild hearts" (80). Just as trees and art mingle, the swallows, dancing in a pattern, yet impulsive in their freedom, move repeatedly through and around the play (121, 129, 192, 202, 209, 212, 224, 242). Other birds enter the language of the play itself: a bird twitters as Queen Elizabeth speaks of the throstle and mavis in the green woods of England (102); Albert, the fool, lists his knowledge of the tit's nest first among his natural secrets (104) and whistles like a bird between his fingers (105); an old crone in the Elizabethan play speaks of gull and heron in her picture of her marshy haunts (108); and the Tudor priest who sums up calls on robin and wren for their obsequies (111).

This rhythm of trees and birds serves to activate the passive spectators and enrich the spectacle: "As they listened and looked—out into the garden—the trees tossing and the birds swirling seemed called out of their private lives, out of their separate avocations, and made to take part" (139). Nature's effect on the dramatic action becomes esthetic in its own right: the trees "barred the music, and massed and hoarded; and prevented what was fluid from overflowing" (213). Ultimately, these symbols are brought together in a great tree of life—an image of natural vitality which crowns the idea of human enterprise established by the pageant:

The whole tree hummed with the whizz [the starlings] made, as if each bird plucked a wire. A whizz, a buzz rose from the bird-buzzing, bird-vibrant, bird-blackened tree. The tree became a rhapsody, a quivering cacophony, a whizz and vibrant rapture, branches, leaves, birds syllabling discordantly life, life, life, without measure, without stop devouring the tree. Then up! Then off! (245)[4]

And this image of life becomes in its turn a further stimulus to art, for Miss La Trobe, seeing the tree where she had been hiding thus transformed, sees it also as the setting for her next play—the drama

[4]Another element of nature with an important role is explored in Stephen D. Fox, "The Fish Pond as Symbolic Center in *Between the Acts*," *Modern Fiction Studies*, XVIII (1972), 467-73.

of conflict and renewal which the Olivers are performing privately at that very moment: "There was the high ground at midnight; there the rock; and two scarcely perceptible figures. Suddenly the tree was pelted with starlings. She set down her glass. She heard the first words" (248).

□

"Of course, there's the whole of English literature to choose from. But how can one choose?" (73). Mrs. Swithin puts the problem in her charming, vague way; the discussion is of choosing a play for the pageant, but she turns it to the subject of her reading. As early as the opening scene, in which Bart Oliver remembers that his mother had given him the works of Byron—and quotes from two well-known lyrics—the characters of *Between the Acts* are as self-conscious as their creator about the presence of English literature in their midst.

At times this is a merely formal presence, as when Isa scans the books of the Pointz Hall library, ranging from *The Faerie Queene* to Yeats, before settling down to a newspaper account of a rape committed by soldiers of the venerable Horse Guards. Alternatively, there is some effort to bring literature to bear upon the self and its concerns: " 'I fear I am not in my perfect mind,' Giles muttered. . . . Words came to the surface—he remembered 'a stricken deer in whose lean flank the world's harsh scorn has struck its thorn. . .' " (103–4)—mingling lines from *King Lear* (act 5, scene 7, 63) and Cowper's *The Task* (book 3, 108). (The rhyming phrases are Giles's invention.) More often, the nation's literary endowment furnishes the fiction with catch phrases imperfectly recalled: "Books: the treasured life-blood of immortal spirits. Poets; the legislators of mankind" (138); mellifluous lines to be mindlessly chanted, like Bart's repetition of the opening lines of Swinburne's "Itylus" (137, 139); and vaguely expressive sentiments: ". . . did you feel when the shower fell, someone wept for us all? There's a poem, *Tears tears tears*, it begins. And goes on *O then the unloosened ocean . . .* but I can't remember the rest" (234) (the nameless speaker refers to feelings mentioned on page 210; the lines are from a non-English writer, Whitman, in "Sea Drift").

The composition of the pageant is not different in kind from the characters' chatter in the way it incorporates fragments of English literature that lie scattered about in modern culture. The play can stand as a minor—and gently satirical—example of the doctrines of Eliot, Pound, and others on the conscious or unconscious assimilation of tradition in the individual artist's talent. The conventions of Elizabethan stagecraft and rhetoric are imitated—even specific lines quoted, e.g., *"Play out the play"* from *I Henry IV*, act 2, scene 4

(107). Incorporated in the play are not only plots, characters, and verbal formulas, but also the classical *topoi* of the genre most appropriate to a pageant, the masque: *"Time, leaning on his sickle, stands amazed. While commerce from her Cornucopia pours the mingled tribute of her different ores. . . . And in the helmet, yellow bees their honey make"* (147) (the latter *topos* is perhaps derived from Robert Greene). And the satire of Victorianism, which ridicules the shibboleths and cant of the era, is largely a parody of literature become cliché, like the descent of Moore's "The Last Rose of Summer" to the level of a popular song (198) or the use of Kipling's "The White Man's Burden" in jingoistic tracts (191).[5]

The full flowering of the pageant's origins in English literature occurs when the characters reappear for a finale and mingle the historical ages by dancing together in their varied costumes. The impression of a unity of historical experience is enforced by their medley (215-16) of literary phrases and fragments of their parts:

. . . I am not (said one) *in my perfect mind* [*Lear*; see also page 103] *. . . Another, Reason am I . . . And I? I'm the old top hat* [a popular song?] *. . . Home is the hunter, home from the hill* [approximating Stevenson's "Requiem"] *. . . Home? Where the miner sweats* [referred to in the pageant on pages 147 and 191], *and the maiden faith is rudely strumpeted* [Shakespeare's sonnet 66; "faith" is substituted for "vertue"]. *. . . Sweet and low; sweet and low, wind of the western sea* [Tennyson's *The Princess*] *. . . Is that a dagger that I see before me* [approximately *Macbeth*, act 2, scene 1, 33] *. . . The owl hoots and the ivy mocks tap-tap-tapping on the pane* [quoted by Giles on page 104]. *. . . Lady I love till I die, leave thy chamber and come . . . Where the worm weaves its winding sheet . . . I'd be a butterfly. I'd be a butterfly* [song by Thomas Haynes Bayly, sung on page 198]. *. . . In thy will is our peace* ["Paradiso," canto 3, 85] *. . . Here, Papa, take your book and read aloud* [not in pageant, but suggested on page 192]. *. . . Hark, hark, the dogs do bark and the beggars . . .* [nursery rhyme].[6]

From these snippets of literature—the lofty and the banal, the universal and the homely, the sentimental in various shades and the sardonic—is made the substance of the pageant. This crescendo of words suggests that the pageant is not a mere pastiche of English

---

[5]A number of these references have been independently identified in an unpublished article by Jean M. Wyatt, who has also commented on other Woolf citations in *"Mrs. Dalloway:* Literary Allusion as Structural Metaphor," *PMLA*, LXXXVIII (1973), 440-51.
[6]The broken-off line ends: "are coming to town"; it is quoted on p. 139 (from number 140 in *The Oxford Dictionary of Nursery Rhymes*). Another nursery rhyme, "Sing a song of sixpence" (number 486), is used as the verbal equivalent of a musical refrain in the pageant, on pp. 137, 146, 211, and 212; it is also imitated by Isa on p. 208. Folk art here plays much the same role as "high" art in making up the tissue of the pageant.

literature but a representation of the collective mind of England, which is composed of just such bits and pieces of language.[7]

What is true for the pageant is true for *Between the Acts* itself, and not merely in the sense that the play makes up a large part of the fiction. At a number of points, the narrative catches up lines of poetry and prose, effectively making them part of its texture, as in the earlier mentioned citation of "Heart of Darkness" on the final page. Elsewhere the mode of incorporation is more elaborate, as when E. M. Forster's *A Passage to India* is imitated: "Beyond that [cloud] was blue, pure blue, black blue: blue that had never filtered down; that had escaped registration" (30). (Part of the penultimate paragraph of Forster's first chapter reads: "By day the blue will pale down. . . . But the core of blue persists, and so it is by night. . . . that farther distance, though beyond colour, last freed itself from blue.") Or the allusion may be so subtle as to defy decisive attribution, as in this scanting of Gertrude Stein's famous line: "She left the sentence unfinished, as if she were of two minds, and they fluttered to right and to left, like pigeons rising from the grass" (91). The theme progressively established by these incorporations is indicated by Mrs. Swithin, as she shows William Dodge over the house: "Then she ran her hand over the sunk books in the wall on the landing, as if they were pan pipes. 'Here are the poets from whom we descend by way of the mind. . .' " (84–85).

Nothing is denied in *Between the Acts*: neither nature, despite the banality of its appearances; nor the sexual drive, which expresses itself almost comically in the Olivers' interest in other characters; nor history, despite the artificiality of the modes in which the men of the past are represented; nor art, which fails to communicate the author's vision and yet renews the artist's will-to-form; nor man himself, thoroughly satirized here and reduced to "scraps, orts, fragments" but capable at moments of approximating the unity that Woolf occasionally posits as a peak of conscious life. This closing fiction, unrevised though it is, can stand as a *summa* of the thematic concerns and experimental modes with which Woolf had been occupied through the course of her career.

□

[7]The composition of a village play is itself a reflection not only of social behavior but of literary practice. Woolf was undoubtedly aware of her friend E. M. Forster's 1934 pageant for the Abinger Church Preservation Fund—the text of which is published in his *Abinger Harvest* collection as part 5. Forster's scenes are mainly historical tableaux rather than literary parodies, but he makes similar use of choral processions, musical transitions, and natural settings. See Renée Watkins, "Survival in Discontinuity—Virginia Woolf's *Between the Acts*," *Massachusetts Review*, x (1969), 357 ff.; this article also points out two possible allusions to Thackeray's *Pendennis* (pp. 357, 363).

At about the time of writing *Between the Acts,* Woolf wrote a prose sketch of an imaginary plane ride, "Flying over London":

Nothing more fantastic could be imagined. . . . the River Thames was as the Romans saw it, as Palaeolithic man saw it, at dawn from a hill shaggy with wood, with the rhinoceros digging his horn into the roots of rhododendrons. So immortally fresh and virginal London looked and England was earth merely, merely the world. . . . There rose a dome, a spire, a factory chimney, a gasometer. Civilization in short emerged; hands and minds worked again; and the wild rhinoceros was chased out of sight for ever. Still we descended. Here was a garden; here a football field. But no human being was yet visible; England looked like a ship that sails unmanned. . . . we rose again like a spirit shaking contamination from its wings, shaking gasometers and factories and football fields from its feet.

It was a moment of renunciation. We prefer the other, we seemed to say. Wraiths and sand dunes and mist; imagination; this we prefer to the mutton and entrails. It was the idea of death that now suggested itself; not being received and welcomed; not immortality but extinction.[8]

But the narrator becomes dissatisfied with this imaginative distancing and wishes to return to earth, renouncing one trait of her art but affirming another:

Everything had changed its values seen from the air. Personality was outside the body, abstract. And one wished to be able to animate the heart, the legs, the arms with it, to do which it would be necessary to be there, so as to collect; so as to give up this arduous game, as one flies through the air, of assembling things that lie on the surface.

[8]*Collected Essays,* IV, 168; and below, 171–72.

afterword

Having examined Virginia Woolf's fictions severally, what comprehensive statement can we make about them that will be true to their infinite variety? One approach is to contemplate the kind of index that would be appropriate to the data of the present study; this decision would imply, if not a whole view of Woolf, at least a gross estimate of the contents of her work. It will quickly be discovered that a list of the proper names mentioned in or associated with the texts—even if extended to include myths, allusions, and conventions—conveys only a fraction of their substance. Although I have taken Woolf to be a learned author and placed her among her myth-minded contemporaries, none of her works stands in need of an allusion index like Weldon Thornton's for *Ulysses*. More appropriate, it seems, would be a motif index, on the model of Clive Hart's for *Finnegans Wake*, which includes single words, names, phrases, quotations, verbal patterns, and mythic figures. Such an index would not only assimilate much of the observable phenomena in Woolf's texts, but would raise questions about the status of these linguistic units and the principles by which they are related to each other. It is my present object to isolate this unit, the Woolfian *motif*, and to describe the principle of *repetition* by which the motif operates in her work. And it is appropriate that this account proceed, initially at least, with reference to *Finnegans Wake*, the work of art in which repetition-with-variation has been raised to a chief principle of composition and, in the same stroke, established as the natural subject-matter of human life: "the seim anew."

Hart's description of this principle may serve as a starting point. After citing a number of German accounts of the *Leitmotiv* (a portion of the Wagnerian heritage), he offers the following definition:

> The main requirement of a true *leitmotiv* [*sic*] is that it should, as its name implies, lead from point to point; it is, in fact, an essentially dynamic device. Reiteration alone is not enough to convert a phrase into a *leitmotiv*. . . . Real *leitmotiv* entails a use of statement and restatement in such a way as to impel the reader to relate part to part; each recurrence of such a motif derives in some necessary way from all its previous appearances and leads on to future resurgences, pointing to correspondences and relationships far beyond those that hold between the individual motif and its immediate context. The full course of such a motif, appearing and disappearing, now in full view, now faintly suggested, must be considered as a whole. . . .[1]

With this principle in mind, Hart distinguishes Joyce's method from, for example, Gertrude Stein's imitations of mechanism and other rigid reproductions of sameness. He also aligns his concept of organically changing repetition with E. M. Forster's "rhythm" and with E. K. Brown's derivative "expanding symbol." These and other theories of fictional form establish repetition as a unifying force that moves, ideally, through all the parts of a text, and as a structural principle that combines similarity and difference in an inevitable reciprocity or dialectic.

Yet when this esthetic rhythm is related to the complexities of repetitive events in the external world, problems arise. While awareness of the interplay of constancy and change in reality goes back to Heraclitus—if not to the *Upanishads*—the perception of the difficulty of representing that interplay in art is of relatively recent date. A keen analysis of some of the issues at stake in describing constancy and change was published by Woolf's sister-in-law, Karin Stephen, in the period during which Woolf's style took shape. It is not necessary to posit either Woolf's underlying orientation toward Bergsonian philosophy or the direct influence of Stephen's book, *The Misuse of Mind* in order to understand her use of motif.[2] But a number of Karin Stephen's formulations of Bergsonian problems have arresting implications for the phenomenon of literary repetition.

---

[1] *Structure and Motif in Finnegans Wake* (London, 1962), pp. 164–65. Hart's entire chapter on *"Leitmotiv"* (pp. 161–81) is of interest; his "Index of Motifs in *Finnegans Wake*" is on pp. 211–47.

[2] *The Misuse of Mind: A Study of Bergson's Attack on Intellectualism* (London and New York, 1922); the quotations below are from pp. 64–65.

In this view, reality (*la durée*) is entirely changeful and free so that there is no real repetition in life, despite appearances:

No 'two' positions in a creative process of duration can have an identical past history, every 'later' one will have more history, every 'earlier' one less. . . . If Bergson is right therefore in saying that abstractions change as a logical series while the actual facts change as a creative process of duration, it follows that, while our descriptions and explanations may contain repetitions the actual fact to which we intend these explanations to apply, cannot.

It is only in our mental constructs that repetitions occur; but if this is the case, what of artistic repetitions? While these cannot be readily called "abstractions," they come into the broad class of "descriptions and explanations." The implication that art, too, suffers from the ineptitude of rational throught in face of reality emerges in the following: "Now the directly known forms a creative duration whose special characteristics are that it is non-logical . . . and does not contain parts which can be repeated over and over, while on the other hand the terms which we have to substitute for it if we want to describe it stand for repetitions and have the logical form. It looks, therefore, as if our descriptions could not, as they stand, be very successful in conveying to others the fact known to us directly, or in recalling it to ourselves." But a way out of the trap of "intellectualism" is broached when an esthetic process is described:

Take a song in which the last line is sung twice over as a refrain: the notes, we say, are repeated, but the second time the line occurs the actual effect produced is different, and that, indeed, is the whole point of a refrain. . . . [the notes'] effect, being a changing process, depends for its flavour upon its position in the whole duration to which it belongs: this flavour grows out of the whole of what has gone before, and since this whole is itself always growing by the addition of more and more 'later stages,' the effect which it goes to produce can never be the same twice over.

If this is so, then the verbal repetitions in a literary work may produce effects like that of a song's refrain, although the discursive accounts of reality in the work may prove inadequate. In other words, literature may represent the creatively changeful repetitions of reality, not by verbal symbols but by the sequences in which those symbols are deployed. We are not here dealing with the imitative tropes through which, for example, poems achieve onomatopoetic effects emulating the repetitions of nature. More broadly, the rhythm of repetition and variation in a work of art may convey the equivalent of constancy and change in human experience. But how precisely would such an equivalence manifest itself, if not by the symbolic or representational means that come under the stigma of "descriptions"? Or, to put the problem as an author with Woolf's pervasive sense of constancy and change might frame it, how to convey that equivalence in terms that are both constant and changeful—to avoid belying one's vision in the very act of uttering it?

Much recent philosophical discussion has centered on this issue, and to proceed without taking account of it would be impractical. The most systematic statement of the philosophical issues posed by recurrent actions—of which the use of literary motifs is a special case— is Gilles Deleuze's *Différence et répétition*.[3] Drawing on, but moving beyond, the classic theories of Kierkegaard's *Repetition*, Nietzsche's eternal return of the same, and Freud's repetition-compulsion, Deleuze posits the existence of two classes of phenomena: *différence libre*, or occasions of differentiation that cannot be qualified by relations of identity, similarity, or even negation; and *répétition complexe*, or occasions of renewed activity that cannot be reduced to mechanical or involuntary organic processes. It is urged that these classes are not distinct, as in the ordinary view of difference and repetition, because the inventive aspect of certain differentiations—what we may call the impulse of freedom or creativity— is akin to the element that distinguishes complex human repetitions from automatic behavior.

Deleuze seeks to isolate a principle of creative repetition distinct from the traditional Platonic conception that judges things as either good or bad copies of the true forms—a principle of repetition which discovers values in things independent of a preexistent norm. This distinctive principle he calls the *simulacre*: here free difference and complex repetition unite in a situation which is neither conceptual analogy, symbolic representation, nor even imaginary recasting of what is initially given. Although he does not apply the term directly, we may call a situation in which this principle of creative repetition obtains a *virtual* one (for his use of the term, see pages 269–70); we may also identify it with the mode of existence in which literary objects—particularly the projected scenes of fictional works—participate.

Deleuze does not, however, arrive at his view of repetition in art by this route but rather by way of psychological phenomena that have been brought to wide attention by Freud. This interpretation of compulsive repetition is, however, strikingly different from Freud's:

---

[3](Paris, 1972 [1968]). The quotations below are from pp. 371 and 375. Deleuze has also discussed some of his key terms in *Logique du sens* (Paris, 1969), particularly in the appendix, "Platon et le simulacre," pp. 292–307.

Quand l'obsédé répète un cérémonial, une fois, deux fois; quand il répète une numération, 1, 2, 3—il procède à une répétition d'éléments en extension, mais qui conjure et traduit une autre répétition, verticale et intensive, celle d'un passé qui se déplace à chaque fois ou à chaque nombre, et se déguise dans l'ensemble des nombres et des fois. . . . On répète deux fois simultanément, mais non pas de la même répétition: une fois mécaniquement et matériellement, en largeur, l'autre fois symboliquement, par simulacre, en profondeur; une fois on répète des parties, une autre fois le tout dont les parties dépendent.

Whether or not this degree of creativity should be accorded to obsessional behavior, the account is strikingly appropriate to the emergence of novel implications from the repeated words of verbal art. There follows one of the most impressive statements of a truth perhaps widely acknowledged but not sufficiently emphasized; not only much of our behavior but also much of our literature is composed of repetitions which operate on this double level—retracing various verbal series which, by their novel associations, simultaneously generate new wholes. Deleuze's account of art follows from this double action:

L'art n'imite pas, mais c'est d'abord parce qu'il répète toutes les répétitions, de part une puissance intérieure (l'imitation est une copie, mais l'art est simulacre, il renverse les copies en simulacres). Même la répétition la plus mécanique, la plus quotidienne, la plus habituelle, la plus stéréotypée trouve sa place dans l'oeuvre d'art, étant toujours déplacée par rapport à l'autres répétitions. . . . Chaque art a ses techniques de répétitions imbriquées, dont le pouvoir critique et révolutionnaire peut atteindre au plus haut point, pour nous conduir des mornes répétitions de l'habitude aux répétitions profondes de la mémoire, puis aux répétitions ultimes de la mort ou se joue notre liberté.

This fusion of repetitive strains into newly formed esthetic wholes—by a process which Deleuze in *Logique du sens* calls *"résonance interne"*[4]—gives us a clue to the dynamic of Woolf's works. Yet even were we to describe the manner by which highly repetitive authors overcome obsession in themselves and ennui in the reader, creating instead novel insight and expressive conviction, we would still lack a clue to the imaginative imperatives that make these authors so highly repetitive—and all authors repetitive to some degree. Various explanations suggest themselves: hypotheses of the

---

[4]"Ce chaos informel, la grande lettre de *Finnegans Wake*, n'est pas n'importe quel chaos: il est puissance d'affirmation, puissance d'affirmer toutes les séries hétérogènes, il 'complique' en lui toutes les séries. . . . Entre ces séries de base se produit une sorte de *résonance interne*; cette résonance induit un *mouvement forcé*, qui déborde les séries elles-mêmes." *Logique du sens*, p. 301.

inherent forms of human thought, from Kant to Lévi-Strauss; instinctual psychological systems, like the archetypes of Jung, or other catalogs of our mental furniture; the literary-historical assemblage of traditions and conventions, a fund of tropes and topics that has recently been revitalized by Auerbach, Frye, and others. Such theories offer satisfying answers to such questions as why a writer repeats what others have written, either by quoting their words or imitating their stylistic traits (which are themselves derivative), or why a writer repeats what he himself has written, whether in the same or in other texts. But these explanations tend to limit the artist's imagination, either by circumscribing his potential stock of concepts and images, or by assuming his tendency to follow the line of least resistance (reusing instead of inventing), or by positing a limited number of things that are to be thought and said in a given cultural tradition. One would appreciate an explanation that envisages positive benefits from repetitiveness, or at least accounts for the special quality generated by highly repetitive texts.

Such an explanation is to be derived from a paper of Freud's, one quite distinct from, and almost independent of, his writing on repetition-compulsion, called *"Das Unheimliche"* ("The 'Uncanny' ": 1919).[5] Freud takes up the well-known psychic phenomenon in which a special feeling surrounds situations (often in particular settings) that have, or seem to have, occurred before. He begins with the observation that this feeling of uncanniness or strangeness attaches to things that are somehow familiar and concludes from an inspired bout of amateur linguistics that *"heimlich* is a word the meaning of which develops in the direction of ambivalence, until it finally coincides with its opposite, *unheimlich. Unheimlich* is in some way or other a subspecies of *heimlich."* The ensuing analysis of E. T. A. Hoffmann's "The Sand-Man" does not get very far beyond Freud's earlier discovery of veiled forms of infantile fantasy in works of art (here, the castration anxiety reawakened by the figure of an evil genius who blinds his victims), except to postulate an instinct to revert to original forms of life, the tendency to return to stasis, womb, or death, which he was concurrently formulating in *Beyond the Pleasure Principle.*

Now Freud, with one of his characteristic swoops of perception, goes on to say:

[5]*The Standard Edition of the Complete Psychological Works of Sigmund Freud,* trans. James Strachey et al. (London, 1953), Vol. xvii. This paper was translated by Alix Strachey, like her husband James a member of Woolf's closest circle of friends. The quotations below are from pp. 226 and 241 respectively.

. . . if psycho-analytic theory is correct in maintaining that every affect belonging to an emotional impulse, whatever its kind, is transformed, if it is repressed, into anxiety, then among instances of frightening things there must be one class in which the frightening element can be shown to be something repressed which *recurs*. This class of frightening things would then constitute the uncanny; and it must be a matter of indifference whether what is uncanny was itself originally frightening or whether it carried some *other* affect.

The sequence of events in such a process seems to be as follows: experience—affect—repression of affect—anxiety—repetition of the same or similar experience—repetition of the anxiety—feeling of the uncanny. What is most striking is the suggestion that the original experience need not have been dreadful to bring about the chain of repression, anxiety, and uncanny reappearance. *Repetition alone* may generate a sense of the uncanny. The original experience drops out of the sequence of later responses, and the mind operates in a self-renewing system of thought and feeling, without direct reference to the past. One way to look at this independent cycle is to regard it as a bondage to the rigid chain of stimulus and response; another way is to consider it a kind of freedom, allowing a distancing from the original events and a conversion of them into a purely imaginative realm of speculation, feeling, and—in some cases—esthetic expression.[6]

Virginia Woolf was, as we have seen, a repetitive writer, both in her thematic concerns and in her means of expression. It is scarcely necessary to cite childhood trauma—the series of deaths in her family, the explosive father, or the "interfering" stepbrother—to see that Woolf was inordinately burdened with her past. Nor is it greatly enlightening to posit a neurotic (or psychotic) complusion to repeat, to return to the same psychic cruxes, when we consider the satisfying formal order she made of her preoccupations in *Jacob's Room, Mrs. Dalloway, The Waves, The Years*, and most of all in *To the Lighthouse*. We know that Woolf dwelt on the past, on the scenes and persons of her childhood and later years; we have also seen that in doing so she used certain images, phrases, and words over and over again. Can we say that the peculiar mixture of eeriness and pleasure

---

[6]A convenient summary of the several modes or motives of repetition of which psychoanalysis is aware is presented in Richard Wollheim, *Sigmund Freud* (New York, 1971), pp. 211–13. These modes include, beyond neurotic compulsion, the pleasures of recall, the possible mastery of what is elusive, and the impulse to restore a prior and more desirable condition—even that of unconscious, inanimate existence. The classic statement of the latter is, of course, *Beyond the Pleasure Principle*, particularly sections 5 and 7.

which emanates from Woolf's fiction is related to that feeling of the uncanny which we have in the presence of the past? Woolf's reworking of persons and places is, of course, different from Wordsworth's return to remembered scenes; her repetition of words and themes is distinct from the reverberations of *"temps"* in the closing pages of Proust's *Recherche.* Nevertheless, these writers are her proper company: she takes her place in the tradition—still alive, although Romantic art has passed—that tells us not only how it feels to be but also how it feels *to have been.* At the same time, there is no avoiding the implication that so powerful an impulse toward the past, now dead, is in line with that temptation to return to a prior state of being that has become known as the "death-instinct."

Yet Woolf's fiction is no mere regression to childhood or death. In the nature of things, an experience can never be exactly repeated, not only because it occurs at another time, another place, but also because the experiencer has become an altered person. The event as replicated in art can only be similar to the original, and achievement of this similarity requires a metaphoric construction by the artist. His is the creative force that assimilates one train of repetitions to another and discovers their relation, endowing them with a new vitality. The spectacle of this creative act should encourage us to believe that a repetitive style may further an art of novelty and freedom—an art, in Deleuze's words, of those *"répétitions ultimes de la mort ou se joue notre liberté."*[7]

[7]After the above was written, there appeared a new study of Woolf that adds to the impression that a great wave of comprehension is washing over this formerly elusive author: Allen McLaurin, *Virginia Woolf: The Echoes Enslaved* (Cambridge, 1973). Part 2, making up almost half the book, is devoted to the problem of "Repetition and Rhythm," and it constitutes a set of theoretical approaches far more elaborate than my own. In his "Introduction to the Problem" (chapter 9), McLaurin cites the works of E. K. Brown, Dorothy Richardson, Gertrude Stein (with a passing reference to Clive Hart on Joyce), D. H. Lawrence, S. Kierkegaard, Hubert Waley, I. M. L. Hunter, Karin Stephen, and Roger Fry—the latter in line with a more general application of Fry's esthetic theories to Woolf.

McLaurin attempts to distinguish between "those works in which there are repetitive devices and those which are self-consciously concerned with repetition itself" (p. 99). He seems to establish as the focus of the latter, "the problem of avoiding deadening habit, of transmuting repetition into a vital rhythm" (p. 101)—cf. Bergson and Lawrence. I cannot follow this argument through all its fleeting appearances in the course of McLaurin's commentary, but I fail to find Woolf concerned with mechanical repetition as a problem to be overcome. It is rather one more element of the natural and social world which she attempts to include in her vision of life—that vision itself assuming the shape of a grand repetitive rhythm.

index

This index includes motifs frequently found in Woolf's fiction; names of writers alluded to or quoted in the novels; literary terms (and authorities) used in my analysis; references to any novel occurring outside the chapter devoted to that work.

index

The Johns Hopkins University Press

This book was composed in Baskerville text and Stettler display type by Jones Composition Company, from a design by Susan Bishop. It was printed on S. D. Warren's 60-lb. 1854 regular paper and bound in Columbia Fiction-ette cloth by Universal Lithographers, Inc.